The Best American Legal Writing 2009

Foreword by
Dahlia Lithwick

PUBLISHING

New York

This publication is designed to provide accurate and authoritative information in regard to the subject matter covered. It is sold with the understanding that the publisher is not engaged in rendering legal, accounting, or other professional service. If legal advice or other expert assistance is required, the services of a competent professional should be sought.

Published by Kaplan Publishing, a division of Kaplan, Inc.
1 Liberty Plaza, 24th Floor
New York, NY 10006

Printed in the United States of America

10 9 8 7 6 5 4 3 2 1

ISBN-13: 978-1-60714-466-3

Kaplan Publishing books are available at special quantity discounts to use for sales promotions, employee premiums, or educational purposes. Please email our Special Sales Department to order or for more information at *kaplanpublishing@kaplan.com*, or write to Kaplan Publishing, 1 Liberty Plaza, 24th Floor, New York, NY 10006.

Table of Contents

Introduction

AMERICANS HAVE A FASCINATION with lawyers and the law that borders on the religious. We can't seem to get enough of John Grisham, Brad Meltzer, *Law and Order, Boston Legal, Ally McBeal* or the attendant promise that justice will be done, and closure will be achieved, in the secular churches that are our courtrooms. On the first day of law school, a classmate of mine remarked that lawyers are modern-day wizards; the last class of individuals with the power to change one thing into another. Never has that observation seemed truer than it did in 2008, with armies of Harry Potters in wingtips toiling to do everything from redefining torture to safeguarding the right to vote in a presidential election. The best legal writing of the past year spotlighted the power of lawyers to perform these great feats of magic, as well as the power of the law itself to being redemption; a form of magic in and of itself.

Great legal writing happens in wonderfully unlikely ways places, and the pieces we've selected reflect the ways in which great writers can make even dull cases, conflicts, and characters leap to life, or use interesting cases and characters to illuminate deeper legal truths. We tried to pick some of the stories that told great stories, that shone a light into complex conflicts, and stories that helped explain to ourselves who we were, in legal and constitutional terms, in 2008.

Not all legal stories are immediately recognizable as such. It's easy to forget, for instance, that in so many ways the story of the 2008 presidential election was also, beneath the surface, a referendum on the Rule of Law. And it's almost impossible to consider the legacy of Barack Obama without recalling that the man began his life as a community lawyer and constitutional law professor. The *New York Times'* Jodi Kantor was quick to recognize that much could be learned about Obama's current legal worldview from his years spent teaching law at the University of Chicago. In a prescient piece of reporting from last year, she discovered that even years ago, then-Professor Barack Obama "was wary of noble theories, students say; instead, they call Mr. Obama a contextualist, willing to look past legal niceties to get results."

Perhaps the most dramatic national legal story of 2008 revolved around President Bush's anti-terror policies, some of which were rapidly rescinded or modified in the early days of the Obama Administration. Stories detailing what really happened at the legal black hole that was Guantanamo Bay, or Abu Ghraib, and how these policies were secretly devised and authorized at the highest levels of government remain the only way most of us can comprehend how dramatically American law was reshaped in the Bush era.

It is no accident that stories of this sort dominate this collection. Historians will someday tell us that while Congress lay supine and the courts awaited further instruction, the war against the war on terror was fought, in the main, by the legal journalists who exposed warrantless wiretapping, abusive interrogation, and other illegal government practices to public scrutiny.

Explosive reporting such as that done by David Rose in September's *Vanity Fair* assessed how and why the United States came to torture its prisoners in the wake of 9/11. Rose wrote that 'it is, perhaps, a little late, more than six years after detainees began to be interrogated at Guantánamo Bay and at the C.I.A.'s black-site prisons, to be asking whether torture works. Yet according to numerous C.I.A. and F.B.I. officials interviewed for this article, at the time this question really mattered, in the months after 9/11, no one seriously addressed it." Rose's conclusions—

that torture does not produce valuable intelligence, but instead wastes time, resources, and moral capital—are shared by most experts in the field. The fact that in 2009 we are still debating whether torture "works" reflects how much the legal and moral world has changed since September of 2001.

Andy Worthington's quirky research into the history of music torture in the War on Terror makes for a fascinating read. Whatever your feelings about Barney the Dinosaur's theme song or Eminem's *Slim Shady* album, the fact that earsplitting, disorienting music was regularly used at prisons in Iraq, Afghanistan and Guantánamo Bay, as part of the US interrogation program, has garnered attention mainly from the performers themselves—who have seemingly been either horrified or deeply moved by their inadvertent government service in the war on terror.

The *New Yorker's* Jeffrey Toobin does for the camp at Guantanamo Bay what David Rose did for Bush Era torture policies. In April of 2008 he traveled to the prison camp to report, rather presciently as it turns out, that "it is easier to talk about closing Guantánamo than to do it." The camp and the military commissions developed to try prisoners there were conceived in haste, but as the Obama Administration has discovered, these policies cannot be reversed quickly, if at all. Toobin handily sums up President Obama's ongoing Guantanamo quandary in quoting the head of the Guantánamo Task Force: "The good news is, we got 'em. The bad news is, we got 'em."

Newsweek's indispensible Michael Isikoff introduced us in December of 2008 to Thomas M. Tamm, the federal lawyer who had divulged the NSA's secret warrantless wiretapping program to the *New York Times*. Readers will have to judge for themselves whether Tamm, whose life is now a shambles, was a traitor or a valiant whistleblower. As Isikoff writes, the distinction between the two can be blurry at the best of times: "In judging Tamm's actions—his decision to reveal what little he knew about a secret domestic spying program that still isn't completely known—it can be hard to decipher right from wrong. Sometimes the thinnest of lines separates the criminal from the hero."

Questions about what happens next with respect to Bush-era anti-terror policies were addressed in a thoughtful essay by Scott Horton, detailing what he characterizes as the crimes committed by members of the Bush Administration and the possible legal actions to be taken against them. Whether or not one agrees with Horton's prescription, the piece was a path-breaking analysis of where to go from here, concluding as it did that "right now, the administration looms large and justice seems distant. That perspective will change significantly with the passage of time."

Race issues continue to plague America, perhaps moreso now than ever before, and some of the finest legal writing of 2008 addressed and reframed racial conflicts head on. Writing in the *Atlantic,* Amy Waldman waded into the dueling narratives constructed around the race-freighted violence that occurred in Jena, Louisiana, in 2007, when a black high school football hero and the rest of the so-called "Jena Six" were aggressively prosecuted for assaulting a white student. The case became iconic for supposedly revealing deep truths about either the innocence of black people and racism of white people in the deep south, or the racism of black people and the misperception of white there. But as Waldman notes, "neither version was correct—and both were. The reality was complex enough that people could assemble a story line, buffet-style, to suit their outlook." Probing the facts beneath the reported stories, Waldman finds a Jena far more complicated than the evidence that had been amassed on blogs and network television.

A.C. Thompson's exploration of the hidden race war that took place in the days after Hurricane Katrina proves a remarkable companion piece to Waldman's study of Jena. It seems a white militia hastily organized itself in Algiers Point to respond to Katrina's alleged looters, and—as white militias are wont to do—promptly shot at and killed unarmed African Americans. Following an 18-month investigation into the attacks, Thompson paints a troubling picture of a racially fragmented New Orleans in the days after the storm, and the simplistic race narrative used to paper it over: "Immediately after the storm, the media portrayed African Americans as looters and thugs—Mayor Ray Nagin, for example, told Oprah Winfrey that 'hundreds of gang members' were marauding through the Superdome. Now it's clear that some of the most serious crimes committed during that time were the work of gun-toting white males."

Without outsized legal characters—the cigar chomping attorneys and the grandiose, power-mad judges—legal writing would be dense and technical, and 2008 was a banner year for stories about larger-than-life lawyers. I defy you to not enjoy every last word of Steve Volk's charming story about a legendary Philadelphia trial attorney and the firm he left to his screw-up son. The screw-up son has turned into an unlikely success story and everything we thought we knew about lawyering has changed. This is the story of a lawyer-son relationship that most of us would recognize—"redolent of anger, vomit and laughable good fortune." It's also a meditation on how the legal profession has changed in a generation and how those changes have led to the demise of a certain type of epic trial attorney.

Judges and their competence have been in the news often recently, with the Supreme Court handing down a landmark decision about the relationship between campaign contributions and the appearance of judicial impropriety. Robert Huber takes a skeptical look at a pack of Philadelphia jurists whose quirks range from incontinence on the bench to berating counsel for bad posture. Huber's observation—that judicial elections have created a system in which money talks and justice walks—is hardly novel. But this is a thorough and merciless depiction of an entire system that cannot help but corrupt the bench—from high priced campaign consultants, party politics, unions, ward leaders, sample ballots, to payoffs and worse.

2008 was also the year the Supreme Court handed down its first major gun decision, striking down the District of Columbia's handgun ban as unconstitutional. Writing about the case in the *Nation*, Daniel Lazare went where even linguistic angels fear to tread: to the text of the Second Amendment for a rollicking close reading of the words themselves: "Surely a mere twenty-seven words, loosely tethered together by three commas and one period, can't be that impenetrable. But they are; and if ever there was a Churchillian 'riddle wrapped in a mystery inside an enigma,' the Second Amendment is it." Lazare ultimately wrestles the Amendment into something resembling submission, but concludes, as he must, that the battle over gun rights in America is actually a conflict over national identity and purpose that only appears to be resolved by the plain meaning of the Constitution. As he puts it: "Although legal academics like to think of the Constitution as a model of reason and balance, the Second Amendment puts us in touch with the document's inner schizophrenic—and, consequently, our own. Thanks to it, we the people know that the people are dangerous. Therefore, we must take up arms against our own authority. We are perennially at war with ourselves and are never more alarmed than when confronted by our own power. The people are tyrannized by the fear of popular tyranny."

Liliana Segura also takes a look at guns, but her inquiry is into the effects of Texas' newly enacted Castle Law—which allows "Texans to not only protect themselves from criminals, but to receive the protection of state law when circumstances dictate that they use deadly force." Texas is one of at least 15 states across the country that has recently enacted laws expanding the circumstances under which we can use deadly force to protect ourselves and our homes. Segura recounts a chilling incident in which a man shot and killed two men he believed to be robbing his neighbor's home. A contemporaneous 911 call has him telling the emergency dispatcher, "Well, here it goes, buddy. You hear the shotgun clicking and I'm going," seconds before pulling the trigger. He appears dispassionate, rational, and chillingly hellbent on killing. Segura says it's too soon to have statistical proof, but it's likely that as a result of these laws we'll see an increase in deadly, "justifiable" violence.

The strange world of criminal law grows ever so slightly stranger with Kevin Carey's *Washington Monthly* exploration of an epidemic of black Baltimore drug dealers using something called the "flesh and blood defense" in court. The flesh and blood defense, as it happens, is a decades-old white supremacist legal theory that's been used by gun nuts, tax protesters, Aryan supremacists, and militia members. Grafting a story that reads like a script from *The Wire*—drug dealers murdering other drug dealers in cold blood—onto an excavation of the roots of the "flesh and blood" defense, Carey finds black gang members cheerfully quoting from web sites like "*www.redemptionservice. com*, which offers maps showing how Satanic runes were secretly incorporated into the street plan of Washington, D.C., and a deluxe package of instructions for renouncing one's social security number for only $3,900, payable by check or money order." In the end, as Carey observes, it hardly matters that "the secret histories and grand conspiracies that have fueled decades of right-wing paranoia, morphing to accommodate one doomed cause after another until finding an unlikely temporary home in a Baltimore lockup, are lies and nothing more." The defense may well have saved these particular criminals' lives.

In yet another piece teasing out the truth behind decades-old mythologies, Heather MacDonald writes provocatively about the campus rape myth, arguing that the liberal feminist orthodoxy that one in every four girls on college campuses is a rape victim is more than just bad data, it's also part of a growth industry of counseling, crisis centers and a point of pride for college administrators. The real truth behind the "campus rape industry?" writes MacDonald: "A booze-fueled hookup culture of one-night, or sometimes just partial-night, stands." MacDonald offers an alternative to the feminists and their sex-is-rape and men-are-subjugators policies: "Maybe these young iconoclasts can take up another discredited idea: college is for learning.

The adults in charge have gone deaf to the siren call of beauty that for centuries lured people to the classics. But fighting male dominance or catering to the libidinal impulses released in the 1960s are sorry substitutes for the pursuit of knowledge. The campus rape and sex industries are signs of how hollow the university has become."

2008 was, yet again, the year of the celebrity divorce. Reese Witherspoon divorced Ryan Phillipe. Madonna ditched Guy Ritchie. Star Jones left Al Reynolds. And by mid-July the divorce trial of Christie Brinkley and Peter Cook—replete with allegations of Cook's Web porn abuse and his adultery with a "fitness model" appeared to have redefined "rock bottom" for high-stakes, high-profile divorce trials. In "McGreevey v. McGreevey", Michael Callahan offers everything you thought you needed to know about former New Jersey Governor Jim McGreevey's divorce litigation. And a lot more that you didn't. But underneath all the salacious details, this piece is a meditation about how anger and public humiliation fuel divorce trials, and probes how two otherwise rational adults might spend months locked in expensive litigation over which Barnes & Noble will be used as the drop off spot for the minor child, and whether or not said minor is to have an American Girl birthday party.

A welcome tonic to the McGreevey madness is Susanna Schrobsdorff's reporting on changes in custody arrangements, away from the traditional "dad-gets-every-other-weekend" approach and toward a more equitable allocation of custodial privileges for divorced fathers. To be sure, as the law shifts away from its traditional preference for custodial mothers, and as complex joint custody arrangements increase, there will be costs, financial, emotional, and otherwise. But research shows that a majority of kids who have grown up in joint physical custody situations are more satisfied than those raised in an "every-other-weekend arrangement." You can read both Callahan and Schrobsdorff together as offering up complimentary cautionary tales about the need for adults to behave like real adults, when there are real children concerned.

Still on the subject of legal dissolution, Ben Hallman reports in the *American Lawyer* on a rare breed of attorneys who can work the legal system at the speed of light: Four senior partners from Weil, Gotshal & Manges somehow managed put together the largest bankruptcy in US history over a few short days in September of 2008. In describing the legal activity that should have occurred over months, Hallman paints a fast-paced picture of high-velocity lawyering, while attempting to explain why the government allowed Lehman Brothers to fail almost overnight. Says one of the lawyers on the Weil, Gotshal dream team, "If the filing didn't spawn Armageddon in the financial markets, it came close. . . But it didn't take an expert to predict what would happen, . . . Just knowledge of simple physics. When a stone starts rolling downhill, it gathers momentum."

Jeffrey Rosen's terrific piece, "Google's Gatekeepers," appeared in the *New York Times Magazine*, and begins with the description of the delicate legal negotiations undertaken by Google's lawyers in response to Turkey's decision to block access to YouTube because it had videos that insulted the founder of modern Turkey, a crime under Turkish law. Rosen uses the thorny Google situation to highlight a paradox of the new media: "Though technology enthusiasts often celebrate the raucous explosion of Web speech, there is less focus on how the Internet is actually regulated, and by whom. As more and more speech migrates online, to blogs and social-networking sites and the like, the ultimate power to decide who has an opportunity to be heard, and what we may say, lies increasingly with Internet service providers." As a practical matter this means a handful of people at a handful of companies "have more influence over the contours of online expression than anyone else on the planet." And while Rosen has no particular objection to Google's current crop of information gatekeepers, he worries, quite rightly, I think, that "they may eventually be replaced with lawyers who are more concerned about corporate profits than about free expression."

Emily Maloney paid a visit to the opening of the National Museum of Crime and Punishment in Washington, D.C. last summer, and came back with a wildly entertaining report. What's not to love about a museum dedicated to heinous crime? Especially if McGruff the crime dog and John Walsh of Fox's *America's Most Wanted* are on hand for the grand opening. But Maloney's doubts begin when she is greeted with a first wall panel warning: "Every 22.2 seconds a violent crime is committed in the United States." Maloney notes that the museum was financed by an Orlando lawyer and produced in conjunction with *America's Most Wanted*. That possibly explains why small children are encouraged to visit a simulated morgue in which they may push a button on a mannequin corpse "and hear about the strangulation wounds, the defensive lacerations, and the gunshot wounds that killed the man." Maloney leaves less than enthusiastic about the museum's relentless *Law and Order* message: "What I didn't know before I arrived and climbed the steps was that the museum itself was going to be curated like TV, selling a simple 'us' versus 'them' concept of crime."

Finally, a gripping narrative that derives new poignancy from the recent murder of Kansas abortion provider, Dr. George Tiller. In a piece for *New York* magazine, Robert Kolker exhaustively traces the unlikely, decades-long friendship between an anti abortion activist and the man, once nicknamed The Trembler, who eventually helped convict him. Kolker unspools a gripping tale: an age-old buddy story complete with a passionate female love interest. Except in this case the female love interest was dear friends with James Kopp, the man who in 1998 gunned down Dr. Barnett Slepian in his own home. The Trembler agreed to cooperate with the FBI, leading to the arrest of Kopp and his friends. This is a story of an ordinary schlemiel who got himself caught up in the double life of the radical pro-life movement.

It's also a story of friendship, forgiveness, and the faces we show our closest friends.

There were too many outstanding articles that didn't find a home in this collection. Possibly enough to produce an anthology of the same shape and size. Groundbreaking work on gun rights, the Supreme Court's rightward tilt, changes to the federal judiciary, the progress of the fight over gay marriage, and many wonderful tales of crime, criminality, and politics were reluctantly put aside.

To the extent there is a common thread in the pieces assembled here it may just be this: Lawbreaking is usually something done swiftly and without much reflection. Whether it's instituting a government-sanctioned torture regime, shooting the guy on your neighbor's lawn, or opening fire on a post-Katrina looter without stopping to check that he is one, people commit reckless acts every day, acts that can turn them into a display at the National Museum of Crime and Punishment. Those of us who write about the law for a living often wish for justice be equally swift and certain: those who abuse prisoners should be punished instantly, those who have sex with young girls at a keg party should be disciplined promptly. And those who litigate American Girl Birthday Parties should be stripped of all custodial rights. But Lady Justice isn't just blind. She's slow too. And deliberate. The very best legal writing reminds us, as Scott Horton suggests, that the legal system is at its maddening, foot-dragging best when the crimes loom large and justice seems most distant.

Teaching Law, Testing Ideas, Obama Stood Slightly Apart

Jodi Kantor

from *The New York Times*

THE YOUNG LAW professor stood apart in too many ways to count. At a school where economic analysis was all the rage, he taught rights, race and gender. Other faculty members dreamed of tenured positions; he turned them down. While most colleagues published by the pound, he never completed a single work of legal scholarship.

At a formal institution, Barack Obama was a loose presence, joking with students about their romantic prospects, using first names, referring to case law one moment and "The Godfather" the next. He was also an enigmatic one, often leaving fellow faculty members guessing about his precise views.

Mr. Obama, now the junior senator from Illinois and the presumptive Democratic presidential nominee, spent 12 years at the University of Chicago Law School. Most aspiring politicians do not dwell in the halls of academia, and few promising young legal thinkers toil in state legislatures. Mr. Obama planted a foot in each, splitting his weeks between an elite law school and the far less rarefied atmosphere of the Illinois Senate.

Before he outraised every other presidential primary candidate in American history, Mr. Obama marched students through the thickets of campaign finance law. Before he helped redraw his own State Senate district, making it whiter and wealthier, he taught districting as a racially fraught study in how power is secured. And before he posed what may be the ultimate test of racial equality—whether Americans will elect a black president—he led students through African-Americans' long fight for equal status.

Standing in his favorite classroom in the austere main building, sharp-witted students looming above him, Mr. Obama refined his public speaking style, his debating abilities, his beliefs.

"He tested his ideas in classrooms," said Dennis Hutchinson, a colleague. Every seminar hour brought a new round of, "Is affirmative action justified? Under what circumstances?" as Mr. Hutchinson put it.

But Mr. Obama's years at the law school are also another chapter—see United States Senate, c. 2006—in which he seemed as intently focused on his own political rise as on the institution itself. Mr. Obama, who declined to be interviewed for this article, was well liked at the law school, yet he was always slightly apart from it, leaving some colleagues feeling a little cheated that he did not fully engage. The Chicago faculty is more rightward-leaning than that of other top law schools, but if teaching alongside some of the most formidable conservative minds in the country had any impact on Mr. Obama, no one can quite point to it.

"I don't think anything that went on in these chambers affected him," said Richard Epstein, a libertarian colleague who says he longed for Mr. Obama to venture beyond his ideological and topical comfort zones. "His entire life, as best I can tell, is one in which he's always been a thoughtful listener and questioner, but he's never stepped up to the plate and taken full swings."

Mr. Obama had other business on his mind, embarking on five political races during his 12 years at the school. Teaching gave him satisfaction, along with a perch and a paycheck, but he was impatient with academic debates over "whether to drop a footnote or not drop a footnote," said Abner J. Mikva, a mentor whose own career has spanned Congress, the federal bench and the same law school.

Douglas Baird, another colleague, remembers once asking Mr. Obama to assess potential candidates for governor.

"First of all, I'm not running for governor, " Mr. Obama told him. "But if I did, I would expect you to support me."

He was a third-year state senator at the time.

Popular and Enigmatic

Mr. Obama arrived at the law school in 1991 thanks to Michael W. McConnell, a conservative scholar who is now a federal appellate judge. As president of The Harvard Law Review, Mr. Obama had impressed Mr. McConnell with editing suggestions on an article; on little more than that, the law school gave him a fellowship, which amounted to an office and a computer, which he used to write his memoir, "Dreams From My Father."

The school had almost no black faculty members, a special embarrassment given its location on the South Side. Its sleek halls bordered a neighborhood crumbling with poverty and neglect. In his 2000 Congressional primary race, Representative Bobby L. Rush, a former Black Panther running for re-election, used Mr. Obama's ties to the school to label him an egghead and an elitist.

At the school, Mr. Obama taught three courses, ascending to senior lecturer, a title otherwise carried only by a few federal judges. His most traditional course was in the due process and equal protection areas of constitutional law. His voting rights class traced the evolution of election law, from the disenfranchisement of blacks to contemporary debates over districting and campaign finance. Mr. Obama was so interested in the subject that he helped Richard Pildes, a professor at New York University, develop a leading casebook in the field.

His most original course, a historical and political seminar as much as a legal one, was on racism and law. Mr. Obama improvised his own textbook, including classic cases like Brown v. Board of Education, and essays by Frederick Douglass, W. E. B. Dubois, the Rev. Dr. Martin Luther King Jr. and Malcolm X, as well as conservative thinkers like Robert H. Bork.

Mr. Obama was especially eager for his charges to understand the horrors of the past, students say. He assigned a 1919 catalog of lynching victims, including some who were first raped or stripped of their ears and fingers, others who were pregnant or lynched with their children, and some whose charred bodies were sold off, bone fragment by bone fragment, to gawkers.

"Are there legal remedies that alleviate not just existing racism, but racism from the past?" Adam Gross, now a public interest lawyer in Chicago, wrote in his class notes in April 1994.

For all the weighty material, Mr. Obama had a disarming touch. He did not belittle students; instead he drew them out, restating and polishing halting answers, students recall. In one class on race, he imitated the way clueless white people talked. "Why are your friends at the housing projects shooting each other?" he asked in a mock-innocent voice.

A favorite theme, said Salil Mehra, now a law professor at Temple University, were the values and cultural touchstones that Americans share. Mr. Obama's case in point: his wife, Michelle, a black woman, loved "The Brady Bunch" so much that she could identify every episode by its opening shots.

As his reputation for frank, exciting discussion spread, enrollment in his classes swelled. Most scores on his teaching evaluations were positive to superlative. Some students started referring to themselves as his groupies. (Mr. Obama, in turn, could play the star. In what even some fans saw as self-absorption, Mr. Obama's hypothetical cases occasionally featured himself. "Take Barack Obama, there's a good-looking guy," he would introduce a twisty legal case.)

Challenging Assumptions

Liberals flocked to his classes, seeking refuge. After all, the professor was a progressive politician who backed child care subsidies and laws against racial profiling, and in a 1996 interview with the school newspaper sounded skeptical of President Bill Clinton's efforts to reach across the aisle.

"On the national level, bipartisanship usually means Democrats ignore the needs of the poor and abandon the idea that government can play a role in issues of poverty, race discrimination, sex discrimination or environmental protection," Mr. Obama said.

But the liberal students did not necessarily find reassurance. "For people who thought they were getting a doctrinal, rah-rah experience, it wasn't that kind of class," said D. Daniel Sokol, a former student who now teaches law at the University of Florida at Gainesville.

For one thing, Mr. Obama's courses chronicled the failure of liberal policies and court-led efforts at social change: the Reconstruction-era amendments that were rendered meaningless by a century of resistance, the way the triumph of Brown gave way to fights over busing, the voting rights laws that crowded blacks into as few districts as possible. He was wary of noble theories, students say; instead, they call Mr. Obama a contextualist, willing to look past legal niceties to get results.

For another, Mr. Obama liked to provoke. He wanted his charges to try arguing that life was better under segregation, that black people were better athletes than white ones.

"I remember thinking, 'You're offending my liberal instincts,'" Mary Ellen Callahan, now a privacy lawyer in Washington, recalled.

In his voting rights course, Mr. Obama taught Lani Guinier's proposals for structuring elections differently to increase minority representation. Opponents attacked those suggestions when Ms. Guinier was nominated as assistant attorney general for civil rights in 1993, costing her the post.

"I think he thought they were good and worth trying," said David Franklin, who now teaches law at DePaul University in Chicago.

But whether out of professorial reserve or budding political caution, Mr. Obama would not say so directly. "He surfaced all the competing points of view on Guinier's proposals with total neutrality and equanimity," Mr. Franklin said. "He just let the class debate the merits of them back and forth."

While students appreciated Mr. Obama's evenhandedness, colleagues sometimes wanted him to take a stand. When two fellow faculty members asked him to support a controversial antigang measure, allowing the Chicago police to disperse and eventually arrest loiterers who had no clear reason to gather, Mr. Obama discussed the issue with unusual thoughtfulness, they say, but gave little sign of who should prevail—the American Civil Liberties Union, which opposed the measure, or the community groups that supported it out of concern about crime.

"He just observed it with a kind of interest," said Daniel Kahan, now a professor at Yale.

Nor could his views be gleaned from scholarship; Mr. Obama has never published any. He was too busy, but also, Mr. Epstein believes, he was unwilling to put his name to anything that could haunt him politically, as Ms. Guinier's writings had hurt her. "He figured out, you lay low," Mr. Epstein said.

The Chicago law faculty is full of intellectually fiery friendships that burn across ideological lines. Three times a week, professors do combat over lunch at a special round table in the university's faculty club, and they share and defend their research in workshop discussions. Mr. Obama rarely attended, even when he was in town.

"I'm not sure he was close to anyone," Mr. Hutchinson said, except for a few liberal constitutional law professors, like Cass Sunstein, now an occasional adviser to his campaign. Mr. Obama was working two other jobs, after all, in the State Senate and at a civil rights law firm.

Several colleagues say Mr. Obama was surely influenced by the ideas swirling around the law school campus: the prevailing market-friendliness, or economic analysis of the impact of laws. But none could say how. "I'm not sure we changed him," Mr. Baird said.

Because he never fully engaged, Mr. Obama "doesn't have the slightest sense of where folks like me are coming from," Mr. Epstein said. "He was a successful teacher and an absentee tenant on the other issues."

Leaving the Classroom

As Mr. Obama built his political career, his so-called groupies became an early core of supporters, handing out leaflets and hosting fund-raisers in their modest apartments.

"Maybe we charged an audacious $20?" said Jesse Ruiz, now a corporate lawyer in Chicago. Mr. Obama was sheepish asking for even that, Mr. Ruiz recalls. With no staff, Mr. Obama would come by the day after a fund-raiser to stuff the proceeds into a backpack.

Mr. Obama never mentioned his humiliating, hopeless campaign against Mr. Rush in class (he lost by a two-to-one margin), though colleagues noticed that he seemed exhausted and was smoking more than usual.

Soon after, the faculty saw an opening and made him its best offer yet: Tenure upon hiring. A handsome salary, more than the $60,000 he was making in the State Senate or the $60,000 he earned teaching part time. A job for Michelle Obama directing the legal clinic.

Your political career is dead, Daniel Fischel, then the dean, said he told Mr. Obama, gently. Mr. Obama turned the offer down. Two years later, he decided to run for the Senate. He canceled his course load and has not taught since.

Now, watching the news, it is dawning on Mr. Obama's former students that he was mining material for his political future even as he taught them.

Byron Rodriguez, a real estate lawyer in San Francisco, recalls his professor's admiration for the soaring but plainspoken speeches of Frederick Douglass.

"No one speaks this way anymore," Mr. Obama told his class, wondering aloud what had happened to the art of political oratory. In particular, Mr. Obama admired Douglass's use of a collective voice that embraced black and white concerns, one that Mr. Obama has now adopted himself.

In class, Mr. Obama sounded many of the same themes he does on the campaign trail, Ms. Callahan said, ticking them off: "self-determinism as opposed to paternalism, strength in numbers, his concept of community development."

But as a professor, students say, Mr. Obama was in the business of complication, showing that even the best-reasoned rules have unintended consequences, that competing legal interests cannot always be resolved, that a rule that promotes justice in one case can be unfair in the next.

So even some former students who are thrilled at Mr. Obama's success wince when they hear him speaking like the politician he has so fully become.

"When you hear him talking about issues, it's at a level so much simpler than the one he's capable of," Mr. Rodriguez said. "He was a lot more fun to listen to back then."

Google's Gatekeepers

Jeffrey Rosen

from *The New York Times Magazine*

IN 2006, THAILAND announced it was blocking access to YouTube for anyone with a Thai I.P. address, and then identified 20 offensive videos for Google to remove as a condition of unblocking the site.

'If your whole game is to increase market share,' says Lawrence Lessig, speaking of Google, 'it's hard to . . . gather data in ways that don't raise privacy concerns or in ways that might help repressive governments to block controversial content.'

In March of last year, Nicole Wong, the deputy general counsel of Google, was notified that there had been a precipitous drop in activity on YouTube in Turkey, and that the press was reporting that the Turkish government was blocking access to YouTube for virtually all Turkish Internet users. Apparently unaware that Google owns YouTube, Turkish officials didn't tell Google about the situation: a Turkish judge had ordered the nation's telecom providers to block access to the site in response to videos that insulted the founder of modern Turkey, Mustafa Kemal Ataturk, which is a crime under Turkish law. Wong scrambled to figure out which videos provoked the court order and made the first in a series of tense telephone calls to Google's counsel in London and Turkey, as angry protesters gathered in Istanbul. Eventually, Wong and several colleagues concluded that the video that sparked the controversy was a parody news broadcast that declared, "Today's news: Kamal Ataturk was gay!" The clip was posted by Greek football fans looking to taunt their Turkish rivals.

Wong and her colleagues asked the Turkish authorities to reconsider their decision, pointing out that the original offending video had already been voluntarily removed by YouTube users. But after the video was taken down, Turkish prosecutors objected to dozens of other YouTube videos that they claimed insulted either Ataturk or "Turkishness." These clips ranged from Kurdish-militia recruitment videos and Kurdish morality plays to additional videos speculating about the sexual orientation of Ataturk, including one superimposing his image on characters from "Queer Eye for the Straight Guy." "I remember one night, I was looking at 67 different Turkish videos at home," Wong told me recently.

After having many of the videos translated into English, Wong and her colleagues set out to determine which ones were, in fact, illegal in Turkey; which violated YouTube's terms of service prohibiting hate speech but allowing political speech; and which constituted expression that Google and YouTube would try to protect. There was a vigorous internal debate among Wong and her colleagues at the top of Google's legal pyramid. Andrew McLaughlin, Google's director of global public policy, took an aggressive civil-libertarian position, arguing that the company should protect as much speech as possible. Kent Walker, Google's general counsel, took a more pragmatic approach, expressing concern for the safety of the dozen or so employees at Google's Turkish office. The responsibility for balancing these and other competing concerns about the controversial content fell to Wong, whose colleagues jokingly call her "the Decider," after George W. Bush's folksy self-description.

Wong decided that Google, by using a technique called I.P. blocking, would prevent access to videos that clearly violated Turkish law, but only in Turkey. For a time, her solution seemed to satisfy the Turkish judges, who restored YouTube access. But last June, as part of a campaign against threats to symbols of Turkish secularism, a Turkish prosecutor made a sweeping demand: that Google block access to the offending videos throughout the world, to protect the rights and sensitivities of Turks living outside the country. Google refused, arguing that one nation's government shouldn't be able to set the limits of speech for Internet users worldwide. Unmoved, the Turkish government today continues to block access to YouTube in Turkey.

THE ONGOING DISPUTE between Google and Turkey reminds us that, throughout history, the development of new media technologies has always altered the way we think about threats to free speech. At the beginning of the 20th century, civil libertarians in America worried most about the danger of the government silencing political speech: think of Eugene V. Debs, the Socialist candidate for President, who was imprisoned in 1919 for publicly protesting American involvement during World War I. But by the late 1960s, after the Supreme Court started to protect unpopular speakers more consistently, some critics worried that free speech in America was threatened less by government suppression than by editorial decisions made by the handful of private mass-media corporations like NBC and CBS that disproportionately controlled public discourse. One legal scholar, Jerome Barron, even argued at the time that the courts should give unorthodox speakers a mandatory right of access to media outlets controlled by giant corporations.

Today the Web might seem like a free-speech panacea: it has given anyone with Internet access the potential to reach a global audience. But though technology enthusiasts often celebrate the raucous explosion of Web speech, there is less focus on how the Internet is actually regulated, and by whom. As more and more speech migrates online, to blogs and social-networking sites and the like, the ultimate power to decide who has an opportunity to be heard, and what we may say, lies increasingly with Internet service providers, search engines and other Internet companies like Google, Yahoo, AOL, Facebook and even eBay.

The most powerful and protean of these Internet gatekeepers is, of course, Google. With control of 63 percent of the world's Internet searches, as well as ownership of YouTube, Google has enormous influence over who can find an audience on the Web around the world. As an acknowledgment of its power, Google has given Nicole Wong a central role in the company's decision-making process about what controversial user-generated content goes down or stays up on YouTube and other applications owned by Google, including Blogger, the blog site; Picasa, the photo-sharing site; and Orkut, the social networking site. Wong and her colleagues also oversee Google's search engine: they decide what controversial material does and doesn't appear on the local search engines that Google maintains in many countries in the world, as well as on Google.com. As a result, Wong and her colleagues arguably have more influence over the contours of online expression than anyone else on the planet.

In response to the rise of online gatekeepers like Wong, some House Democrats and Republicans have introduced a bipartisan bill called the Global Online Freedom Act, which would require that Internet companies disclose to a newly created office in the State Department all material filtered in response to demands by foreign governments. Google and other leading Internet companies have sought modifications to the bill, arguing that, without the flexibility to negotiate (as Wong did with Turkey), they can't protect the safety of local employees and that they may get kicked out of repressive countries, where they believe even a restricted version of their services does more good than harm. For the past two years, Google, Yahoo and Microsoft, along with other international Internet companies, have been meeting regularly with human rights and civil-liberties advocacy groups to agree on voluntary standards for resisting worldwide censorship requests. At the end of last month, the Internet companies and the advocacy groups announced the Global Network Initiative, a series of principles for protecting global free expression and privacy.

Voluntary self-regulation means that, for the foreseeable future, Wong and her colleagues will continue to exercise extraordinary power over global speech online. Which raises a perennial but increasingly urgent question: Can we trust a corporation to be good—even a corporation whose informal motto is "Don't be evil"?

"To love Google, you have to be a little bit of a monarchist, you have to have faith in the way people traditionally felt about the king," Tim Wu, a Columbia law professor and a former scholar in residence at Google, told me recently. "One reason they're good at the moment is they live and die on trust, and as soon as you lose trust in Google, it's over for them." Google's claim on our trust is a fragile thing. After all, it's hard to be a company whose mission is to give people all the information they want and to insist at the same time on deciding what information they get.

THE HEADQUARTERS OF YouTube are in a former Gap building in San Bruno, Calif., just a few miles from the San Francisco International Airport. In the lobby, looming over massage chairs, giant plasma-screen TVs show popular videos and scroll news stories related to YouTube. The day I arrived to interview the YouTube management about how the site regulates controversial speech, most of the headlines, as it happens, had to do with precisely that topic. Two teenagers who posted a video of themselves throwing a soft drink at a Taco Bell employee were ordered by a Florida judge to post an apology on YouTube. The British culture secretary had just called on YouTube to carry warnings on clips that contain foul language.

The volume of videos posted on YouTube is formidable—Google estimates that something like 13 hours of content are uploaded every minute. YouTube users can flag a video if they think it violates YouTube's community guidelines, which prohibit sexually explicit videos, graphic violence and hate speech. Once flagged, a video is vetted by YouTube's internal reviewers at facilities around the world who decide whether to take it down, leave it up or send it up the YouTube hierarchy for more specialized review. When I spoke with Micah Schaffer, a YouTube policy analyst, he refused to say how many reviewers the company employs. But I was allowed to walk around the office to see if I could spot any of them. I passed one 20-something YouTube employee after another—all sitting in cubicles and wearing the same unofficial uniform of T-shirt and jeans. The internal reviewers were identifiable, I was told, only by the snippets of porn flickering on their laptops.

The idea of a 20-something with a laptop in San Bruno (or anywhere else, for that matter) interpreting community guidelines for tens of millions of users might not instill faith in YouTube's vetting process. But the most controversial user flags or requests from foreign governments make their way up the chain of command to the headquarters of Google, in Mountain View, Calif., where they may ultimately be reviewed by Wong, McLaughlin and Walker.

Recently, I spent several days talking to Wong and her colleagues at the so-called Googleplex, which has the feeling of a bucolic and extraordinarily well-financed theme camp. As we sat around a conference table, they told me about their debates as they wrestled with hard cases like the dispute in Turkey, as well as the experiences that have informed their thinking about free speech. Walker, the general counsel, wrote for *The Harvard Crimson* as an undergraduate and considered becoming a journalist before going into law; McLaughlin, the head of global public policy, became a fellow at Harvard's Berkman Center for Internet and Society after working on the successful Supreme Court challenge to part of the federal Communications Decency Act. And Wong, a soft-spoken and extremely well organized woman, has a joint degree in law and journalism from Berkeley and told me she aspired to be a journalist as a child because of her aunt, a reporter for *The Los Angeles Times*.

I asked Wong what was the best analogy for her role at Google. Was she acting like a judge? An editor? "I don't think it's either of those," she said. "I definitely am not trying to pass judgment on anything. I'm taking my best guess at what will allow our products to move forward in a country, and that's not a judge role, more an enabling role." She stressed the importance for Google of bringing its own open culture to foreign countries while still taking into account local laws, customs and attitudes. "What is the mandate? It's 'Be everywhere, get arrested nowhere and thrive in as many places as possible.'" So far, no Google employees have been arrested on Wong's watch, though some have been detained.

When Google was founded, 10 years ago, it wasn't at all obvious whether the proprietors of search engines would obey the local laws of the countries in which they did business—and whether they would remove links from search results in response to requests from foreign governments. This began to change in 2000, when a French Jew surfed a Yahoo auction site to look for collections of Nazi memorabilia, which violated a French law banning the sale and display of anything that incites racism. After a French judge determined that it was feasible for Yahoo to identify 90 percent of its French users by analyzing their I.P. addresses and to screen the material from the users, he ordered Yahoo to make reasonable efforts to block French users from accessing the prohibited content or else to face fines and the seizure of income from Yahoo's French subsidiary. In January 2001, Yahoo banned the sale of Nazi memorabilia on its Web sites.

The Yahoo case was a landmark. It made clear that search engines like Google and Yahoo could be held liable outside the United States for indexing or directing users to content after having been notified that it was illegal in a foreign country. In the United States, by contrast, Internet service providers are protected from most lawsuits involving having hosted or linked to illegal user-generated content. As a consequence of these differing standards, Google has considerably less flexibility overseas than it does in the United States about content on its sites, and its "information must be free" ethos is being tested abroad.

For example, on the German and French default Google search engines, Google.de and Google.fr, you can't find Holocaust-denial sites that can be found on Google.com, because Holocaust denial is illegal in Germany and France. In the wake of the Yahoo decision, Google decided to comply with governmental requests to take down links on its national search engines to material that clearly violates national laws. (In the interest of disclosure, however, Google has agreed to report all the links it takes down in response to government demands to chillingeffects.com, a Web site run by Harvard's Berkman Center that keeps a record of censored online materials.)

Of course, not every overseas case presents a clear violation of national law. In 2006, for example, protesters at a Google office in India demanded the removal of content on Orkut, the social networking site, that criticized Shiv Sena, a hard-line Hindu political party popular in Mumbai. Wong eventually decided to take down an Orkut group dedicated to attacking Shivaji, revered as a deity by the Shiv Sena Party, because it violated Orkut terms of service by criticizing a religion, but she decided not to take down another group because it merely criticized a political party. "If stuff is clearly illegal, we take that down, but if it's on the edge, you might push a country a little bit," Wong told me. "Free-speech law is always built on the edge, and in each country, the question is: Can you define what the edge is?"

INITIALLY, GOOGLE'S POLICY of removing links to clearly illegal material on its foreign search engines seemed to work. But things changed significantly after Google bought and expanded YouTube in 2006. Once YouTube was available in more than 20 countries and in 14 languages, users began flagging hundreds of videos that they saw as violations of local community standards, and governments around the globe demanded that certain videos be blocked for violating their laws. Google's solution was similar to the one the French judge urged on Yahoo: it agreed to block users in a particular country from accessing videos that were clearly illegal under local law. But that policy still left complicated judgment calls in murkier cases.

In late 2000, for example, Wong and her colleagues debated what to do about a series of videos that insulted the king of Thailand, where a lèse-majesté law makes criticisms of the king a criminal offense. Wong recalls hearing from an employee in Asia that the Thai government had announced that it was blocking access to YouTube for anyone with a Thai I.P. address. Soon after, a Thai government official sent Wong a list of the U.R.L.'s of 20 offensive videos that he demanded Google remove as a condition of unblocking the site. Some of the videos were sexually explicit or involved hate speech and thus clearly violated the YouTube terms of service. Some ridiculed the king—by depicting him with his feet on his head, for example—and were clearly illegal under Thai law but not U.S. law. And others—criticizing the Thai lèse-majesté law itself—weren't illegal in Thailand but offended the government.

After an extensive debate with McLaughlin and Walker, Wong concluded that since the lèse-majesté law had broad democratic support in Thailand, it would be better to remove the videos that obviously violated Thai law while refusing to remove the videos that offended the government but didn't seem to be illegal. All three told me they were reassured by the fact that Google could accommodate the Thai government by blocking just the videos that were clearly illegal in Thailand (and blocking those for Thai users only), leaving them free to exercise their independent judgment about videos closer to the line. The Thai government was apparently able to live with this solution.

Over the past couple of years, Google and its various applications have been blocked, to different degrees, by 24 countries. Blogger is blocked in Pakistan, for example, and Orkut in Saudi Arabia. Meanwhile, governments are increasingly pressuring telecom companies like Comcast and Verizon to block controversial speech at the network level. Europe and the U.S. recently agreed to require Internet service providers to identify and block child pornography, and in Europe there are growing demands for network-wide blocking of terrorist-incitement videos. As a result, Wong and her colleagues said they worried that Google's ability to make case-by-case decisions about what links and videos are accessible through Google's sites may be slowly circumvented, as countries are requiring the companies that give us access to the Internet to build top-down censorship into the network pipes.

It's NOT ONLY foreign countries that are eager to restrict speech on Google and YouTube. Last May, Senator Joseph Lieberman's staff contacted Google and demanded that the company remove from YouTube dozens of what he described as jihadist videos. (Around the same time, Google was under pressure from "Operation YouTube Smackdown," a grass-roots Web campaign by conservative bloggers and advocates to flag videos and ask YouTube to remove them.) After viewing the videos one by one, Wong and her colleagues removed some of the videos but refused to remove those that they decided didn't violate YouTube guidelines. Lieberman wasn't satisfied. In an angry follow-up letter to Eric Schmidt, the C.E.O. of Google, Lieberman demanded that all content he characterized as being "produced by Islamist terrorist organizations" be immediately removed from YouTube as a matter of corporate judgment—even videos that didn't feature hate speech or violent content or violate U.S. law. Wong and her colleagues responded by saying, "YouTube encourages free speech and defends everyone's right to express unpopular points of view." In September, Google and YouTube announced new guidelines prohibiting videos "intended to incite violence."

In addition to Lieberman, another outspoken critic of supposed liberal bias at YouTube and Google is Michelle Malkin, the conservative columnist and blogger. Malkin became something of a cause célèbre among YouTube critics in 2006, when she created a two-minute movie called "First, They Came" in the wake of the violent response to the Danish anti-Muhammad cartoons. After showing pictures of the victims of jihadist violence (like the Dutch filmmaker Theo Van Gogh) and signs declaring "Behead Those Who Insult Islam," the video asks, "Who's next?" and displays the dates of terrorist attacks in America, London, Madrid, and Bali.

Nearly seven months after she posted the video, Malkin told me she was "flabbergasted" to receive an email message from YouTube saying the video had been removed for its "inappropriate content." When Malkin asked why the video was removed, she received no response, and when she posted a video appealing to YouTube to reinstate it, that video, too, was deleted with what she calls the "false claim" that it had been removed at her request. Malkin remains dissatisfied with YouTube's response. "I'm completely flummoxed about what their standards are," she said. "The standards need to be clear, they need to be consistent and they need to be more responsive."

I watched the "First, They Came" video, which struck me as powerful political commentary that contains neither hate speech nor graphic violence, and I asked why it was taken down. According to a YouTube spokesman, the takedown was a routine one that hadn't been reviewed by higher-ups. The spokesman said he couldn't comment on particular cases, but he forwarded a link to Malkin's current YouTube channel, noting that it contains 55 anti-jihadist videos similar to "First, They Came," none of which have been taken down. ("First, They Came" can now be found on Malkin's YouTube channel, too.)

The removal of Malkin's video may have been an innocent mistake. But it serves as a reminder that one person's principled political protest is another person's hate speech, and distinguishing between the two in hard cases is a lot to ask of a low-level YouTube reviewer. In addition, the publicity that attended the removal of Malkin's video only underscores the fact that in the vast majority of cases in which material is taken down, the decision to do so is never explained or contested. The video goes down, and that's the end of it.

Yet even in everyday cases, it's often no easier to determine whether the content of a video is actually objectionable. When I visited YouTube, the management showed me a flagged French video of a man doubled over. Was he coughing? Or in pain? Or playacting? It was hard to say. The YouTube managers said they might send the item to a team of French-language reviewers for further inspection, but if the team decided to take down the video, its reasons would most likely never become public.

As THE LAW professor Tim Wu told me, to trust Google, you have to be something of a monarchist, willing to trust the near-sovereign discretion of Wong and her colleagues. That's especially true in light of the Global Network Initiative, the set of voluntary principles for protecting free expression and privacy endorsed last month by leading Internet companies like Google and leading human rights and online-advocacy groups like the Center for Democracy and Technology. Google and other companies say they hope that by acting collectively, they can be more effective in resisting censorship requests from repressive governments and, when that isn't possible, create a trail of accountability.

Google is indeed more friendly to free speech than the governments of most of the countries in which it operates. But even many of those who are impressed by Wong and her colleagues say the Google "Decider" model is impractical in the long run, because, as broadband use expands rapidly, it will be unrealistic to expect such a small group of people to make ad hoc decisions about permissible speech for the entire world. "It's a 24-hour potential problem, every moment of the day, and because of what the foreign governments can do, like put people in jail, it creates a series of issues that are very, very difficult to deal with," Ambassador David Gross, the U.S. coordinator for International Communications and Information Policy at the State Department, told me. I asked Wong whether she thought the Decider model was feasible in the long term, and to my surprise, she said no. "I think the Decider model is an inconsistent model because the Internet is big and Google isn't the only one making the decisions," she told me.

When I pressed Wong and her colleagues about who they thought should make these decisions, they said they would be happiest, of course, if more countries would adopt U.S.-style free-speech protections. Knowing that that is unlikely, they said they would prefer that countries around the world set up accountable bodies that provide direct guidance about what controversial content to restrict. As an example of his preferred alternative, Andrew McLaughlin pointed to Germany, which has established a state agency that gathers the U.R.L.'s of sites hosting Nazi and violent content illegal under German law and gives the list to an industry body, which then passes it on to Google so that it can block the material on its German site. (Whenever Google blocks material there or on its other foreign sites, it indicates in the search results that it has done so.)

It is striking—and revealing—that Wong and her colleagues would prefer to put themselves out of business. But it is worth noting that even if Google's suggestion were adopted, and governments around the world began to set up national review boards that told Google what content to remove, then those review boards might protect far less free speech than Google's lawyers have. When I raised this concern, McLaughlin said he hoped that the growing trends to censor speech, at the network level and elsewhere, would be resisted by millions of individual users who would agitate against censorship as they experienced the benefits of free speech.

There's much to be said for McLaughlin's optimism about online free-speech activism. Consider recent experiences in Turkey, where a grass-roots "censuring the censors" movement led more than 400 Turkish bloggers to shutter their Web sites in solidarity with mainstream sites that were banned for carrying content that, among other things, insulted Turkey's founding father. In America, and around the world, the boundaries of free speech have always been shaped more by political activism than by judicial decisions or laws. But what is left out of McLaughlin's vision is uncertainty about one question: the future ethics and behavior of gatekeepers like Google itself.

"Right now, we're trusting Google because it's good, but of course, we run the risk that the day will come when Google goes bad," Wu told me. In his view, that day might come when Google allowed its automated Web crawlers, or search bots, to be used for law-enforcement and national-security purposes. "Under pressure to fight terrorism or to pacify repressive governments, Google could track everything we've searched for, everything we're writing on gmail, everything we're writing on Google docs, to figure out who we are and what we do," he said. "It would make the Internet a much scarier place for free expression." The question of free speech online isn't just about what a company like Google lets us read or see; it's also about what it does with what we write, search and view.

Wu's fears that violations of privacy could chill free speech are grounded in recent history: in China in 2004, Yahoo turned over to the Chinese government important account information connected to the email address of Shi Tao, a Chinese dissident who was imprisoned as a result. Yahoo has since come to realize that the best way of resisting subpoenas from repressive governments is to ensure that private data can't be turned over, even if a government demands it. In some countries, I was told by Michael Samway, who heads Yahoo's human rights efforts, Yahoo is now able to store communications data and search queries offshore and limits access of local employees, so Yahoo can't be forced to turn over this information even if it is ordered to do so.

Isolating, or better still, purging data is the best way of protecting privacy and free expression in the Internet age: it's the only way of guaranteeing that government officials can't force companies like Google and Yahoo to turn over information that allows individuals to be identified. Google, which refused to discuss its data-purging policies on the record, has raised the suspicion of advocacy groups like Privacy International. Google announced in September that it would anonymize all the I.P. addresses on its server logs after nine months. Until that time, however, it will continue to store a wealth of personal information about our search results and viewing habits—in part to improve its targeted advertising and therefore its profits. As Wu suggests, it would be a catastrophe for privacy and free speech if this information fell into the wrong hands.

"The idea that the user is sovereign has transformed the meaning of free speech," Wu said enthusiastically about the Internet age. But Google is not just a neutral platform for sovereign users; it is also a company in the advertising and media business. In the future, Wu said, it might slant its search results to favor its own media applications or to bury its competitors. If Google allowed its search results to be biased for economic reasons, it would transform the way we think about Google as a neutral free-speech tool. The only editor is supposed to be a neutral algorithm. But that would make it all the more insidious if the search algorithm were to become biased.

"During the heyday of Microsoft, people feared that the owners of the operating systems could leverage their monopolies to protect their own products against competitors," says the Internet scholar Lawrence Lessig of Stanford Law School. "That dynamic is tiny compared to what people fear about Google. They have enormous control over a platform of all the world's data, and everything they do is designed to improve their control of the underlying data. If your whole game is to increase market share, it's hard to do good, and to gather data in ways that don't raise privacy concerns or that might help repressive governments to block controversial content."

Given their clashing and sometimes self-contradictory missions—to obey local laws, repressive or not, and to ensure that information knows no bounds; to do no evil and to be everywhere in a sometimes evil world—Wong and her colleagues at Google seem to be working impressively to put the company's long-term commitment to free expression above its short-term financial interests. But they won't be at Google forever, and if history is any guide, they may eventually be replaced with lawyers who are more concerned about corporate profits than about free expression. "We're at the dawn of a new technology," Walker told me, referring not simply to Google but also to the many different ways we now interact online. "And when people try to come up with the best metaphors to describe it, all the metaphors run out. We've built this spaceship, but we really don't know where it will take us."

Tortured Reasoning

David Rose

from *Vanity Fair*

George W. Bush defended harsh interrogations by pointing to intelligence breakthroughs, but a surprising number of counterterrorist officials say that, apart from being wrong, torture just doesn't work. Delving into two high-profile cases, the author exposes the tactical costs of prisoner abuse.

BY THE LAST days of March 2002, more than six months after 9/11, President George W. Bush's promise "to hunt down and to find those folks who committed this act" was starting to sound a little hollow. True, Afghanistan had been invaded and the Taliban toppled from power. But Osama bin Laden had vanished from the caves of Tora Bora, and none of his key al-Qaeda lieutenants were in U.S. captivity. Intelligence about what the terrorists might be planning next was almost nonexistent. "The panic in the executive branch was palpable," recalls Mike Scheuer, the former C.I.A. official who set up and ran the agency's Alec Station, the unit devoted to tracking bin Laden.

Early in the morning of March 28, in the moonlit police-barracks yard in Faisalabad, Pakistan, hopes were high that this worrisome intelligence deficit was about to be corrected. Some 300 armed personnel waited in silence: 10 three-man teams of Americans, drawn equally from the C.I.A. and the F.B.I., together with much greater numbers from Pakistan's police force and Inter-services Intelligence (ISI). In order to maximize their chances of surprise, they planned to hit 10 addresses simultaneously. One of them, they believed, was a safe house containing a man whose name had been familiar to U.S. analysts for years: Zayn al-Abidin Muhammad Hussein, a 30-year-old Saudi Arabian better known as Abu Zubaydah. "I'd followed him for a decade," Scheuer says. "If there was one guy you could call a 'hub,' he was it."

The plan called for the police to go in first, followed by the Americans and ISI men, whose job would be to gather laptops, documents, and other physical evidence. A few moments before three a.m., the crackle of gunfire erupted. Abu Zubaydah had been shot and wounded, but was alive and in custody. As those who had planned it had hoped, his capture was to prove an epochal event—but in ways they had not envisaged.

Four months after Abu Zubaydah's capture, two lawyers from the Department of Justice, John Yoo and Jay Bybee, delivered their notorious memo on torture, which stated that coercive treatment that fell short of causing suffering equivalent to the pain of organ failure or death was not legally torture, an analysis that—as far as the U.S. government was concerned—sanctioned the abusive treatment of detainees at the C.I.A.'s secret prisons and at Guantánamo Bay. But, as Jane Mayer writes in her recent book, *The Dark Side* (Doubleday), Abu Zubaydah had been subjected to coercive interrogation techniques well before that, becoming the first U.S. prisoner in the Global War on Terror to undergo waterboarding.

The case of Abu Zubaydah is a suitable place to begin answering some pressing but little-considered questions. Putting aside all legal and ethical issues (not to mention the P.R. ramifications), does such treatment—categorized unhesitatingly by the

International Committee of the Red Cross as torture—actually work, in the sense of providing reliable, actionable intelligence? Is it superior to other interrogation methods, and if they had the choice, free of moral qualms or the fear of prosecution, would interrogators use it freely?

President Bush has said it works extremely well, insisting it has been a vital weapon in America's counterterrorist arsenal. Vice President Dick Cheney and C.I.A. director Michael Hayden have made similar assertions. In fact, time and again, Bush has been given opportunities to distance his administration from the use of coercive methods but has stood steadfastly by their use. His most detailed exposition came in a White House announcement on September 6, 2006, when he said such tactics had led to the capture of top al-Qaeda operatives and had thwarted a number of planned attacks, including plots to strike U.S. Marines in Djibouti, fly planes into office towers in London, and detonate a radioactive "dirty" bomb in America. "Were it not for this program, our intelligence community believes that al-Qaeda and its allies would have succeeded in launching another attack against the American homeland. By giving us information about terrorist plans we could not get anywhere else, this program has saved innocent lives."

Really? In researching this article, I spoke to numerous counterterrorist officials from agencies on both sides of the Atlantic. Their conclusion is unanimous: not only have coercive methods failed to generate significant and actionable intelligence, they have also caused the squandering of resources on a massive scale through false leads, chimerical plots, and unnecessary safety alerts—with Abu Zubaydah's case one of the most glaring examples.

Here, they say, far from exposing a deadly plot, all torture did was lead to more torture of his supposed accomplices while also providing some misleading "information" that boosted the administration's argument for invading Iraq.

Everything that was to go wrong with the interrogation of Abu Zubaydah flowed from a first, fatal misjudgment. Although his name had long been familiar to the C.I.A., that did not make him an operational terrorist planner or, as Bush put it in September 2006, "a senior terrorist leader and a trusted associate of Osama bin Laden." Instead, Scheuer says, he was "the main cog in the way they organized," a point of contact for Islamists from many parts of the globe seeking combat training in the Afghan camps. However, only a tiny percentage would ever be tapped for recruitment by al-Qaeda.

According to Scheuer, Abu Zubaydah "never swore *bayat* [al-Qaeda's oath of allegiance] to bin Laden," and the enemy he focused on was Israel, not the U.S. After Abu Zubaydah's capture, Dan Coleman, an F.B.I. counterterrorist veteran, had the job of combing through Abu Zubaydah's journals and other documents seized from his Faisalabad safe house. He confirms Scheuer's assessment. "Abu Zubaydah was like a receptionist, like the guy at the front desk here," says Coleman, gesturing toward the desk clerk in the lobby of the Virginia hotel where we have met. "He takes their papers, he sends them out. It's an important position, but he's not recruiting or planning." It was also significant that he was not well versed in al-Qaeda's tight internal-security methods: "That was why his name had been cropping up for years."

Declassified reports of legal interviews with Abu Zubaydah at his current residence, Guantánamo Bay, suggest that he lacked the capacity to do much more. In the early 1990s, fighting in the Afghan civil war that followed the Soviet withdrawal, he was injured so badly that he could not speak for almost two years. "I tried to become al-Qaeda," Abu Zubaydah told his lawyer, Brent Mickum, "but they said, 'No, you are illiterate and can't even remember how to shoot.'" Coleman found Abu Zubaydah's diary to be startlingly useless. "There's nothing in there that refers to anything outside his head, not even when he saw something on the news, not about any al-Qaeda attack, not even 9/11," he says.

"All it does is reveal someone in torment. Based on what I saw of his personality, he could not be what they say he was."

In May 2008, a report by Glenn Fine, the Department of Justice inspector general, stated that, as he recovered in the hospital from the bullet wounds sustained when he was captured, Abu Zubaydah began to cooperate with two F.B.I. agents. It was a promising start, but "within a few days," wrote Fine, he was handed over to the C.I.A., whose agents soon reported that he was providing only "throw-away information" and that, according to Fine, they "needed to diminish his capacity to resist." His new interrogators continued to question him by very different means at so-called black-site prisons in Thailand and Eastern Europe. They were determined to prove he was much more important than the innkeeper of a safe house.

Bush discussed Abu Zubaydah's treatment in his 2006 announcement. "As his questioning proceeded, it became clear that he had received training on how to resist interrogation. And so the C.I.A. used an alternative set of procedures…. The procedures were tough, and they were safe, and lawful, and necessary." Soon, Bush went on, Abu Zubaydah "began to provide information on key al-Qaeda operatives, including information that helped us find and capture more of those responsible for the attacks on September 11." Among them, Bush said, were Khalid Sheikh Mohammed, the alleged 9/11 mastermind, and his fellow conspirator Ramzi Binalshibh. In fact, Binalshibh was not arrested for another six months and K.S.M. not for another year. In K.S.M.'s case, the lead came from an informant motivated by a $25 million reward.

As for K.S.M. himself, who (as Jane Mayer writes) was waterboarded, reportedly hung for hours on end from his wrists, beaten, and subjected to other agonies for weeks, Bush said he provided "many details of other plots to kill innocent Americans." K.S.M. was certainly knowledgeable. It would be surprising if he gave up nothing of value. But according to a former senior C.I.A. official, who read all the interrogation reports on K.S.M.,

"90 percent of it was total fucking bullshit." A former Pentagon analyst adds: "K.S.M. produced no actionable intelligence. He was trying to tell us how stupid we were."

It is, perhaps, a little late, more than six years after detainees began to be interrogated at Guantánamo Bay and at the C.I.A.'s black-site prisons, to be asking whether torture works. Yet according to numerous C.I.A. and F.B.I. officials interviewed for this article, at the time this question really mattered, in the months after 9/11, no one seriously addressed it. Those who advocated a policy that would lead America to deploy methods it had always previously abhorred simply assumed they would be worthwhile. Non-governmental advocates of torture, such as the Harvard legal scholar Alan Dershowitz, have emphasized the "ticking bomb" scenario: the hypothetical circumstance when only torture will make the captured terrorist reveal where he—or his colleagues—has planted the timed nuclear device. Inside the C.I.A., says a retired senior officer who was privy to the agency's internal debate, there was hardly any argument about the value of coercive methods: "Nobody in intelligence believes in the ticking bomb. It's just a way of framing the debate for public consumption. That is not an intelligence reality."

There is, alas, no shortage of evidence from earlier times that torture produces bad intelligence. "It is incredible what people say under the compulsion of torture," wrote the German Jesuit Friedrich von Spee in 1631, "and how many lies they will tell about themselves and about others; in the end, whatever the torturers want to be true, is true."

The unreliability of intelligence acquired by torture was taken as a given in the early years of the C.I.A., whose 1963 kubark interrogation manual stated: "Intense pain is quite likely to produce false confessions, concocted as a means of escaping from distress. A time-consuming delay results, while investigation is conducted and the admissions are proven untrue. During this respite the interrogatee can pull himself together. He may even use the time to think up new, more complex 'admissions' that take still longer to disprove."

A 1957 study by Albert Biderman, an Air Force sociologist, described how brainwashing had been achieved by depriving prisoners of sleep, exposing them to cold, and forcing them into agonizing "stress positions" for long periods. In July 2008, *The New York Times* reported that Biderman's work formed the basis of a 2002 interrogators' training class at Guantánamo Bay. That the methods it described had once been used to generate Communist propaganda had apparently been forgotten.

Experience derived from 1990s terrorism cases also casts doubt on torture's value. For example, in March 1993, F.B.I. agents flew to Cairo to take charge of an Egyptian named Mahmud Abouhalima, who would be convicted for having bombed the World Trade Center a month earlier. Abouhalima had already been tortured by Egyptian intelligence agents for 10 days, and had the wounds to prove it. As U.S. investigators should have swiftly realized, his statements in Egypt were worthless, among them claims that the bombing was sponsored by Iranian businessmen, although, apparently, their sworn enemy, Iraq, had also played a part.

In the fall of 2001, publications such as *Newsweek, The Washington Post,* and *The Wall Street Journal* ran articles suggesting torture might be essential to prevent further attacks. All cited the case of Abdul Hakim Murad, a Pakistani terrorist in possession of explosives arrested in the Philippines in January 1995, who was later convicted in New York. According to Dershowitz, his coerced confessions about the "Bojinka" plot, to blow up 11 airliners over the Pacific, supported the claim that "torture sometimes does work and can sometimes prevent major disasters."

Murad was certainly tortured. At his trial in 1996, transcripts of his interrogation by the Philippines National Police contained pauses and gasps, which his lawyer claimed were the result of his enduring a procedure much like waterboarding. But did it really pay intelligence dividends? With Murad's arrest, the plot was blown. As Professor Stephanie Athey of Lasell College noted in a 2007 article, Dershowitz's claim that the torture prevented a major disaster is false. A computer seized in Murad's apartment held details of the flights he planned to attack, detonator-timer settings, and photos of some of his co-conspirators, together with their aliases, so enabling their subsequent arrest. It was this, Mike Scheuer says, not Murad's interrogation, that provided more useful intelligence.

Equally significant was what Murad didn't give up under torture. Bojinka was partly the brainchild of none other than Khalid Sheikh Mohammed, later alleged to be the chief planner of 9/11. He had been living in the Philippines, but apparently Murad said nothing that might have helped his interrogators find him: he was not captured until 2003.

On April 10, 2002, 13 days after Abu Zubaydah's capture, in Faisalabad, a 23-year-old Ethiopian named Binyam Mohamed was detained at the airport in Karachi, Pakistan, attempting to board a flight to London, where he had been living for seven years. Information about the case drawn up by the British security service M.I.5, and obtained by *Vanity Fair*, suggests that if Mohamed was a terrorist his tradecraft was unimpressive: he was stopped because he was using a passport that obviously belonged to someone else, his friend Fouad Zouaoui—the second time that Mohamed had tried to leave Pakistan on Zouaoui's papers. He also had a heroin problem.

In notes by his attorney, Clive Stafford Smith, made from days of interviews with him at Guantánamo, the picture that emerges is one more of naïveté than wickedness. He said he went to Pakistan, and then Afghanistan, in June 2001, partly because he wanted to kick his drug habit (arguably, the world's biggest source of opium was not an ideal place) and partly to ascertain whether Taliban-controlled Afghanistan was a "good Islamic country." In any event, there is no dispute that he fled across the border into Pakistan as soon as he could after 9/11.

The first 10 days of Mohamed's detention, at Landi prison, near Karachi, were not, on his account, comfortable, but he was not tortured or abused. But after he was moved to a Pakistani security jail, around April 20, he began to be abused. A few days later, when he was questioned for the first time by U.S. agents, his treatment worsened dramatically.

"They seemed to think I was some kind of top al-Qaeda person," Mohamed said. "How? It was less than six months since I converted to Islam, and before that I was using drugs!" After the Americans' visit, Mohamed said, he was hung by his wrists for hours on end, so that his feet barely touched the ground. Suspended thus, he said, he was beaten regularly by Pakistani guards. He said he was also threatened with a gun.

U.S. interest in Mohamed appears to have been triggered by an unlucky coincidence. It so happened that in the period in early April before Abu Zubaydah's torture began, when he was starting to cooperate with the F.B.I., he gave up the name of one of those who had passed through his safe house en route to an Afghan camp—that of Jose Padilla, a former Chicago gang member. "He probably remembered Padilla because he was a U.S. citizen, and that was rare," says the former F.B.I. al-Qaeda specialist Dan Coleman.

Mohamed has maintained that if he had ever met Padilla it would have been a fleeting, chance encounter, perhaps when they both fled Afghanistan, and he has no memory of it. But the first time Mohamed tried to fly to London via Zurich, around April 4, Padilla was booked on the same flight. Their ultimate destinations were different: Padilla planned to spend time in Egypt before returning to Chicago. But the fact they were starting their journeys together, says an F.B.I. agent who attended official briefings about the case, convinced American agencies that they shared some joint purpose. "It was simply that—flight coincidence," he says. "I never saw any evidence that Padilla and Mohamed met."

By late April, Abu Zubaydah was being tortured and giving up details of a plot that sounded truly terrifying: a plan for Padilla to build and detonate a radioactive dirty bomb in America. But even at the outset, some who worked in U.S. counterterrorism were skeptical. "If there is a dirty bomb, you'd better take it seriously, because as bad as 9/11 was, a dirty bomb would be a hundred times worse," says the former F.B.I. agent who attended the case briefings. "It was clear that Padilla had some form of training, that he was a sympathizer. But to claim he really had a plan to do a dirty bomb? That's tough. You show me he knew how to go and get it. That he knew how to make it. They never had that."

Convinced that the dirty-bomb plot was real, those interrogating Binyam Mohamed assumed that he must be part of it, and if he could not fill in missing details, he must have been covering up. Agents such as the F.B.I.'s Jack Cloonan, who spent years fighting al-Qaeda before his retirement in 2002, had learned that it had an impressive "quality-control system," which meant "they looked for people with the right makeup, they did their own due diligence, and they would not pick weak guys"—not, typically, heroin addicts. But no one was listening to these agents.

M.I.5 seems to have shared the C.I.A.'s groupthink. Sources in London say that its agents also assumed that anything Mohamed said to try to defend himself must be a lie. One admission he did make was that he had seen a Web site with instructions on how to make a hydrogen bomb, but he was apparently claiming it was a joke. The intelligence agencies believed this was a smoking gun, notwithstanding Mohamed's bizarre statement that the instructions included mixing bleach with uranium-238 in a bucket and rotating it around one's head for 45 minutes. Neither the British nor the Americans thought Mohamed's claim that the Web site was a joke was credible: his "confession" to reading instructions about building nuclear weapons on the Internet was cited in Mohamed's Guantánamo charge sheet. Yet it *was* a joke: such a Web site, with instructions about how to refine bomb-grade uranium with bleach and a bucket, has been doing the rounds on the World Wide Web since at least 1994. In 2005, the conservative columnist Michelle Malkin cited it in her blog as evidence of al-Qaeda's deadly intentions. She was swiftly disabused by readers, who, unlike the C.I.A. and M.I.5, immediately recognized it as satire.

But even M.I.5 couldn't help but notice "glaring inconsistencies" among the different accounts of the plot being given by those getting interrogated. And instead of asking whether the plot was real, the investigators seem to have assumed that the different accounts of those being interrogated were merely an attempt to protect al-Qaeda operations.

Clive Stafford Smith believes that the weakness of the dirty-bomb charge against Padilla may well explain what happened to Binyam Mohamed: "Maybe what they were trying to do was turn him into a prosecution witness." After all, he had already confessed in Pakistan, under torture that had been, in comparison with what was to come, relatively mild. But on July 21, 2002, as the plane's flight log later confirmed, he was flown aboard a Gulfstream V jet chartered by the C.I.A. to Rabat, in Morocco. There he was to spend the next 18 months.

With the help of Stafford Smith, he later assembled a diary describing his treatment there. Amid numerous beatings in Rabat, Mohamed wrote, "They'd ask me a question. I'd say one thing. They'd say it was a lie. I'd say another. They'd say it was a lie. I could not work out what they wanted to hear." He also said the Moroccans repeatedly cut his chest and genitals with a razor. Finally he was subjected to further harsh treatment in the "Dark Prison" near Kabul, Afghanistan, after being spirited away on another C.I.A. flight in January 2004.

After another nine months, he was brought to Guantánamo, where he remains. He filed a habeas corpus lawsuit in federal court in the District of Columbia, a claim that there was no credible reason for his continued detention, and in its attempt to defend this, the administration in October 2008 dropped all mention of the dirty-bomb plot. In Guantánamo's parallel quasi-legal world of military commissions, where the rules make it much harder to exclude evidence derived from torture, the Pentagon in May 2008 issued a charge sheet against Mohamed. It said that having trained in various al-Qaeda camps and taken instruction from bin Laden, Mohamed "reviewed technical information concerning the construction of an improvised radioactive bomb" with K.S.M. and decided with Padilla to detonate one in America.

In October, the charges were withdrawn, after the prosecutor, Lieutenant Colonel Darrel Vandeveld, resigned. Later he told the BBC he had concerns at the repeated suppression of evidence that could prove prisoners' innocence. Meanwhile, as of December 2008, Mohamed's lawyers were fighting separate court cases to force the U.S. government in Washington and the British government in London to disclose all the information they have about Mohamed's treatment. (Coincidentally, my sister, Dinah Rose, Q.C., is representing Mohamed in the London case.) Stafford Smith is bound by Draconian restrictions that prevent him from offering any but the blandest comments about the evidence in his client's case. He says, "I know of no evidence against him other than his own confessions, all of which are the bitter fruit of his abuse."

"There was no dirty-bomb plot. I'm sure it was just Abu Zubaydah trying to get them excited," says the F.B.I.'s Dan Coleman. "There's never been any corroboration except the confessions of Binyam Mohamed under torture. No one was willing to take their time." But, in the words of the former C.I.A. official Mike Scheuer, "That dirty-bomb business put the fear of God into these people in the administration." As a result, he says, "they may well have sent Binyam Mohamed somewhere where the authorities would do things we wouldn't—or couldn't."

On June 10, 2002, then attorney general John Ashcroft interrupted a visit to Moscow to speak to reporters: "I am pleased to announce today a significant step forward in the war on terrorism. We have captured a known terrorist who was exploring a plan to build and explode a radiological dispersion device, or 'dirty bomb,' in the United States." He meant Jose Padilla, who had been arrested as he flew into Chicago on May 8. The president, Ashcroft said, had designated Padilla an "enemy combatant," and he had been removed from civilian custody to a navy brig. In due course, Ashcroft said, he would be tried by a military commission.

"Let me be clear: we know from multiple independent and corroborating sources that Abdullah Al Mujahir [Padilla's nom de guerre] was closely associated with al-Qaeda and that ... he was involved in planning future terrorist attacks on innocent American civilians in the United States," Ashcroft said. Had his dirty bomb gone off, it could have caused "mass death and injury."

The shakiness of Ashcroft's "multiple independent and corroborating sources" claim was demonstrated by an affidavit from an F.B.I. agent, Joe Ennis, in support of Padilla's detention. Referring to Binyam Mohamed as "Subject-1," it said that his "wife" had told law-enforcement authorities that he "would often become emotional and cry when he discussed his willingness to die for his God." Strangely enough, Mohamed was and remains unmarried.

Mohamed, the affidavit said, "has not been completely candid about his association with Al Qaeda, and his own terrorist activities," and was trying to "mislead or confuse U.S. law enforcement." But it was clear that after weeks of abuse he had started to crack. According to Ennis, he had already told his interrogators that he and Padilla had "researched the construction of a uranium-enhanced explosive device"; that Padilla had been to meetings with al-Qaeda officials; and that he believed Padilla had been ordered to return to America.

In the brig, Padilla's attorneys claimed, he too was tortured. He was deprived of all contact with the outside world for two and a half years, and, according to one court filing, "He would be shackled and manacled, with a belly chain, for hours in his cell. Noxious fumes would be introduced to his room causing his eyes and nose to run. The temperature of his cell would be manipulated, making the cell extremely cold for long stretches of time." Chained in agonizing "stress positions" repeatedly, he was also allegedly "threatened with imminent execution.... Often he had to endure multiple interrogators who would scream, shake, and otherwise assault [him]."

The government did not deny these assertions, only the claim that they amounted to torture. Donna Newman, Padilla's attorney before he was taken to the brig, says that afterward "he was not the same person. Beforehand, he was engaged in his case; he asked pertinent questions. When I saw him again, he hardly said a word. He had no interest in what was happening, even though his case was nearing the Supreme Court."

Under this pressure, Padilla produced ever more elaborate confessions. Former deputy attorney general James Comey said in June 2004 that Padilla spoke of discussing the dirty bomb with Khalid Sheikh Mohammed, of an instruction from K.S.M. to blow up apartments by filling them with gas and igniting it, and of a dinner party with Binyam Mohamed, K.S.M., and al-Qaeda bigwigs the night before he left Pakistan.

Very senior officials had a lot invested in Padilla. But in November 2005, three days before the Justice Department was to file a brief before the Supreme Court in response to his lawyers' claim that his treatment was unconstitutional, the administration returned him to civilian custody. With all mention of the dirty-bomb plot deleted, he stood trial in Florida on far less serious charges of conspiracy to murder, maim, and kidnap, and providing material support to terrorist organizations, and in January 2008 he was sentenced to 17 years and four months in prison. "The dirty-bomb plot was simply not credible," Jack Cloonan says. "The government would never have given up that case if there was any hint of credibility to it. Padilla didn't stand trial for it, because there was no evidence to support it."

On March 27, 2007, Abu Zubaydah was able to make a rare public statement, at a "Combatant Status-Review Tribunal" at Guantánamo—a military hearing convened to determine whether he should continue to be detained. Everything he said about the details of his treatment was redacted from the unclassified record. But a few relevant remarks remain: "I was nearly before half die plus [because] what they do [to] torture me. There I was not afraid from die because I do believe I will be shahid [martyr], but as God make me as a human and I weak, so they say yes, I say okay, I do I do, but leave me. They say no, we don't want to. You to admit you do this, we want you to give us more information ... they want what's after more information about more operations, so I can't. They keep torturing me."

The tribunal president, a colonel whose name is redacted, asked him: "So I understand that during this treatment, you said things to make them stop and then those statements were actually untrue, is that correct?" Abu Zubaydah replied: "Yes."

Some of those statements, say two senior intelligence analysts who worked on them at the time, concerned the issue that in the spring of 2002 interested the Bush administration more than almost any other—the supposed operational relationship between al-Qaeda and Iraq. Given his true position in the jihadist hierarchy, Abu Zubaydah "would not have known that if it was true," says Coleman. "But you can lead people down a course and make them say anything."

Some of what he did say was leaked by the administration: for example, the claim that bin Laden and his ally Abu Musab al-Zarqawi were working directly with Saddam Hussein to destabilize the autonomous Kurdish region in northern Iraq. There was much more, says the analyst who worked at the Pentagon: "I first saw the reports soon after Abu Zubaydah's capture. There was a lot of stuff about the nuts and bolts of al-Qaeda's supposed relationship with the Iraqi Intelligence Service. The intelligence community was lapping this up, and so was the administration, obviously. Abu Zubaydah was saying Iraq and al-Qaeda had an operational relationship. It was everything the administration hoped it would be."

Within the administration, Abu Zubaydah's interrogation was "an important chapter," the second analyst says: overall, his interrogation "product" was deemed to be more significant than the claims made by Ibn al-Shaykh al-Libi, another al-Qaeda captive, who in early 2002 was tortured in Egypt at the C.I.A.'s behest. After all, Abu Zubaydah was being interviewed by Americans. Like the former Pentagon official, this official had no idea that Abu Zubaydah had been tortured.

"As soon as I learned that the reports had come from torture, once my anger had subsided I understood the damage it had done," the Pentagon analyst says. "I was so angry, knowing that the higher-ups in the administration knew he was tortured, and that the information he was giving up was tainted by the torture, and that it became one reason to attack Iraq."

One result of Abu Zubaydah's torture was that the F.B.I.'s assistant director for counterterrorism, Pasquale D'Amuro, persuaded Director Robert Mueller that the bureau should play no part in future C.I.A. interrogations that used extreme techniques forbidden by the F.B.I. The Justice Department's Glenn Fine indicated in a statement before the U.S. Senate that the main reason was that the agency's techniques would "not be effective in obtaining accurate information."

If torture doesn't work, what does? The evidence suggests that when the Bush administration decided to ignore many of America's most experienced counterterrorist agents and go for torture in 2001 and 2002, it shut down rich sources of intelligence. In the biggest terrorist case of the 1990s, the bombings of the U.S. Embassies in Kenya and Tanzania in 1998 that killed more than 220 people, the F.B.I.'s Cloonan and his colleagues were able to persuade three of the main conspirators not only to talk to them but also to give prosecution testimony in court. Here Morocco, the U.S. ally where Binyam Mohamed was sent to be tortured in 2002, provided assistance of a very different order.

Eighteen months after the attacks, Cloonan traced L'Houssaine Kherchtou, also known as Joe the Moroccan, an al-Qaeda operative who had played a key role, to his hiding place, in Sudan. The Moroccans concocted a story to lure him home, and when he arrived in Rabat he was arrested.

After reports of Abu Zubaydah's torture, F.B.I. director Robert Mueller agreed that the bureau should play no part in future C.I.A. interrogations that use extreme techniques.

Cloonan says, "We all went to a beautiful safe house outside of town, with gazelles bouncing around in the grounds and three solid meals fit for a king each day. We all sat on sofas in a big room—me, Ali Soufan [an F.B.I. colleague], Pat Fitzgerald [the U.S. attorney then in charge of a special counterterrorist section in New York], a C.I.A. guy, and two Moroccan colonels. The Moroccans said he'd never talk. He never shut up for 10 days." Cloonan had done his homework: "His wife needed money for medical treatment in Khartoum, and al-Qaeda had failed to provide it." That gave Cloonan his "in."

The intelligence Kherchtou provided, at a time when U.S. knowledge about al-Qaeda was still perfunctory, was invaluable. "He told us about a lot of things," says Cloonan. "We learned how they recruited people, their front organizations, how they used NGOs, false passports, what they thought about kidnapping, how they developed targets, did their surveillance, a day in the life of Osama bin Laden, what weapons they used, what vehicles they drove, who was the principal liaison with the Sudanese government, that there was a relationship between al-Qaeda and Hezbollah, how they did their training exercises, their finances, and their membership."

Finally Fitzgerald offered Kherchtou a deal: if he came to New York, pleaded guilty, and testified against the bombers, Fitzgerald would ask the judge to treat him leniently. At first, it looked as if he was going to turn it down. Then, Cloonan says, "I said, 'Joe, you understand English, so I'd like you to go out and pray on this with your two Moroccan brothers.' I thought Fitzy was going to give birth. Joe went out and prayed and came back and said yes." Kherchtou is now in the federal witness-protection program. Thanks in part to his testimony, four of his onetime associates are serving life.

To reach a final calculus of the Bush administration's use of torture will take years. It will require access to a large body of material that for now remains classified, and the weighing not just of information gained against false or missed leads but of the wider consequences: of the damage done to America's influence with its friends, and of the encouragement provided to its enemies. Even harder to quantify is the damage done to institutions and their morale, especially the C.I.A.

"We were done a tremendous disservice by the administration," one official says. "We had no background in this; it's not something we do. They stuck us with a totally unwelcome job and left us hanging out to dry. I'm worried that the next administration is going to prosecute the guys who got involved, and there won't be any presidential pardons at the end of it. It would be O.K. if it were John Ashcroft or Alberto Gonzales. But it won't be. It'll be some poor G.S.-13 who was just trying to do his job."

At the F.B.I., says a seasoned counterterrorist agent, following false leads generated through torture has caused waste and exhaustion. "At least 30 percent of the F.B.I.'s time, maybe 50 percent, in counterterrorism has been spent chasing leads that were bullshit. There are 'lead squads' in every office trying to filter them. But that's ineffective, because there's always that 'What if?' syndrome. I remember a claim that there was a plot to poison candy bought in bulk from Costco. You follow it because someone wants to cover himself. It has a chilling effect. You get burned out, you get jaded. And you think, Why am I chasing all this stuff that isn't true? That leads to a greater problem—that you'll miss the one that is true. The job is 24-7 anyway. It's not like a bank job. But torture has made it harder."

Several of those I interviewed point out the dearth of specific claims the administration has proffered. "The proponents of torture say, 'Look at the body of information that has been obtained by these methods.' But if K.S.M. and Abu Zubaydah did give up stuff, we would have heard the details," says Cloonan. "What we got was pabulum." A former C.I.A. officer adds: "Why can't they say what the good stuff from Abu Zubaydah or K.S.M. is? It's not as if this is sensitive material from a secret, vulnerable source. You're not blowing your source but validating your program. They say they can't do this, even though five or six years have passed, because it's a 'continuing operation.' But has it really taken so long to check it all out?"

Officials who analyzed Abu Zubaydah's interrogation reports say that the reports were afforded the highest value within the Bush administration not because of the many American lives they were going to save but because they could be cited repeatedly against those who doubted the wisdom of ousting Saddam by force.

"We didn't know he'd been waterboarded and tortured when we did that analysis, and the reports were marked as credible as they could be," the former Pentagon analyst tells me. "The White House knew he'd been tortured. I didn't, though I was supposed to be evaluating that intelligence." To draw conclusions about the importance of what Abu Zubaydah said without knowing this crucial piece of the background nullified the value of his work. "It seems to me they were using torture to achieve a political objective. I cannot believe that the president and vice president did not know who was being waterboarded, and what was being given up."

One of the most specific claims Bush made in 2006 was that secret black-site C.I.A. interrogations "helped foil a plot to hijack passenger planes and fly them into Heathrow [airport] and London's Canary Wharf." Could that be true?

One man who knows is Peter Clarke, head of Scotland Yard's Anti-terrorist Branch from the spring of 2002 until May 2008, and as such the U.K.'s chief counterterrorist official, who succeeded in stopping several jihadist attacks that were in advanced stages of planning. Clarke, who has not publicly discussed this issue before, says it is possible that al-Qaeda had considered some project along the lines suggested by Bush, but if so it was nowhere near fruition. "It wasn't at an advanced stage in the sense that there were people here in the U.K. doing it. If they had been, I'd have arrested them."

Perhaps the most dangerous of the plots disrupted on Clarke's watch was through Operation Crevice, the 2004 bust of a gang of seven who had 1.3 tons of homemade explosive material, with which they had intended to blow up targets including a nightclub and a shopping mall. But the lead that led to Crevice came not from torture, Clarke says, but an electronic intercept. He says he can think of only one arrest made by his team that could be said to have been partly the result of C.I.A. interrogations—that of Dhiren Barot, sentenced to life, in 2006, for conspiracy to murder stemming from his plan to attack a range of British targets. But even here, the original lead, reportedly given up by K.S.M., was vague. "All we had was a nom de guerre, Esa al-Hindi, and the claim that he was a serious player and a Brit," Clarke says. "We had no idea who he was. It took weeks and months of painstaking work to identify and find him."

In an interview in London in April 2008, I remind F.B.I. director Robert Mueller of the attacks planned against targets on American soil since 9/11 that his agents have disrupted: for example, a plot to kill soldiers at Fort Dix, New Jersey, and another to wreak mayhem at army recruiting centers and synagogues in and around Torrance, California. These and other homegrown conspiracies were foiled by regular police work. The F.B.I. learned of the Fort Dix plot from a Circuit City store where a technician raised the alarm when asked to copy firearms-training videos, while the Torrance cell was rounded up when cops probed the backgrounds of two of its members after they allegedly robbed a local gas station.

I ask Mueller: So far as he is aware, have any attacks on America been disrupted thanks to intelligence obtained through what the administration still calls "enhanced techniques"?

"I'm really reluctant to answer that," Mueller says. He pauses, looks at an aide, and then says quietly, declining to elaborate: "I don't believe that has been the case."

Gun Rights and Our National Identity Crisis

Daniel Lazare

from *The Nation*

LIKE THE THIRD Amendment against the peacetime quartering of soldiers in private homes, the Second Amendment used to be one of those obscure constitutional provisions that Americans could safely ignore. Legal opinion was agreed: this relic of the late eighteenth century did not confer an individual right "to keep and bear arms," only a collective right on the part of the states to maintain well-regulated militias in the form of local units of the National Guard. While a few gun nuts insisted on their Second Amendment right to turn their homes into mini-arsenals, everyone else knew they were deluded. Everyone knew this because the Supreme Court had supposedly settled the matter by unanimously dismissing any suggestion of an individual right in 1939.

But now everyone knows something else. Ever since a University of Texas law professor named Sanford Levinson published a seminal article, "The Embarrassing Second Amendment," in the *Yale Law Journal* in 1989, the legal academy has had to take another look at a provision that Laurence Tribe, the doyen of liberal constitutionalists, described ten years earlier as having no effect on gun control and as "merely ancillary to other constitutional guarantees of state sovereignty." Now such comfy notions arc out the window as the National Rifle Association's view that the Second Amendment confers an individual right to own guns gains ground. While some scholars, such as Mark Tushnet, author of the new study *Out of Range*, argue that an individual-rights reading still allows for extensive gun control, others are frank enough to admit they're not sure what this oddly constructed amendment does and does not allow (although they'll still hazard a guess). As a prominent constitutional scholar named William Van Alstyne once remarked, "No provision in the Constitution causes one to stumble quite so much on a first reading, or second, or third reading." It is as if the legal academy, shaking its head over the First Amendment, suddenly could not make up its mind as to whether that hallowed text protected free speech or prohibited it.

What's going on here? Surely a mere twenty-seven words, loosely tethered together by three commas and one period, can't be that impenetrable. But they are; and if ever there was a Churchillian "riddle wrapped in a mystery inside an enigma," the Second Amendment is it.

Perhaps the best way to begin unraveling this puzzle is to think of the amendment not as a law but, with apologies to Tom Peyer and Hart Seely, as a bit of blank verse:

> *A well regulated Militia,*
> *being necessary to the security of a free State,*
> *the right of the people to keep and bear Arms,*
> *shall not be infringed.*

It's rhythmic and also somewhat strange, as proper modern verse should be. As to what it actually means, the questions begin with "well regulated" in line one. The phrase is confusing because when Americans hear the word "regulation" or any of its cognates, they usually think of government restrictions on individual liberty. But if a government-regulated militia is necessary for a free society (the meaning, presumably, of "a free State"), then how can the amendment mandate an individual right that the same government must not infringe? It is as if the amendment were telling government to intervene and not intervene at the same time.

This is certainly a head-scratcher. Yet the questions go on. Another concerns line two, which, while asserting that the militia is "necessary to the security of a free State," does not pause to explain why. Perhaps the connection was self-evident in the eighteenth century, but it is certainly not in the twenty-first. Today, we can think of a lot of things that are important to the survival of a free society: democratic expression, honest and fair elections, a good educational system, and a sound and equitable economy. So why does the amendment "privilege" a well-regulated militia above all others?

Finally, there are the questions posed by lines three and four. Why "keep and bear" rather than just "bear"? What does "Arms" mean—muskets, pistols, assault rifles, grenade launchers, nukes? Finally, concerning the phrase "the right of the people to keep and bear Arms," the individualist interpretation holds that eighteenth-century Anglo-Americans viewed this as part of a natural right of armed resistance against tyranny. But if this was the case, why put it in writing? After all, Americans were well armed in the aftermath of the Revolutionary War and hair-trigger sensitive to any new tyrannical threat. Why, then, approve an amendment acknowledging the obvious? After asking Americans to ratify a new plan of government, why did the founders then request that they assert their right to overthrow it?

Questions like these are the subject of Tushnet's *Out of Range*. With the Supreme Court poised to issue its first gun-rights decision in nearly seven decades in *District of Columbia v. Heller*, a case the Court heard on March 18 and that involves one of the most sweeping citywide gun bans in the country, Tushnet's brief but dense primer on the Second Amendment and its relationship to the gun-control battles of the last quarter-century could not be more timely. Unfortunately, it also could not be more frustrating. Tushnet, a professor at Harvard Law School, suffers from an excess of caution. Understandably, he is determined not to be one of those overconfident types who, as he puts it, are just "blowing smoke" in claiming to know precisely what the Second Amendment means. As a consequence, he advances a couple of possibilities as to what it might mean, explains why one interpretation may have an edge over the other and then announces that the whole question may be beside the point, since it has little to do with reducing gun-related crime. In fact, he argues that the long-running debate over the Second Amendment may be really about something else—not about what the Second Amendment means, or about how to reduce violence, but . . . about how we understand ourselves as Americans. Get that straight, and the fights over the Second Amendment would go away. But, of course, we can't get our national self-understanding straight, because we are always trying to figure out who we are, and revising our self-understandings. And so the battle over the Second Amendment will continue.

Like a patient on a psychiatrist's couch, Americans thus talk about the Second Amendment to avoid talking about peskier matters, in this case highly sensitive topics having to do with national identity and purpose. So we keep talking because we don't know how to stop.

But this is unfair, since Americans have no choice but to talk about a law they can neither change (thanks to the highly restrictive amending clause in Article V of the Constitution) nor even fully understand (thanks to the pervasive ambiguity of its twenty-seven words). Still, *Out of Range* attempts to explain the inexplicable by approaching the Second Amendment from two angles: its original meaning at the time of its adoption as part of the Bill of Rights in 1791 and the meaning it has acquired through judicial interpretation and political practice in the centuries since.

In purely historical terms, Tushnet says, the answer on balance seems more or less clear. Lines one and two, which compose something of a preamble, are plainly the product of an eighteenth-century ideology known as civic republicanism, a school of thought almost paranoid in its tendency to see tyranny forever lurking around the corner. Tushnet's discussion of this school is somewhat cursory (as he admits), but a host of historians, from Bernard Bailyn to Isaac Kramnick, have described it as consisting of a series of polarities between political power, on the one hand, and the people, on the other. If the people are soft, lazy and corrupt, they will easily succumb to a tyrant's rule. Conversely, if they are proud, brave and alert, then would-be oppressors, sensing that the people are keen to defend their liberties, will back off. While a popular militia is important in this respect, no less important are the values, habits and attitudes that accompany it—vigor, courage, a martial spirit ("keep and bear" turns out to be a military term), plus a steely determination born of the knowledge that "those who expect to reap the blessings of freedom," to quote Tom Paine, "must, like men, undergo the fatigue of supporting it."

All of which suggests a broad reading of the Second Amendment, one that holds that a well-regulated militia is not the only social benefit that arises from widespread gun ownership but merely one of many. As Tushnet puts it, "Once each of us has the right to keep and bear arms, we can use the right however we want—but always preserving the possibility that we will use it to defend against government oppression." Guns are good in their own right because guns, military training and liberty are all inextricably linked.

But what about "well regulated"—surely that phrase suggests a government-controlled militia along the lines of today's National Guard? Not quite. In eighteenth-century parlance, regulation could take the form of a militia either spontaneously created by individuals or decreed by the state. Tushnet points out that the financially distressed farmers who participated in Daniel Shays's agrarian uprising in western Massachusetts in 1786 called themselves "regulators." Even though Tushnet doesn't mention it, the North Carolina frontiersmen who rose up against unfair colonial tax policies some twenty years earlier did so as well. Hence, there was nothing strange or inconsistent about regulation mustered from below by individuals rather than enforced from above by the state. Indeed, the Virginia Ratifying Convention in 1788 implied as much when it declared "that the people have the right to keep and bear arms [and] that a well regulated militia composed of the body of the people trained to arms is the proper, natural, and safe defense of a free state." Such a militia would be well regulated to the degree it was composed of the people as a whole.

This is no doubt the sort of thinking one would expect of a postrevolutionary society in which the people had just used their weapons to overthrow one government and were leery of laying them aside as another was taking shape. But the notion that "we the people" would reserve the right to take up arms against a government that "we" had just created seems contradictory. After all, if it's a people's government, who would the people revolt against—themselves? Still, Americans clearly believed in a natural right of revolution in the event that power was misused or usurped, and they further believed that their Constitution should acknowledge as much. In a document festooned with checks and balances, this was to be the ultimate check, one directed against government tout court.

While one can quarrel about the details, it would thus appear that the NRA has been correct all along concerning the Second Amendment's original intent to guarantee an individual right to bear arms. But Tushnet adds that there is also the question of how the amendment has come to be understood in the years since. Once the Constitution was ratified and the new Republic began taking its first wobbly steps, three things happened: militias fell by the wayside as Americans discovered they had better ways to spend their time than drilling on the village green; politicians and the police took fright when guns began showing up in the hands of people they didn't like, such as newly freed blacks or left-wing radicals; and public safety became more and more of a concern as urbanization rose.

Thus, Supreme Court Justice Joseph Story complained in 1833 about "a growing indifference to any system of militia discipline, and a strong disposition, from a sense of its burthens, to be rid of all regulations." In 1879 the Illinois state legislature outlawed private militias after 400 or so German socialists paraded through Chicago with swords and guns, while the Supreme Court's 1939 decision *United States v. Miller* upheld a ban on sawed-off shotguns on the grounds that such weapons had nothing to do with maintaining a well-regulated militia. However scattershot, various gun-control measures have proliferated since the 1930s, prohibiting certain types of firearms (Tommy guns), forbidding certain people from owning them (felons and fugitives), establishing "gun-free school zones" and so on, all based on a collective-right reading holding that government has free rein to do what it wishes to maintain public safety. By the time Tribe published his famous textbook, *American Constitutional Law*, in 1978, any concept of an individual right to bear arms had effectively disappeared. The Second Amendment, *American Constitutional Law* announced, was irrelevant when it came to "purely private conduct" in the form of gun ownership. Gun control could therefore go forward unimpeded.

In retrospect, Tribe's textbook was plainly the high-water mark for the "collective right" interpretation. Eleven years later, Levinson published his *Yale Law Journal* article, complaining that "for too long, most members of the legal academy have treated the Second Amendment as the equivalent of an embarrassing relative, whose mention brings a quick change of subject to other, more respectable, family members." In fact, intellectual honesty dictated that they recognize there was more to the amendment than they had been willing to admit.

While Tribe has since come around to the individual-rights point of view (the 2000 edition of American Constitutional Law contains a ten-page reconsideration of the subject), he is now among those arguing that, notwithstanding such a right, fire- arms are still "subject to reasonable regulation in the interest of public safety" and that "laws that ban certain types of weapons, that require safety devices on others and that otherwise impose strict controls on guns can pass Constitutional scrutiny." Tush- net agrees, noting that the Pennsylvania State Constitutional Convention declared in 1788 that "no law shall be passed for disarming the people . . . unless for crimes committed, or real danger of public injury from individuals," a clear indication that public safety was a concern even in the Republic's earliest days. He observes that, in what has been called "America's first gun control movement," state legislatures followed up in the 1810s with laws against concealed weapons, bowie knives and the like for the same reason. Today, there is no shortage of gun-control laws even in states that recognize a constitutional right to bear arms, yet the courts have not seen a conflict. "Indeed," says Tushnet, "it's hard to identify a gun-control policy that has not been upheld against challenges based on state constitutional guarantees of an individual right to keep and bear arms."

In other words, we can all relax. Given its current conserva- tive lineup, the Supreme Court will almost certainly uphold an individual right to bear arms in *District of Columbia v. Heller.* But while gun prohibition or equally sweeping licensing laws will probably not be permissible, lesser forms of gun control are still acceptable. Thus, things will continue pretty much unchanged. Lawyers will go back to arguing whether banning assault weap- ons passes constitutional muster, while the NRA will go back to complaining that we are all on a slippery slope to tyranny. Moms will march for gun control, hunters will campaign against it and "cold dead hands" bumper stickers will continue to proliferate on pickups. *Plus ça change, plus c'est la même Scheiss.*

Or so Tushnet suggests, although some of us may not be so sanguine. The problem may be an excessively narrow reading of the Second Amendment and the broader Constitution of which it is a part. Law professors, not surprisingly, tend to think of the Constitution as the law. But it is also a plan of government and a blueprint shaping American thought on such topics as democracy, civil liberties and popular sovereignty. Hence, while an individualist reading of the Second Amendment will certainly affect gun control in some fashion, that is not all it will affect. It will also send a powerfully coded message about the proper relationship between the people and their government and the nature of political authority. It is this aspect of the Second Amendment as opposed to its strictly legal dimension that seems most important.

Indeed, the closer one looks at the Second Amendment, the more significant its political ramifications seem. Its structure, for example, is oddly parallel to that of the larger Constitution, with a preamble (lines one and two) advancing a rationale of sorts and then a body, or gist (lines three and four), stating what is to be done. Other than the famous one beginning with "We the people," this is arguably the only such preamble in the entire document and certainly the only one in the Bill of Rights. The logical parallels are also curious. The larger Constitution opens by declaring that the people have unlimited power to alter their political circumstances so as to "promote the general welfare and secure the blessings of liberty to ourselves and our posterity." It seems that "we the people" can do whatever we want to improve our situation, including tossing out one constitution (the Articles of Confederation) and ordaining a new one. But the body of the Constitution goes on to say something completely different by declaring in Article V that a supposedly sovereign people is decidedly unsovereign when it comes to modifying the plan of government made in its name. (With just thirteen states representing as little as five percent of the US population able to veto any amendment, the US Constitution is among the hardest to change on earth.) By the same token, the mini-constitution that is the Second Amendment opens by declaring a people in arms to be the ultimate guarantor of freedom, but then it goes on to say that the people's government lacks the freedom to alter individual gun rights. Since the 1930s liberals have succeeded in circumventing the first restriction via the miracle of judicial interpretation, a modern form of transubstantiation that allows them to alter the essence of the Constitution without changing so much as a comma. But a return to an individual-rights reading of the Second Amendment would mean a rollback of free-form judicial review. By returning the amendment to its original meaning, such a reading couldn't help but strengthen the old civic-republican view of an expansive state as a threat to liberty.

This is profoundly reactionary and profoundly confusing. Are the people sovereign or not? Are they the protectors of liberty or a threat? The answer, according to the Big-C and little-c constitution, is both. Although legal academics like to think of the Constitution as a model of reason and balance, the Second Amendment puts us in touch with the document's inner schizophrenic—and, consequently, our own. Thanks to it, we the people know that the people are dangerous. Therefore, we must take up arms against our own authority. We are perennially at war with ourselves and are never more alarmed than when confronted by our own power. The people are tyrannized by the fear of popular tyranny.

Richard Feldman's *Ricochet*, an insider account of how conservatives have used the Second Amendment to clobber liberals on gun control and more, is evidence of what this schizophrenia means on the most down-to-earth political level. *Ricochet* is long —too long—on details about the inner workings of the NRA, the purges, the plots and the Machiavellian maneuvers of executive vice president Wayne LaPierre. Still, it has its moments. The most relevant concerns a campaign Feldman helped engineer in New Jersey in July 1990 to punish then-Governor Tom Florio, a Democrat, for pushing through a ban on assault weapons a few months earlier. When Florio announced a major tax increase to plug a deficit in the state budget, a Pat Buchanan-style "pitchfork rebellion"—led by a letter carrier named John Budzash and a title searcher named Pat Ralston—erupted across the middle of the state. Feldman, eager for revenge and experienced as a field operative when it came to populist campaigns of this type, sprang into action. Working behind the scenes, he established contact with Hands Across New Jersey, as the tax protesters called themselves, funneling them money, advising on strategy and grooming their press releases. "But unlike what I'd helped produce for the NRA, we had to give the Hands documents a rough edge," he recalls. "I always made sure to misspell at least one word, 'frivilous' or 'wastefull.'" The group's biggest PR coup was distributing thousands of rolls of "Flush Florio" toilet paper to protest the governor's proposal to slap a seven percent sales tax on such items, a tactic that frightened the state's Democratic establishment to the core. Senator Bill Bradley did his best to duck the controversy but barely squeaked through to re-election, while Florio lost to Republican Christine Todd Whitman three years later. It was an example of the sort of right-wing populism that would continue to build throughout the 1990s, crippling the Clinton Administration and paving the way for the Bush/ Cheney coup d'état in December 2000.

Hands Across New Jersey could not have done it without the NRA, and the NRA could not have done it without the Second Amendment. On the surface, tax hikes and gun control would seem to have as little to do with each other as horticulture and professional wrestling. But eighteenth-century civic republican-ism, the ideology bound up with an individualist reading of the Second Amendment, provided the necessary link by portraying both as the products of overweening government. In the face of such "tyranny," the message to protesters was plain: take down those muskets, so to speak, and sally forth to meet the redcoats. Don't think, don't analyze, don't engage in any of the other sober measures needed to sort out the fiscal mess. Just turn the clock back to the eighteenth century, pack your musket with "Flush Florio" wadding and fire away! Needless to say, atavistic protests like these were sadly irrelevant in terms of the financial pressures that, in a politically fragmented, traffic-bound state like New Jersey, were growing ever more acute. Yes, the protesters succeeded in throwing out some bums (and ushering in even worse ones). But with the current governor, Democrat Jon Corzine, now struggling to resolve a 10 percent budget gap, the crisis has only deepened.

After the disaster of the Bush years, it would seem that the right-wing populism embodied by Hands Across New Jersey has burned itself out. But given the collapse of the liberal-collectivist reading of the Second Amendment and the Supreme Court's likely embrace of an individual right, it could conceivably gain a new lease on life—just as the country is grappling with a major recession, the worst housing crisis since the 1930s and a wave of municipal bankruptcies, all problems that call for a collective government response. But an incoherent Constitution dating from the days of the French monarchy, the Venetian republic and the Holy Roman Empire is now sending an increasingly strong message that firm and concerted action of this sort is the very definition of tyranny and must be resisted to the hilt. Once again, Americans must take aim—at themselves! Tushnet's question concerning "how we understand ourselves as Americans" thus becomes somewhat easier to answer: Americans are people at the mercy of eighteenth-century attitudes they don't know how to escape.

The Legacy

Steve Volk

from Philadelphia Magazine

Jim Beasley Sr., a legendary, boot-stomping Philadelphia Lawyer, left his firm in the hands of his ne'er-do-well son. But now Beasley Jr.'s quiet approach is not only winning big cases, but signaling a new era in the city's courtrooms.

WHILE HIS OLD man worked, the Kid usually spent the day screwing up. He skipped school. He chewed tobacco in the back of class. He learned Spanish like a knucklehead, retaining little more than that *cállate* means "shut up." His path seemed set from the time he was 12 years old. He was forced to repeat the seventh grade and was asked to leave Penn Charter in 10th.

Meanwhile, the old man was a legend, humping cases as a plaintiff's attorney in city courtrooms. He won multimillion-dollar verdicts with regularity. And he did it with a Spartan's dedication to combat. While the Kid complained about serving 45 hours of summer-school detention for being a no-account fuckup, the Legend put in 45 hours by Thursday afternoon. Then he kept right on working. He outshone opposing attorneys, wrestled control of the courtroom away from presiding judges, and ran roughshod to victories.

The Philadelphia Lawyer is a hoary cliché now. But it has been invoked as a compliment and a pejorative, a means of describing an intellectual strong man who twists not metal, but facts. Whatever. A Philadelphia Lawyer is suspect until he's needed. Then, he's your best friend. And the Legend was the ultimate Philadelphia Lawyer.

The Legend was so great, he excelled even at recreation. He raced cars. He jammed himself into the tight little barrel of a World War II fighter plane. He cheated death, pinwheeling through tight corkscrew spirals like a *Top Gun* pilot. But his performance suffered at home. When the Kid finished last in his first motocross race, the Legend said, "What's the matter with you? I won all my races!"

The Legend was lying. Right to his son's face. But the Kid wouldn't learn that until years later. So instead he figured that somehow, everything had gone wrong. Somehow he was born a loser to a father who always won. And when the Legend's headlights hit the front window, long after dinner each weekday night, his children fled before he could reach the front door. Two daughters and the boy bounded up the stairs rather than see their dad—tired, inebriated, and always on the lookout for someone or something to criticize.

In his mid-20s, though, the Kid did something that might have seemed unthinkable to the boy he once was. He decided to become a trial attorney. "Don't," the Legend warned him. "People will always compare you to me."

The Legend was right. But miraculously, so was the boy. The courtroom is where he belongs. And watching him work now, as a man bearing the legacy of the Philadelphia Lawyer, is an opportunity to see how the nature of being a lawyer in this town has changed.

The shoot-'em-up cowboy tactics of the father have given way to the subtler skills of the son. And all these years later, the

Kid is no longer scrambling out of his father's headlights. He is standing where everyone can see him—even in the courtroom, where the glare is brightest. And the incredible thing is, he looks like the right man for his time.

It's a hot summer day in June. Jim Beasley Jr., the Kid, is bent over a cardboard box and working it open quickly, like a child stricken with Christmas fever. He has been waiting for this moment through much of the trial—the chance to introduce Exhibit P-51, the object in the box.

The case began a week earlier. Beasley's client is Robert Black, an internist in the UPenn health system. Black underwent cancer-related prostate surgery in his late 40s. He walked away impotent. He and his wife waited five sexless years for him to be declared cancer-free. Then he opted for an inflatable penile prosthesis. The device includes a fluid reservoir, two inflatable plastic rods and a tiny pump. Squeezing the pump in one of his testicles would push fluid from the reservoir into the rods inside his penis. *Hallelujah.* An erection. But he suffered complications. The three-ounce fluid reservoir wound up stuffed inside his bladder before he ever left the hospital. He remains impotent today. He hasn't had sex with his wife in seven years.

Beasley took the case knowing it would be difficult to win. Bladder injuries are common enough among penile implant patients that they present no grounds for a lawsuit. His only claim is that a weeklong delay in diagnosing the problem is worth punishing. He also took the case knowing that the defendant, Terrence Malloy, is one of the most accomplished penile-implant surgeons in the country.

So . . . what's in that box? In a sense, what's in the box doesn't matter. The box is a MacGuffin—the term film director Alfred Hitchcock coined to describe the briefcase every character wants to possess, the safe every film thief wants to crack. The MacGuffin is the reason the characters in the film behave as they do. The MacGuffin takes on the sum total of all our hopes and fears. And once the MacGuffin is secure, the film is over.

For Jim Beasley Jr., then, the object in the box must have something to do with his father.

BEASLEY SR. GOT to the top—that's his name on Temple's Beasley School of Law—after starting at the bottom. His own father died when he was just 14 years old, and his early work history included stints as a bus driver and a motorcycle cop. But once he finished law school, he discovered the courtroom was really where he belonged. In a long, distinguished career, he won more than 100 cases with verdicts of at least a million dollars.

He died in September 2004 at 78 years old, just 13 days after being diagnosed with cancer, prompting one of the city's other legendary attorneys, Richard Sprague, to declare: "He was the sun around which we planets revolved."

Before he passed, the Legend was working with one of his former clients, Ralph Cipriano, on writing a book about his best cases. But after the Legend died, Beasley Jr. opened up his father's entire life to the reporter. The result, *Courtroom Cowboy*, scheduled to be released by Lawrence Teacher Books later this fall, is a raw, red and bleeding love letter from a son to his dad. The elder Beasley is revealed as an emotionally stunted product of the World War II generation. He cheated on his wife and lorded over his kids. The chapter on his divorce from Beasley Jr.'s mother—which took eight years in court to resolve—is a vivid painting of a man on fire. The Legend was consumed with his legal career; his family was an afterthought. But at the end, in his final few years of life, the senior Beasley rehabilitates himself. He grows to treasure his family. He remarries Jim Jr.'s mother, Helen. And then he's gone. The sun around which the planets rotated, eradicated.

Beasley Jr. inherited his father's empire—a law firm specializing in medical malpractice cases, and the well-appointed mansion at 11th and Walnut streets that houses the firm—and he now owns a handful of airplanes father and son enjoyed piloting together.

But what he would probably like most is the chance to hear his father say "I'm proud of you." The Legend was sparing with praise, and the junior Beasley gave him little reason to be generous. His teenage years were a constant rebellion of unapproved keg parties at his dad's place and righteous bong hits. He started to pull his act together in his senior year, and in college he met his wife, whose tender ministrations helped propel him all the way through a medical degree. He thought about being a research geneticist before deciding he needed a profession that was more . . . *aggressive*. He has that streak in him, just like the Legend. He has even surpassed his father as a stunt pilot, performing in an annual air show each summer in Atlantic City in the cockpit of a World War II plane. But practicing law is different, of course. Because mastering the law is what his father was famous for.

DAY ONE OF the trial, Beasley calls the first witness, Robert Black. Beasley is dressed in a tan suit and sits behind a table piled with paperwork. His witness is clearly anxious. Several times, Black begins answering questions Beasley has yet to ask.

"Be cool," Beasley tells him.

Gradually, he calms. Then Beasley, still sitting at the plaintiff's table, asks him the most sensitive question: "Could you describe your ability to be intimate with your wife now?"

Black's response spares nothing. "If you were to look at me right now, I look like a seven-year-old boy, except I have pubic hair," he says. "I have a penis about three inches long, and with stimulation, it does nothing."

To compound indignities, after he returned to work Black found out that some of his colleagues had accessed his computerized medical records, violating the HIPAA Act for a cheap jolly. (We changed Black's name for this story at his request.)

Through it all, Beasley's performance is conspicuous mostly for his seeming absence. He remains seated the entire time. His co-counsel actually sits closer to the jury box, rendering Beasley a kind of disembodied voice in the courtroom. But when Black drops the bomb about his shrunken, non-working member, the moment is even more powerful, more intimate, because Beasley is sitting. It is as if the wounded internist is sharing a moment alone with the jury.

As the trial progresses, Beasley rarely stands, drawing a stark contrast between himself and his chief opponent in the case, Adrian King. In total, the defense includes three attorneys, one to represent UPenn and the other two to represent Malloy. But it's King, in particular, who sucks all the air from the room. Ostensibly representing Penn, the 60–something, elfin-small former Marine defends Malloy, too—arching his thick eyebrows in cartoonish fashion, gesturing violently at the plaintiff and saying his name, *Doctor Black*, as if uttering these syllables requires him to fish-hook his own testes and give the line a yank.

King's theatrical, carpet-bombing performance is more reminiscent of Jim Beasley Sr. than is that of the Legend's own son. But that should come as no surprise. A Philadelphia Lawyer approaches trial work like an actor, finding a character for the courtroom that fits his own personality. Father and son are different attorneys because they are different men. Beasley Sr. was known to prowl the courtroom like a big-game hunter (which he also was—the Legend's legend knows no bounds). He wore cowboy boots into court, called the jurors "folks," and in his later years sported a dignified shock of long gray locks, lending him the air of a country sheriff. He was salty in combat, once refusing a settlement offer from King with the admonition: "Tell your client to take the same amount of money you just offered me in dollar bills—and shove it up his ass."

In contrast, though Jim Beasley Jr. looks lean and fit like his father, his persona is more nerd than stunt pilot. He wears computer-geek eyeglasses perched on his thin, pointed nose.

His dark brown hair is cut conservatively short. And his voice is pitched at a higher register. In court, his combative questions are masked by his friendly, almost passive demeanor. And for that, juries tend to like him. But the differences between Junior's style and his father's aren't solely about the chasm between their personalities. Ask anybody in the Philadelphia legal world, and you'll hear that even Jim Beasley Sr. couldn't be Jim Beasley Sr. today.

When the senior Beasley first stood before a judge and jury, lawyers spent most of their days in courtrooms. Cases rarely settled. The discovery process had yet to evolve into the foul, paper-generating beast it's become today. This meant that lawyers essentially walked into court blind, unsure what witnesses might say. For Beasley Sr., this was an advantage. Having worked as a cop and driven a bus, the old man had skills no law school could teach. He looked at witnesses and determined what questions to ask by instinct.

Today, the Kid—and, by extension, every other attorney in Philadelphia—clambers over a vast mountain of paperwork before entering the court. Cases settle more often than not. The discovery process is so comprehensive that Beasley Jr. knows pretty much everything a witness will say. And he faces a jury made more sophisticated, or cynical, by decades of courtroom TV dramas. Courtrooms are still theaters, of a sort. But Beasley's direct examination of Robert Black was theater of a remarkably subtle kind.

Because the junior Beasley lacks his father's commanding presence and long list of accomplishments, he is easy to underestimate. "What do you want to write about him for?" one prominent attorney asked me. "What has he ever done? His father was a legend. He built all that, working cases. The kid just had it handed to him."

But the junior Beasley is a lawyer for his times. And against all odds, the buzz on the Beasley firm seems to be changing. Both Dick Sprague and high-flying criminal defense attorney

Fred Perri say they're hearing from local judges that this Junior-led Beasley firm is once again receiving a lot of referrals. This, too, shouldn't come as a surprise. In a sense, the firm was passed from father to son in the Legend's last trial, a 2004 medical malpractice case. Senior tried wrangling the judge for control of the courtroom, his usual method of forcibly beating a path to victory. But the jury wasn't with ahim. He lost. He was diagnosed with cancer directly afterward.

His sudden end marked the passage of his older, freewheeling brand of lawyering. And the final act of an eccentric, brawling old man.

Nineteen Seventy-eight
The Legend flies his family to San Diego.

Being a child of poverty, the multimillionaire refuses to equip his private airplane with the necessary upgrades to soar at higher altitudes. He flies in the same manner he lives his life: turbulently, at a height of 4,000 feet, chain–smoking Tiparillos. Behind him, his wife, two daughters and son rattle in the silver metal tube and choke upon his exhalations. Before long, they take turns puking into plastic bags. And they beg the Legend to find some calmer altitude for flying.

This is the usual scene whenever the Beasley family takes to the air. But on this particular trip, after the Kid pukes, he convinces his father to take an unplanned detour. "C'mon, Dad," the 11-year-old boy says. "Take a left."

There's a historical plane collection in Harlingen, Texas, which means traveling some 500 miles off course. The Kid wants to see a World War II-era plane—"The coolest plane ever," he tells his father—of which he's building models at home: the P-51 Mustang, one of the most famous fighter planes in aviation history. The then-52-year-old Beasley Sr. not only flies his family to Texas. He buys the P-51, for $140,000.

Many of the Kid's stories about the Legend are like this— redolent of anger, vomit and laughable good fortune. This one is particularly special because the warplane is a passion father and son grow to share, and flying an activity they bond over between problems. And over the years, there are always problems.

When the Kid got fat, for instance, the Legend's response was brutal. "Stop eating," he said. "Fat shit." The Kid spent his nights in the basement, lifting weights to scour the fat away, feeling helpless as he listened to his father yell at his mother upstairs. And one afternoon he came home to find all the furniture gone. "Dad," he said, phoning his father, "I think we've been robbed."

The reality was that his mother had moved out, unable to live with a Legend.

In *Robert Black v. Terrence Malloy*, the defense called a series of medical residents to try and refute the plaintiff's testimony. But they seemed to focus mostly on the color of Black's urine. He maintained in his testimony that it was often bright red and thick with clots it pained him to pass, suggesting that doctors should have quickly discovered his injured bladder. The residents testified that his urine was usually clear and sometimes "light rosé," a reference to a gradation of red wine, suggesting that there was no evidence of bladder injury at all.

Beasley's cross-examination of the defendant, Terrence Malloy, promises to be more interesting. In Malloy, Beasley is to face an experienced witness who also holds a distinct advantage. Modern juries want *Gladiator*-style combat, but they don't consider the match between lawyer and witness a fair fight. Beasley knows: If Malloy gets sharp with him, he'll enjoy more room to maneuver. He might even be able to retrieve the exhibit from its box.

But the doctor never rattles. Beasley questions him for maybe half an hour. Working carefully, he pins him into claiming that the fluid reservoir "eroded" into Black's bladder without producing any signs or symptoms. Black had testified that he bled and suffered intense pain.

"If there was erosion," Beasley asks, "would you not expect that the patient would suffer from considerable lower abdominal pain?"

"He may or may not," replies Malloy.

Without a hint of impatience, Beasley refers the doctor back to his deposition in the case. "Dr. Malloy," he begins, "on page 24 of your deposition I asked, 'What are the signs and symptoms of an erosion?'"

Malloy's wrinkled fingers sift through a copy of his deposition on the stand.

"You testified," Beasley begins again, "that 'You would have considerable lower abdominal pain if there was an erosion,' correct?"

The jury's eyes flit from Beasley to the witness. "Yes," Malloy admits.

In a television show, the plaintiff's attorney would further probe this discrepancy. But in real life, asking another question on the subject would risk the jury's ire and give the witness the opportunity to clean up his mess. Beasley's father almost certainly would have appeared combative. Once, in fact, the senior Beasley blasted Malloy on the stand, accusing him of "being willing to come into court and say anything" he had to—a claim Malloy vehemently denied.

But having won a point from Malloy, the junior Beasley merely nods and moves on to another topic. He has removed a pound of the doctor's flesh without spilling any blood. Later, he'll acknowledge his pleasure with the day's events. But in the courtroom, his facial expression never changes. And he never pulls the exhibit out of the box. The entire exchange shows him working a case in his own way, subtlety winning over flamboyance, the Kid not giving in to the Legend, a mirror for how lawyering itself has evolved.

AFTER HAVING BEEN separated from -Beasley's mother for 18 years, the elder Beasley turned up one day at age 73 on his ex-wife's doorstep, wearing his trademark boots and a long leather coat. They remarried less than three years later. He also reconciled with his children, though for Beasley Jr. there is still some air of mystery surrounding the changes his father made. He doesn't know if the old man had truly grown wiser, mellower, more -loving—or if the cancer eating his body had slowed him down.

Today, however, the Beasley firm's website includes a video tribute to his dad. It's an oddly intimate thing to have included there, but disquietingly beautiful. Images of the father flicker in a slow reveal as the mournful acoustic ballad "I Just Don't Think I'll Ever Get Over You" plays. Toward the end, Beasley Jr. ascends the grand staircase of what was once his father's firm and leans into the doorway of what used to be the Legend's office. His flair for the theatrical is not so great, but his expectant expression and deferential posture indicate that he expects to see his father, somehow, still sitting there.

SOMETIMES A TRIAL'S most important turns occur at the unlikeliest times. In the case of *Black v. Malloy*, that's exactly what happens.

The witness's name is Victor Carpiniello, and he is called by the defense to bolster the claim that there is no evidence the hospital should have discovered Black's bladder damage sooner. It will be the first time—just as the story of this trial is coming to a close—that Beasley himself will stand out. Carpiniello has created an opening of sorts by claiming he remembers his single visit with Black. And Black, he says, never complained to him of pain.

"How many patients do you typically see a week?" asks Beasley.

"Eighty to 100," replies Carpiniello.

"So if it's 80 or 100 a week," replies Beasley, "how many weeks are there in a year?"

"*Fifty-two*," Carpiniello replies, his voice grown suddenly thick and condescending. Beasley privately celebrates, because Carpiniello has cracked the veneer of civility between them. But his voice remains calm, kind.

"So," he says, "that's 5,200 patients from July of '05 to July of '06, is that fair to say?"

"If that's the math," replies Carpiniello, still talking down to his questioner, "yes."

So Beasley does the math: 5,000 patients a year times nearly three years. "That's almost 14,000 patients," he calculates. "You remember Dr. Black specifically, 14,000 patients ago?"

"Absolutely," replies Carpiniello.

The jurors openly smirk in their seats. "Mr. King showed you this document," says Beasley, holding up a single sheet of paper. "It says 'urine, light rosé.'"

By now, the jury has repeatedly heard what "rosé" means in the context of a hospital. But like a comedian setting up his punch line, Beasley retraces his steps. "What's 'rosé' mean?" he asks.

"Rosé is a descriptive term relating to wine color," replies Carpiniello.

"Wine color," the attorney repeats. He puts his fingers to his chin, as if pondering Carpiniello's response. It's a simple action, and a kind of ruse—a means of buying an extra second to make his calculations, which run something like this: When a jury wishes the questioning would stop, the spirit of the room dims. When a jury expects that something important or dramatic is about to happen, the energy shoots higher. Beasley's father always used to tell him that working as a plaintiff's attorney required him to be director, producer and one of the principal actors in a play. So with the words "wine color" still hanging in the air, Beasley finally decides to open the box.

Striding quickly around the jurors' stand, he crouches down on the floor, seizes the box's cardboard flaps, and opens them quickly. When he stands again, he holds a bottle of rosé wine triumphantly aloft in his right hand. "Like this?" he asks.

The red liquid shines vividly under the harsh light of the courtroom, like fresh blood. And the bottle, like any good prop, speaks: If this was the color of Robert Black's urine, why didn't the hospital take swifter action?

Some of the jurors smile; others laugh appreciatively. The judge, smiling, says, "I think we're all going to lose our appetites."

After deliberations, the jury will return with a 10-2 verdict in favor of the plaintiff, awarding Black and his wife $650,000 in damages. The Kid wins the case, grandstanding with a wine bottle in the space afforded him by all his earlier restraint. And he acknowledged his father in the process. "I will call this," he says, still holding the bottle in his hands, "Exhibit P-51."

The P-51 was the warplane he talked his father into detouring 500 miles to Texas to see, the plane he and his father both enjoyed flying so much over the years.

Jim Beasley Jr., the Kid, may be a very different man from the Legend—a much more attentive father to his own four children, and a less famous attorney. And what it takes to be a Philadelphia Lawyer has definitely changed since his father's day. But the Kid feels sure that the Legend, under the same circumstances, would have brought the wine bottle to court. And so, as a tribute to him, he brings a new Exhibit P-51 to every case. He tries to choose something unusual, something colorful—-something as flamboyant as a brilliant attorney corkscrewing through the weekend sunlight in a fighter plane—as a means of remembering the old man and keeping him alive in court. The jury never knows it. But they've just seen a son honor his father. They've just seen the Kid honor a Legend that modern times, and his own temperament, will never allow him to be.

Mercenary for Justice

Robert Kolker

from *New York Magazine*

Pro-life zealot James Kopp murdered an upstate abortion doctor in 1998. And he might well have escaped the FBI if not for an informant whose desire for the big reward money led him to betray a lifelong friend. In the following chronicle, the informant tells his story for the first time, offering the inside account of how the abortion war's most notorious assassin was finally taken down.

DENNIS MALVASI WAS the kind of kid everyone else wanted to be—the funny one, the street-smart one, the handsome one with a natural swagger. The Brooklyn neighborhood he grew up in was one of the worst slums in the city; East New York in the mid-sixties was a gangland, perpetually on the brink of a race riot. But Dennis always seemed above it all, despite being worse off than most. He had eleven brothers and sisters, with three fathers between them. His mother was so poor she sent him for a time to an orphanage upstate. Maybe it was knowing so many unwanted children that explains what happened later.

Dennis entered the Vietnam War just after the Tet Offensive. He was 17 but so eager to enlist that he found a stranger in the street to sign his parental-consent form. He served one tour as a field radio operator, drawing VC fire on a number of occasions, then turned around and re-upped for a second. As a soldier, "I felt really alive, really wanted," is how Dennis put it. Life at home was harder. He was arrested for being in a street fight—"hanging around," he'd later say, "with some very dangerous people." He tried to become an actor, joining an Off–Off Broadway troupe on the Lower East Side, even winning some acclaim. But in 1975, he got stopped and frisked by a police officer on a subway platform. He was carrying a .25-caliber pistol. It was his second felony. He was sent upstate to prison for two years.

Dennis couldn't get over the idea that he was behind bars while draft evaders received clemency. His anguished letters from jail were dated with the years he served in Vietnam, as if to will himself back in time. Some time after he got out, he became secretive—taking messages from a beeper, having his mail delivered to bars, getting jobs and a driver's license under assumed names. He missed being in action and got licensed as a pyrotechnics expert to work with explosives. Then he started spending time with a group called Our Lady of the Roses, a Catholic fringe group that raged on about the evils of Vatican II and the sinfulness of modern life. The foulest of sacrileges, they believed, was abortion.

Dennis wasn't a churchgoing Catholic, but he'd never believed in abortion. "Here's the truth. Look. This is a life," he once said, pointing to a picture of a fetus in a training book for paramedics. Now he complained to one friend about how he'd defended his country and was called a baby-killer while others were murdering the unborn with impunity.

On December 10, 1985, a small pipe bomb ignited inside a vacant men's room at the Manhattan Women's Medical Center on East 23rd Street. Eleven months later, another homemade explosive, this one with a half-stick of dynamite, blew a hole through the wall of the Eastern Women's Center on 30th Street. Two weeks after that, police found an unexploded bomb with three sticks of dynamite inside a sofa at a clinic on Queens Boulevard. Finally, on December 14, 1986, the bomb squad burst into the smoke-filled Second Avenue headquarters of Planned Parenthood to find a carpet fire started by a small incendiary device, not far from a larger bomb with fifteen sticks of dynamite, enough to destroy the front of the building had it not been defused in time. The attack had the hallmarks of a highly motivated professional: blasting caps, timers, batteries, and a Catholic medal of St. Benedict. Dennis Malvasi was New York City's first abortion-clinic bomber.

Joseph had come to Brooklyn with his family in the sixties when he was 14 years old. His parents were *shtetl* Jews who had stayed in Poland during the war, fighting the Nazis, only to leave in 1960 when some kids went after Joseph with a straight razor, claiming that his parents had killed Christ. His family found a tenement in the only slightly less dangerous neighborhood of East New York. His father worked as a leather cutter, his mother as a seamstress. Joseph was prone to fainting spells and panic attacks, and had to learn to speak English without a lisp. Even his friends called him the Trembler. He tried playing the clown but was too cloying and needy. "I was the water boy," Joseph remembers. "I was in the background."

Joseph, whose identity has been protected here for reasons that will become clear, can't remember when he first met Dennis. It was 1964 or '65, out on the street, playing skelly or picking up girls. He remembers Dennis as very friendly and very poor. "We hung out, but it was, 'Hi, how're you doing?' We didn't develop a closeness." Within a few years, Dennis had enlisted and Joseph had been drafted, and the two lost touch. As a noncitizen, Joseph served Stateside, then spent the seventies leading a small, dead-end sort of life. He was a process server for the courts, a collection agent, a driver, and, finally, a counselor to veterans for the State Department of Labor. It was there, in 1985, that Joseph got a call from a friend, asking if he would look after a down-on-his-luck Vietnam veteran from the old neighborhood named Dennis Malvasi.

They met again on a sunny afternoon at a pretzel stand outside Saint Patrick's Cathedral. Within minutes they found they knew a lot of the same people, and Joseph was enthralled. Here was someone from the old days who'd gone on to become a war hero, someone who made him feel like a big shot just by knowing him. "It was the same old Dennis," Joseph remembers. "Easygoing: 'Everything's going to be all right.' A sweetheart. He stood up for this country and the war. I looked up to him—respected him for doing it."

Dennis spent the early weeks of 1987 hiding from the police—and laughing over the phone (though not with Joseph) about what a bad job the cops were doing finding him. The manhunt might have gone on longer if Cardinal O'Connor hadn't appeared on the news in late February, delivering a plea for Dennis, who was publicly identified as the main suspect, to give himself up. The next day, Dennis, wearing an eyepatch and sunglasses, walked unnoticed into the Church Street headquarters of the Bureau of Alcohol, Tobacco, and Firearms. "It's hard to turn down the cardinal," he said. Then he asked for a lawyer.

Dennis pleaded guilty to two of the attacks, and the other two charges were dropped; largely because no one had been seriously hurt, he was sentenced to just seven years. Behind bars, he grew more defiant. "History will show that abortion in New York State was nothing more than the dissipation of the black and Puerto Rican populace," Dennis said in his one jailhouse interview.

One day in 1992, Joseph got a call from someone he and Dennis both knew. The two men hadn't been in touch since the conviction. "Dennis is coming out," their friend said. "Take him in."

They made a point of never talking about what Dennis had done. "We made a pact," Joseph remembers. "I said, 'Look, don't drag me into your world. What you have done in the past, it's history.' He promised me, 'Yes,' and that's it. I took his word for it. But Dennis had two different lives."

So, eventually, would Joseph.

Joseph remembers the first few months after Dennis got out as an idyll. They lived near each other in Brooklyn again, goofing off like they were kids. Joseph bought Dennis a used Oldsmobile, co-signed for his credit card, helped him find odd jobs. Taking care of Dennis made Joseph feel like the important one. They chased women, too—until one day Dennis dropped by Joseph's place with a woman dressed in a simple long skirt, like a Mennonite. She seemed about 30, a decade younger than Dennis, and was plain-looking, with long dark hair and dark skin, and green eyes.

"This is Rose," Dennis said. "She's gonna be my wife." Rose was the nickname of Loretta Marra.

Loretta was the closest thing the radical pro-life movement had to Joan of Arc: a compelling, innocent-seeming young woman speaking out against the evils of abortion. She was born into the movement. Her father was a Fordham philosophy professor named William Marra who ran as a third-party right-to-life candidate for president in 1988. From an early age, she began speaking at demonstrations and chaining herself to other protesters outside clinics in America and Europe. Her good friend and perhaps closest spiritual ally in the abortion war was a man named James Charles Kopp.

A biology graduate student from Pasadena, California, who abandoned his career to devote his life to saving the unborn, Kopp had been a regular at clinic protests throughout the eighties. He went to work for Randall Terry, who founded Operation Rescue, and crossed paths with Michael Bray, a central figure in the Army of God. His first major contribution to the cause was the invention of handmade, Kryptonite-lock-style shackles that could block clinic entrances for hours. He met Loretta's father at a protest in Florida in the summer of 1986, when she was just 23. Friends said Kopp and Loretta were instant soul mates, almost finishing each other's thoughts. Some say Kopp was in love with her.

Loretta and Dennis were married in 1994. Two years later, Loretta delivered a baby boy named Louis. A second son—James—was born in April 1999. The couple lived secretly, Joseph says, using fake driver's licenses, dodging Dennis's probation officer, keeping anyone from seeing the inside of their apartment. According to Joseph, Loretta once persuaded Dennis to quit a job after she noticed that one of the company's contracts was with a hospital that performed abortions. Joseph didn't know until years later that their wedding had never been recorded with the state and that Loretta had delivered both her boys in Canada. And he didn't know that even after Loretta and Dennis got married, Loretta had kept in touch with her friend James Kopp.

Sometime in 1998, Dennis came to Joseph's apartment carrying a large sack. Joseph looked inside. It was a rifle.

"What the fuck?! Are you for real?"

"I've gotta store it," Dennis said, "for a friend."

The nation's most notorious abortion-related murder had taken patience. James Kopp visited the woods behind the house on the outskirts of Buffalo for days—wrapping his Russian-made SKS in vinyl and stowing it in a tube he'd planted in the ground, then covering the tube with leaves until he came back, waiting for the right moment. Finally, at 9:55 P.M. on Friday, October 23, 1998, Kopp got the shot he wanted. The abortion doctor was standing in the kitchen, microwaving a bowl of soup. Kopp pulled the trigger. The bullet shattered a window and hit the doctor in the back.

"I think I've been shot," Barnett Slepian said.

"Don't be ridiculous," said his wife, Lynne.

He bled to death before he could get to the hospital.

Slepian's death instantly galvanized the abortion debate: Pro-choice supporters cried out for justice; militant pro-life advocates proclaimed that justice had been done. Bill Clinton called the killing a "tragic and brutal act." The Justice Department launched an international manhunt for the sniper. But Kopp had a carefully thought-out getaway plan. He dyed his hair blond to match a fake driver's license, and a friend drove him to the Mexican border. Within weeks, he flew to London undetected; from there he'd move on to Ireland. But Kopp had one stroke of bad luck. A woman who lived near the Slepians told the police about a man she'd seen while jogging who had seemed out of place. She'd even written down his car's license-plate number.

On November 4, a material-witness warrant was issued for James Kopp, with a $500,000 reward offered for information; by the time Kopp was indicted, the reward had been raised to $1 million. FBI agents raced to search all the places he had lived over the years and to interview friends. Near the top of their list was Loretta Marra. They found her pager number in the phone records of another friend of Kopp's but still couldn't locate her. They went to her father's funeral in December, but she didn't show up. Their best move, they decided, was to somehow get to Dennis Malvasi.

In the spring of 1999, Joseph says he was in the parking lot of a shopping center on Ralph Avenue when a van rolled up next to him and stopped. The van door slid open.

"We want to talk to you."

"Forget it," he said, and kept walking.

Joseph knew Dennis was still on parole. He figured this must be about him. So he told him about the van a few days later. "I was followed," he said. "You better watch it." Dennis smiled cryptically and thanked him.

A few weeks passed, then it happened again—this time an SUV pulled up beside Joseph while he was parking his car.

"Can we talk now? It doesn't have to be here. We don't expect you to trust us."

"No," Joseph said. "I don't want to get involved"—though he had no idea what Dennis might have done.

In mid-September, Joseph was hanging out in Marine Park, making conversation with a plainclothes detective he knew named Julio.

"There was a killing in Buffalo," Julio said.

"Yeah?" said Joseph.

Julio told Joseph that the victim had been an abortion doctor.

Joseph's mind flooded. *Dennis.*

Days later, on September 27, 1999, Joseph found himself sitting in the back of an SUV with tinted windows parked at a Toys"R"Us near the Kings Plaza mall on Flatbush Avenue. Julio was there, to make him feel comfortable. And in the driver's seat was a man in a dark suit. The man was smiling. "How," asked the man, "would you like to have $1 million in your pocket?"

A few days later, face-to-face with FBI agents in an airless downtown hotel room, Joseph panicked. He started making demands, insisting that no one call him by his real name. He even made up a pseudonym on the fly: Jack, from a framed poster he saw on the wall, Steele, from *Remington Steele*. He still wasn't ready to cooperate, but the agents kept pursuing him, asking to meet again and again, and in October, a new agent called. "Would you give me a try?" asked Michael Osborn of the New York office. Osborn told Joseph that all he wanted to know was what Loretta and Dennis knew about the case. He was respectful; he even called him Jack Steele.

Joseph was running out of reasons to say no. He knew they'd never stop asking. Maybe, he told himself, there was an angle here: If Dennis was clean, no harm done; if Dennis did happen to know who did this, he would help solve a murder and go home a millionaire.

So he said yes.

Joseph insists his decision wasn't about abortion. It was about murder. "Pro-life? I got no problem with that. But murdering someone? I got a problem with that regardless who they are."

Then there was the money—or as Joseph calls it, "the incentive."

"Want me to lie to you and tell you no?" Joseph says. "I'd be lying to myself."

The bureau wanted to bug everything—Dennis's place on Chestnut Street, Joseph's car—so they could listen as Joseph tried to get Dennis and Loretta to reveal where Kopp was. But until they could get warrants, Joseph would be their eyes and ears. The agents provided Joseph with cash for entertaining Dennis and Loretta. He was already buying them meals almost every day; now the FBI was picking up the tab. Joseph would tag along with Dennis to trash cans where he got rid of reams of paper so the FBI could search through them once Joseph tipped them off. Later, Osborn suggested that Joseph give Dennis a bunch of prepaid phone cards that the FBI could trace. In time, the FBI knew about every call Dennis and Loretta made or received. Joseph once sat with Dennis and Loretta at his place as they watched a *60 Minutes* segment about the hunt for Kopp, waiting for them to give something up. They said nothing the agents could use.

About a month into his surveillance, the three of them were in Dennis's car, heading home from a Chinese buffet in Canarsie. Loretta's cell rang. She picked it up and gasped.

"It's him! It's him!"

"Pull over," Dennis said.

Joseph might have guessed they were talking about Kopp, but he wasn't sure. He tried to act uninterested. "Dennis, do me a favor, man. Just drop me off." That night, he called Michael Osborn and told him what had happened. All he got were questions—what did Loretta say? Who was she talking to? They needed more.

By the end of 1999, Kopp had made his way from London to Dublin, calling himself Timothy Guttler, walking the streets, even hanging out in well-traveled spots like Bewleys coffee shop. The following July, he took the name Sean O'Briain, a name he'd seen on a local tombstone. Kopp wanted eventually to return to Canada or America—perhaps just to be around the people he loved, perhaps to come out of what he called "retirement." Throughout his exile, he wrote letters—at times lighthearted and jokey, at times sentimental—to his friends Dennis Malvasi and Loretta Marra at 385 Chestnut Street in Brooklyn.

Joseph, meanwhile, spent the next year hinting to Dennis and Loretta that he wanted to join their cause. Joseph would tell Michael Osborn he was going on car trips with Dennis and Loretta, and the FBI would loan him cars with bugs; he'd tell Dennis and Loretta his own car was in the shop. According to FBI transcripts from Jon Wells's book about the Kopp case, *Sniper*, Joseph (referred to in the book as a "confidential source") and Loretta were talking on one car trip about gumming the locks of clinic entrances with glue—a tactic used to stop abortions, if only for a few hours.

Joseph brought up the Slepian murder.

"You think the shooter was trying to kill him?" he asked.

"You're always out there to maim," she said.

"What's Jim's opinion on that?" he asked—slipping in a mention of Kopp's name.

"I know he feels bad for Slepian's children," she said. "But he knows Slepian was not an innocent person, either. He was, morally, a guilty person."

Joseph couldn't think of a way to ask Loretta where Kopp was hiding. Instead, he brought up Dennis's clinic bombings. That was when Loretta told Joseph that she thought Dennis never should have surrendered to the cardinal. "In my opinion, Dennis had an obligation *not* to obey him," Loretta said. "O'Connor's request was a sinful command."

On another trip, Joseph remembers asking Loretta, "Would you really have the fortitude to kill a human being?"

"I think I'd be capable of killing," she said, "for God and a higher good."

After Joseph and Loretta came home, Osborn pushed Joseph to go inside Dennis and Loretta's apartment; they'd always made excuses whenever Joseph tried to enter. Joseph went on a shopping spree and came over on the pretext of delivering presents. "They had a little room, nothing much," he remembers. "They slept on the freakin' floor." When Loretta stepped out to a bodega, Joseph started to play with little Louis. Joseph pointed to a picture on a shelf of James Kopp with a cross on it.

"Who's this guy?" Joseph asked.

"Oh, that's Uncle Jim," said Louis.

"You saw him?"

"Yeah."

"Where?"

"In our old house," Joseph remembers the boy saying. He meant the place his parents had moved from on Linden Boulevard. "He came up to see us once."

On the Friday night after one car trip, Loretta picked up Joseph at his apartment for his first clinic action. Joseph was married now, and he told his wife, Rachel, that he was going out to play cards. When he opened Loretta's car door, he saw she was wearing fatigues. She'd gone to three different stores to buy toothpicks, glue, and a dark cap for Joseph. They drove across Brooklyn to a doctor's office on Church Avenue that they had cased during the day. Loretta parked. In Joseph's hand was a toothpick dripping with glue. He opened the car door, and walked out into the rain.

When he got to the clinic, Joseph picked up his cell phone and called Osborn.

"Michael," said Joseph, "I have a toothpick. I have Krazy Glue. I'm gluing it."

"You're not gonna glue it," the agent said.

"Michael, I don't know what I'm gonna do."

"You're not gluing it. You're breaking the law."

Joseph laughed. "Come on!" he said. "A little won't hurt."

A pause. Then Joseph reassured him.

"Michael, I'm dropping the glue."

Some glue dripped on Joseph's fanny pack. A happy accident; now he'd have something to show Loretta. "Look at this!" he said, back in the car. "It's all over me!"

Loretta couldn't contain herself. She called Dennis. "Dennis, we did it, we did it!" All the way home and through the next day, it was all she could talk about.

Kopp started making plans to leave Ireland toward the end of 2000, perhaps for Germany. He was issued an Irish passport under the name John O'Brien in November, and applied for a driver's license under the name Daniel Joseph O'Sullivan in December. But to travel, Kopp needed money, and Dennis and Loretta happened on a way to raise some.

In January 2001, Dennis and Loretta drove south on the New Jersey Turnpike to attend the annual White Rose Banquet in Bowie, Maryland—the ultimate radical pro-life trade show. Created by Army of God's Michael Bray to mark the anniversary of *Roe v. Wade*, the White Rose featured speakers paying tribute to people jailed for attacking abortion clinics. (The name White Rose was borrowed from a group of German resisters to the Nazis.) Dennis, an A-list celebrity in this circle ever since the New York clinic bombings, agreed to be one of that year's honorees. To raise money, he would auction off a wristwatch he'd used as a timing device in his attacks.

Dennis and Loretta invited Joseph to come with them on the trip. Milling around the banquet room, Joseph got his first look at the stars of the pro-life movement. There was Donald Spitz from Army of God, who called Barnett Slepian a "serial murderer" and his assassin a "hero." There was Chuck Spingola, who wrote, "I believe James Kopp was serving Jesus the righteous, if and when he killed the baby-butcher Slepian, ending his abhorrent and satanic lust for innocent blood." And there was the Reverend Matt Trewhella, founder of Missionaries to the Pre-Born, who once said, "This Christmas, I want you to do the most loving thing. I want you to buy each of your children an SKS rifle and 500 rounds of ammunition." Joseph remembers watching the banquet room fill up with women in long skirts, men in ties and jackets, and children—"little blonde girls, 11,

12 years old. You could hear the kids preaching hate against the animals who killed babies."

Then came the speeches. "They were preaching hate to faggots," Joseph says. Later, Bray and Spitz brought up the Jews—Dennis shot Joseph a look.

"Don't say a fucking word," he said.

Joseph was silent.

Loretta never set foot inside the hall. There was media there, so she stayed away, afraid of being recognized. She did, however, help write Dennis's keynote speech in the car on the way down. "One favorite [saying] is, 'Violence never solves anything,'" he told the crowd. "Of course it does. It solves all kinds of problems. And just men have used it as a tool throughout history." Dennis ended by saluting "the noble work of supporting your local baby-defender, from lock-gluers to bombers ... arsonists, and snipers. Your help makes all the difference in the world—to the babies themselves."

On the way home, Joseph decided to push a little harder. He talked with Dennis about what it might take to meet the man who killed Barnett Slepian.

Dennis looked at Joseph.

"Maybe," Dennis said. For $4,000 or $5,000, he suggested, Joseph could have a picture taken with him.

"How about $10,000?" said Joseph.

"Maybe you'll have a dinner with him."

"If you need the money that bad," Joseph said, "how about we go to Atlantic City? You know how good I am. I gamble, I give you the money."

On February 3, Dennis and Loretta and Joseph and Rachel drove to the Trump Taj Mahal. The FBI bugged Joseph's van for the trip—and even paid for the hotel rooms. Listening in on the car ride, the FBI learned that Loretta used a Yahoo! account to communicate with Kopp. At the Taj, Rachel went shopping, Dennis stayed upstairs with the boys, and Joseph and Loretta went to the casino to gamble.

After a short time, Loretta left the table to see Luciano Pavarotti perform at the Taj's theater. Loretta had given Joseph her things to hang on to. For the next two hours, Joseph was alone with Loretta Marra's wallet. Joseph rifled through everything, searching for addresses, phone numbers, anything that could lead to Kopp. His heart pounding, he called Michael Osborn from a pay phone. To make the search seem legal, he said the wallet had fallen to the ground accidentally.

"I read every single note," Joseph says, "and one of the numbers was in Ireland. It was James Kopp's phone number in Ireland."

The FBI secured a warrant for the Yahoo! account, giving them a window into almost every communication between Kopp and his friends. They learned that Kopp was planning a return to the U.S. or Canada, and on March 21, they spotted a message from Kopp saying he was not in Germany but in Dinan, France. All they needed was an exact location to make the arrest. The FBI listened on bugs as Loretta and Dennis fretted about the logistics of bringing Jim Kopp home: money, phone calls, emails, wiring instructions, travel from Montreal into the States.

Dennis was unusually nervous. "You shouldn't stay online so long," he said. "Who else is using the account? And who established it? We have to get rid of the papers. I'll wrap them in newspapers and throw them in the recycling boxes in the subway."

On March 24, Kopp emailed Loretta three times about wiring arrangements: "Can't get the $20 without the control number. Send the number on the email account right way [*sic*] and then send $50 after that and $600 after that." That same day, Loretta called Joseph. "I need you to come down here. Dennis is not here. I want to send some money."

With her children in the back seat, Loretta and Joseph drove through a drizzling early-spring snow to a Western Union office near Jamaica Avenue. Loretta had everything written down.

She handed him a sheet of paper with the address of a Western Union collection point in Dinan, France.

"Do me a favor," she said. "I'm here with the kids. Why don't you take this in?"

Joseph was shaking. Here was hard evidence linking Dennis and Loretta to Kopp—and a written record of where Kopp would have to be if he wanted to pick up his money. He could see now the whole thing would be over soon. He handed the forms to the clerk.

"Could you send $300?" And then, trying to sound nonchalant, "Could you make a copy, please, for me?"

Joseph folded over the copied papers a billion times and stuffed them into his sock, right under his foot. He put his boot back on and pushed his foot and almost cried out. It felt like a rock. Later, Joseph would call Osborn and read him the information. He thought he could hear the whole Earth stop on the other end of the line. He imagined Osborn was happy.

Back in the car, Loretta seemed to understand that Joseph had crossed a line of some sort. "We're both into it," she told him. "Anything that happens, we're in it now together."

Five days later, on March 29, 2001, Joseph was supposed to meet with Dennis and Loretta for breakfast. As he was about to leave his apartment, his phone rang. It was Osborn.

"Where you going?"

"I'm going to meet Dennis."

"Where is *she*?" Meaning Loretta.

"He says she's at the laundromat," said Joseph. "She's doing laundry."

"Under no condition go to see Dennis today."

Joseph called another friend right away, taking him up on an offer he'd made to spend the day in Brighton Beach. The friend picked him up at about 10 A.M. On the way, the news radio station ticked off the headlines: James Kopp, the suspected abortion assassin, had been captured in Dinan, France.

Joseph's phone rang. Dennis.

"Help me, help me! The FBI's all over! They're on the roofs!"

They'd already picked up Loretta on the way home from the laundromat. Now they were on their way in to get him.

Joseph hung up.

The cell rang again.

"Please help me! *Help me!* I got people—I got cops all over!"

Joseph hung up again.

It took two years of legal wrangling, but on March 18, 2003, James Kopp was convicted of the murder of Barnett Slepian. He was sentenced to 25 years to life in prison. In 2007, he was convicted for the federal offense of blocking access to an abortion clinic and received a life sentence without parole. Dennis and Loretta were jailed, too, for more than two years, as their cases slogged through the courts. At first they seemed likely to face up to ten years each for obstruction of justice and five other counts, but eventually they were just indicted for harboring a fugitive, carrying sentences of only a few years. The prosecutor tried to link Dennis more closely to the murder, claiming they had a witness who had spotted him in Barnett Slepian's neighborhood less than two weeks after the killing, perhaps to retrieve the gun. But the judge declined to hear this witness and on August 21, 2003, sentenced Dennis and Loretta to time served. They were free.

On their way out of the courthouse, a reporter asked Dennis if he was still part of the anti-abortion movement. "I am an abolitionist," Dennis said. "I have never been a member of the anti-abortion movement. So I don't know what you're talking about."

Dennis's close friend Abe Laufgas says that Dennis and Loretta are now living "somewhere around" Newark, in a slum not so different from the East New York of Dennis's youth. They're reunited with their boys (a sister of Loretta's took care of them while they were in jail) and have a third child, a girl named

Lydia. The family lives largely off the grid, says Laufgas—no cell phones, no real names. Dennis repairs computers—"nothing you'd call a steady job," Laufgas says. Money is tight. "They won't take welfare from the state, 'cause then the kids can't be home-tutored, and then the state's going to tell them what to do. They're still revolutionaries, you know?"

They're also still in touch with their friends from White Rose. "As a matter of fact, I was in touch with Loretta just a week ago," Michael Bray of Army of God told me in June. They had been hashing out a theological matter. "I was working on a new catechism. It's for children. Just a fresh look at what the Christian faith is now. And I had her review it for me. Because I know she's sharp."

Last year, Loretta attended a court appearance of Kopp's and was spotted by a reporter. "My life will never be normal," she snapped. "Not when this country is bathed in the blood of millions of children. All I can smell is the stench—the stench of the blood."

James Kopp is now several years into his sentence at a federal prison in West Virginia. Not that long ago, he was asked why Loretta and Dennis named their second child James. "You'll have to ask Loretta," he said with a smile.

Joseph is 62 now—round but solid, balding and tan, almost always grinning and fidgeting. Since 2002, he's been living with Rachel in a Spanish-modern villa in a well-manicured gated community in Florida, having collected most of the $1 million reward for information leading to Kopp's capture. He isn't in a witness-protection program—as an informant, not a witness, he was never offered that option—but he's trying to live as if he were. He and Rachel aren't listed in public phone or address records, and he makes ample use of caller I.D. Fearing reprisals by pro-life activists, he asked to change his name and his wife's for this story.

When I visited Joseph earlier this year, he walked me through his place, showing off his five bedrooms, five flat-screens, a small pool, and the garden he tends during the day while Rachel works. Much of the time, he admits, he's bored out of his mind. The only thing to do here is play golf. "I've never played golf in my life," he says, laughing. "I'm from Brooklyn."

He and Dennis haven't spoken since that phone call, the day of Dennis's arrest. But Dennis did try to reach out to him from prison. At his dining-room table, Joseph sifts through cartons of old papers and finds the letters—more than a dozen from Dennis, all in longhand. One early letter is long, scorching, accusatory: "You cannot imagine the stunning blow and crushing spirit we have undergone by all this suffering and betrayal," Dennis wrote.

But months later, once a plea seemed likely for him and Loretta, Dennis's tone grew a little warmer. "It's taken me all this time to stop being mad at you," Dennis wrote. "But actually if I were you I would have done the same thing proberly [*sic*], so I really can't be mad at you anymore."

The strangest letter came in March 2003, just after Kopp was convicted, but before Dennis and Loretta knew their own fate: "Congratulations! You deserve that money—all of it . . . Don't let them screw you out of your money. I would be more than happy to testify on your behalf." It was the last letter Dennis sent. Joseph would like to think that Dennis was trying to be nice—that he really wants the best for him. But Rachel thinks he was just trying to get into Joseph's head.

Abe Laufgas says that he believes Dennis has forgiven Joseph now—at least somewhat. "He knows how Joseph was and how Joseph is, and he figured that the Feds put pressure on him. And Joseph cracked. He cracks very easy." When Dennis talks about Joseph now, Laufgas says, he calls him by that old nickname, the Trembler.

After all this time, Joseph still has trouble reconciling the Dennis who was his friend with the Dennis who bombed abortion clinics. I asked him several times why Dennis did what he did. "I don't know," he said. But he may have happened on an answer in *Performing in Brooklyn*, a screenplay Dennis wrote back in 1997 about his life. Before I leave, Joseph gives me a copy. The cinematic version of Dennis Malvasi (or "Danny" in the script) is a pro-life action hero—part Rambo, part Randall Terry. Trained in Vietnam to be a killing machine, Danny comes home to a world he doesn't understand. He rips off some guys who are criminals anyway, and goes on the run from the police, all while performing onstage in plays. Danny's life changes forever, though, when he discovers the remains of aborted fetuses in a Dumpster outside a women's health clinic. He has a flashback to Vietnam, the sight of bullets tearing the womb of a pregnant villager, her baby spilling out onto the ground next to her corpse. Danny goes to confession for the first time in years, and the priest tells him he'd been blessed with a moment of grace: He's been a soldier for the military and then a soldier of fortune. Now he'll be a soldier of Christ. That's when the bombings start.

In the screenplay, as in life, the cardinal comes forward to plead with our hero to surrender. But in Dennis's script, the cardinal is a patsy, duped by law enforcement to lure Danny into the hands of a malevolent government. The movie of Dennis's life concludes with the hero walking into the trap, but at least his conscience is clear. "I've always followed my heart," Danny says at the end, on his way to prison. The cardinal is wrong. Danny—Dennis—is a martyr.

Camp Justice

Jeffrey Toobin

from *The New Yorker*

Everyone wants to close Guantánamo, but what will happen to the detainees?

AN ADVERSE RULING from the Supreme Court may be less a legal setback for Bush than a political opportunity for the Republicans.

The future of the detention facility on the American naval base at Guantánamo Bay, Cuba, inspires an unusual degree of bipartisan consensus, at least in theory. All three remaining candidates for President, the Republican John McCain and the Democrats Hillary Clinton and Barack Obama, have called for Guantánamo to be closed. So have Condoleezza Rice, the Secretary of State, and Robert M. Gates, the Secretary of Defense; after touring Guantánamo in January, Admiral Mike Mullen, the chairman of the Joint Chiefs of Staff, said, "I'd like to see it shut down." At a news conference in 2006, President Bush said, "I'd like to close Guantánamo."

Still, Guantánamo is bustling. Although the number of detainees has fallen from a high of around six hundred and eighty to around two hundred and seventy-five, the base is gearing up for what could become a series of military commissions—criminal trials of detainees. The first is scheduled to begin in May. On a dusty plaza surrounded by barbed wire on an abandoned airfield, contractors are finishing a metal warehouse-type building, which will house a new, highly secure courtroom. On the former runways, more than a hundred semi-permanent tents have been erected, in which lawyers, journalists, and support staffs will work and sleep (six to a tent) during the trials. The tent city has been named Camp Justice. The Bush Administration, instead of closing Guantánamo, is trying to rebrand it—as a successor to Nuremberg rather than as a twin of Abu Ghraib.

The commission trials will be the latest act in a complex legal drama that began shortly after September 11, 2001. A few weeks after the attacks on the World Trade Center and the Pentagon, the United States invaded Afghanistan, and on November 13, 2001, President Bush issued an order establishing military commissions to prosecute war crimes by members and affiliates of Al Qaeda. On January 11, 2002, the first prisoners from Afghanistan reached Guantánamo, which was at the time a sleepy Navy facility used for refuelling Coast Guard vessels. The Bush Administration made it clear that it did not believe that the detainees were entitled to any Geneva-convention protections. Then as now, the Bush Administration asserted that they could be held until the "cessation of hostilities," meaning not the war in Afghanistan but the "global war on terror"—that is, indefinitely.

From the moment Guantánamo opened, it has been a target of criticism around the world. In 2005, the Amnesty International secretary-general said that "Guantánamo has become the gulag of our times, entrenching the notion that people can be detained without any recourse to the law." There were allegations of excessively harsh interrogation practices at the detention center in its first years of operation, and the Army's own reporting has substantiated at least one case of abusive treatment. There have been four apparent suicides at the camp and many more attempts. Even staunch American allies, like Tony Blair, in Great Britain, and Angela Merkel, in Germany, have criticized the facility. As McCain said in 2007, "Guantánamo Bay has become an image throughout the world which has hurt our reputation." It is that sort of damage, as much as what has gone on at Guantánamo, that has prompted the calls for the closing of the facility.

Administration officials hope that the military commissions will change Guantánamo's reputation, but that seems unlikely. To date, the commissions have been an abject failure; in more than six years, they have adjudicated just one case—a plea bargain for David Hicks, a former kangaroo skinner from Australia. In March 2007, after more than five years in custody, he pleaded guilty to "material support to terrorism," and was sentenced to nine months; he was returned to Australia, where he served out his sentence, and has now been released. Charges have been filed against fifteen detainees, but even if these cases come to trial—and considerable legal obstacles remain—many more prisoners will be left in limbo, without any charges pending against them or any foreseeable prospect of release. As the clatter of construction work shows, it is easier to talk about closing Guantánamo than to do it. Even shuttering it would not settle the most fundamental question raised by this notorious prison: what to do with its inmates. And attempts to resolve that dilemma are increasingly likely to play a role in the Presidential election.

Four times a week, a twelve-seat propeller plane belonging to Air Sunshine, a small airline based in Florida, lands at Guantánamo. The flight from Fort Lauderdale, just three hundred miles away, takes three hours, because the American airliner must avoid Cuban airspace. More than two thousand people work there; most are Navy and Army personnel, and about twelve per cent are civilian contractors. As in many military bases around the world, the local commanders compensate for Guantánamo's isolation with a kind of hyper-Americanism. There are half a dozen fast-food restaurants, two outdoor movie theatres, miniature golf, and a bedraggled, but playable, nine-hole course. The roads are full of "Gitmo specials"—broken-down heaps that are traded to newcomers by people at the end of their tours.

Heading west from the base's townlike center, you pass the first of its infamous landmarks—Camp X-Ray. A connected series of open-air cages surrounded by barbed wire, X-Ray was the destination for Guantánamo's first prisoners. Photographs of these orange-suited detainees, many hunched over in awkward positions, became emblems of the base. The number of prisoners quickly exceeded the capacity of Camp X-Ray, and it was closed in April, 2002. Base leaders have long wanted to tear down the camp, but a federal judge, who is presiding over one of the many pending cases regarding Guantánamo, ordered X-Ray preserved as possible evidence. So the camp remains, filled with trash and overgrown with weeds.

Fifteen minutes farther down the road, overlooking a particularly beautiful rocky beach, is Camp Delta, the prison complex for the remaining detainees. When I first visited Guantánamo, in late 2003, most of the detainees were held in three areas of Camp Delta, Camps 1, 2, and 3, which look like higher-tech versions of Camp X-Ray. The detainees spent their days and nights in open-air cells, which were topped by metal roofs and surrounded by layers of barbed wire. Now, with fewer prisoners, these camps appear almost empty. (The camp authorities will not specify how many people are in each camp.)

About two dozen "highly compliant" prisoners are being held in Camp 4, which features a dusty courtyard in which inmates can move freely during the day and dormitory-style sleeping arrangements. The prisoners in Camp 4 also have access to a small library for books and movies (a National Geographic film about Alaska is popular), and they can take classes to learn to read and write Pashto, Arabic, and English.

The biggest change to Guantánamo has been the completion of Camp 5, in 2005, and Camp 6, the following year. Most of the detainees now reside there. They are modern federal-prison structures, brick-for-brick copies of a pair of existing facilities, one in Terre Haute, Indiana, and the other in Lenawee, Michigan. The scenes inside, for better or worse, resemble those at most Supermax facilities. The prisoners spend about twenty-two hours a day inside climate-controlled, eight-foot-by-twelve-foot cells, with no televisions or radios, and generally leave only for showers or for recreation in small open-air cages.

Painted on the floor of all cells are arrows pointing toward Mecca, and through the cell doors the detainees can hear each other pray five times a day. Each tier of cells appoints a prayer leader who gets a sign—"Imam"—on his door. About two years ago, there were a hundred detainees on hunger strikes demanding an end to their terms, or at least a finite sentence; the number has declined to about ten, although one inmate has been refusing food for more than eight hundred days, and another for nine hundred days. (These prisoners are force-fed twice daily, via a tube through the nose.) Interview rooms for interrogations are outfitted with blue couches for the detainees. Camp 6 had been intended as a medium-security alternative to Camp 5, but after a series of near-riots by the detainees, in 2006, it, too, was converted to maximum-security status. The so-called "high value" defendants are held at Camp 7. This is a secret location at the base and is never shown to reporters.

In a trailer "inside the wire," adjacent to Camp 4, I spoke with Bruce Vargo, the Army colonel who runs the detention facility. "I think any facility matures over time, and I think that we've continued maturing and offering more programs to them, like the library," he told me. "But they are still very dangerous men, and they take every opportunity they can. There are still assaults that take place weekly on the guards. Every day we have 'splashings,' so I made sure the guards have face shields to protect themselves from feces and urine."

The catchphrase that Vargo and others at Guantánamo often used when describing their work was "safe and humane care and custody." It was clear, however, that winning hearts and minds is not part of the agenda. "They wouldn't be the type of people they are without being driven," Vargo said. "They obviously are very intent on pursuing their cause. They will let you know that this place is just an extension of the battlefield." He went on, "I would not say that we are building a fan base for the U.S. here. We are keeping bad guys off the battlefield."

Vargo's comments reflect the unchanging perspective of the Bush Administration, which holds that these detainees are, in the words of former Secretary of Defense Donald Rumsfeld, "the worst of a very bad lot"—incorrigible soldiers in an unending war. But, in the absence of any meaningful due process, there is no proof that they are. Benjamin Wittes, a fellow at the Brookings Institution, has made a comprehensive review of the prisoners for his forthcoming book, "Law and the Long War." For a period in 2006 when Camp Delta held about five hundred prisoners, Wittes examined all the available data—including the military's assertions about the prisoners and any statements that they themselves made—and estimated that about a third of the detainees could reasonably be said to be terrorists or enemy fighters.

The legal battle over Guantánamo has followed a trajectory similar to the political fortunes of the Bush Administration as a whole. The first court challenges by lawyers representing detainees were filed by the Center for Constitutional Rights, the left-leaning legal-advocacy group in New York, and Joseph Margulies, a civil-liberties attorney. Now, however, the anti-Guantánamo cause has gone mainstream, and Air Sunshine flights often ferry attorneys from white-shoe law firms to visit their detained clients. Almost all the remaining detainees who want attorneys are represented by American counsel.

Initially, government lawyers asserted that because the detainees were held outside the United States they had no right to challenge their status in American courtrooms, or even to file writs of habeas corpus. The Presidential order of November 13, 2001, said that the detainees "shall not be privileged to seek any remedy or maintain any proceeding, directly or indirectly . . . in any court of the United States." But, in 2004, the Supreme Court ruled, in Rasul v. Bush, that, because the Guantánamo base was under the exclusive control of the U.S. military, the detainees were effectively on American soil and had the right to bring habeas-corpus petitions in federal court. As Justice John Paul Stevens said in his opinion, the federal courts "have jurisdiction to determine the legality of the Executive's potentially indefinite detention of individuals who claim to be wholly innocent of wrongdoing."

In response to Rasul, the Department of Defense created a Combatant Status Review Tribunal, an administrative proceeding to justify each detainee's "enemy combatant" status. According to the rules, however, the detainees are not entitled to counsel, are not allowed to see all the evidence against them, and receive only the opportunity to be present and, if they choose, to respond to unclassified charges against them.

These days, the review tribunals are conducted in a windowless double-wide trailer inside the wire, under the supervision of a Navy captain named Ken Garber. These are not trials but a rough cross between grand-jury and probable-cause hearings. Three officers preside over each tribunal, and they can recommend continued detention or transfer to another country. There is only a limited right to appeal, but each detainee receives an annual review of his status in another hearing. "We look at two questions," Garber told me above the hum of the air-conditioners. "Are they still a threat? Do they still have intelligence value? A yes to either one is enough to keep them." The tribunals have been widely criticized as one-sided—Eugene R. Fidell, a noted American expert on military law, has called them a "sham"—and, according to Garber, last year only thirteen per cent of the detainees agreed to participate in or attend their own annual review hearings.

The commissions, which were meant to serve as criminal trials for the detainees, have so far proved to be even more dubious. After the Rasul case, in 2004, the military began pretrial proceedings in the first of the military commissions. One defendant, Salim Ahmed Hamdan, who was alleged to be a driver and bodyguard for Osama bin Laden, challenged the procedures for the commissions, and in June 2006, he won his case before the Supreme Court. In another opinion by Stevens, the Court held Bush's order of November 13, 2001, as it related to military commissions, to be invalid, because the President could not create the commissions without the explicit assent of Congress. Stevens also rejected Bush's long-standing contention that the Geneva conventions did not apply to the detainees.

Bush's response to the ruling was notable both for what it revealed about the Administration's stance on Guantánamo and for what it might mean for the politics of 2008. Far from being chastened by another rebuke from the Justices, Bush used the Hamdan case to return to the subject of the September 11th attacks and to challenge Congress to ratify his aggressive approach. In a carefully choreographed ceremony in the White House on September 6, 2006, Bush made a surprise statement. "We're now approaching the five-year anniversary of the 9/11 attacks—and the families of those murdered that day have waited patiently for justice," he said. "So I'm announcing today that Khalid Sheikh Mohammed, Abu Zubaydah, Ramzi bin al-Shibh, and eleven other terrorists in C.I.A. custody have been transferred to the United States Naval Base at Guantánamo Bay." All had previously been held in secret C.I.A. prisons. Despite the skepticism that Bush and his team had expressed about Guantánamo, the President had, by placing the nation's most notorious terrorist suspects there, given the detention facility a new vote of confidence.

Bush also announced that he was sending a bill to Congress to re-create the military commissions that the Supreme Court had just struck down. "As soon as Congress acts to authorize the military commissions I have proposed, the men our intelligence officials believe orchestrated the deaths of nearly three thousand Americans on September 11, 2001, can face justice," he said. In other words, at the height of the midterm campaign season, Bush forced Congress to weigh the legal legacy of 9/11, his favored political terrain, and turned the commissions from an abstract debate about constitutional rights into a matter of getting Khalid Sheikh Mohammed to trial. It was a winning gambit, for a little more than a month later, on October 17, 2006, Bush signed the Military Commissions Act into law.

The Military Commissions Act was promptly challenged, and the Supreme Court is expected to rule on the case shortly. The act's most vulnerable point, from a constitutional perspective, is a provision barring the detainees from filing writs of habeas corpus. The Administration argues that, even if detainees have rights under the Constitution to habeas corpus, the procedures in place at Guantánamo are an adequate substitute; lawyers for the detainees argue that the Administration has fallen far short of justifying the extreme step of suspending habeas corpus. Last December, at the oral argument of the current Supreme Court case, which is known as *Boumediene v. Bush,* a majority of the Justices—among them Anthony Kennedy, the Court's swing vote—seemed skeptical of the Administration's position, and the Court will likely strike down at least part of the Commissions Act. Again, it appears, a rebuke from the Court will prompt not a retreat by the Bush Administration but another attempt to double-down on its aggressive approach to the detainees. The Court's ruling, in that sense, could be less a legal setback for the President than a political opportunity for his party.

Near Camp Justice, the authorities will use the "pink palace," an old air-traffic-control terminal, for the trials of detainees regarded as minor figures. But the big trials, like that of Khalid

Sheikh Mohammed, will take place in the new metal building, in what for the most part resembles a modern federal courtroom in the United States. The defendants will sit at the end of long defense-counsel tables, next to their interpreters, and all counsel will have computers where the evidence and legal filings in the case can be displayed. The jurors, who will all be military personnel, will also have their own terminals. The law requires at least twelve jurors in capital cases, and at least five in commissions where the penalty is less than death. (In February, the Administration announced that it would seek the death penalty on charges against Mohammed and five others; last week, it added a capital case against Ahmed Khalfan Ghailani for his alleged role in the 1998 bombing of the American Embassy in Tanzania.)

In the new courtroom, I spoke to Brigadier General Thomas W. Hartmann, the legal adviser to the Office of Military Commissions, in the Pentagon, and, as such, the chief Administration defender of the commission process. Hartmann, an Air Force Reservist, is in civilian life general counsel to a Connecticut-based energy company. "When this is over, I'd like people to say these trials were conducted as fairly and as consistently as possible, and we followed the rule of law," he told me, as we sat at one of the prosecution tables.

Hartmann said that the commission procedures mirrored those of courts-martial. "There will be no secret evidence—defendants will see all of the evidence presented to the jury against them," he said. "If the prosecution wants to use hearsay evidence, it has to give notice to the defense and a hearing has to be held to see if it's reliable." Proof beyond a reasonable doubt is required for conviction, and defendants are given a military counsel (and also may hire an attorney), and they do not have to testify, with no inference to be drawn against them if they do not. Death sentences must be unanimous; two-thirds or three-quarters may be sufficient for conviction of lesser offenses.

But there is a heads-I-win, tails-you-lose quality to the proceedings. If a defendant is acquitted, he need not be released;

he can simply be returned to detainee status at Guantánamo, to remain in custody until the end of the war on terror—raising the question of what sort of recourse the proceedings really provide.

"What's unusual about what we're doing is that we're having the commissions before the end of the war," Hartmann told me. "The Nuremberg trials were after World War Two, so there was no possibility of the defendants going back to the battlefield. We still have that problem. We are trying these alleged war criminals during the war. So, in order to protect our troops in the field, in general we are not going to release anyone who poses a danger until the war is over." By this reasoning, even those Guantánamo detainees who are acquitted of the charges against them are analogous to Nazi war criminals.

The commissions are not, however, the only way for detainees to be released. In the past year or so, the U.S. government has engaged in extensive diplomatic efforts to find acceptable homes for detainees of lesser interest. Hundreds of prisoners have left this way; Saudi Arabia alone took about a hundred last year. In a rather forlorn attempt to control the detainees' future behavior, each of those released is asked to sign a form that promises, among other things, that he "will not affiliate himself with al Qaeda or its Taliban supporters" and he "will not engage in, assist, or conspire to commit any acts of terrorism." If detainees refuse to sign, they are released anyway. According to critics, the release of so many detainees in such a short period amounts to an admission by the Administration that the detainees were never as dangerous as had been claimed. "Now that it's clear that Guantánamo is such an embarrassment, they are just shipping as many of them out the door as they can, and just keeping enough of them to save face," Clive Stafford Smith, who has long represented detainees at Guantánamo, said. "It's a political process that has little to do with terrorism."

Of the two hundred and seventy-five or so detainees now in Guantánamo, about sixty have been approved for transfer, if countries can be found to take them. (This issue is complicated by the fact that the United States has not been able to negotiate handovers to some countries, notably Yemen. Other detainees say that they will be tortured in their home country; cases involving Algerian and Tunisian nationals making this claim are pending in federal court in Washington.) Of the remaining detainees, Hartmann anticipates that there is sufficient evidence to bring commissions against only between sixty and eighty. In sum, there are more than a hundred and thirty detainees for whom Administration officials acknowledge they have no plan, except indefinite detention without trial.

The design of the courtroom itself suggests another problem with the commissions. For trials in America, journalists and other members of the public sit inside the courtroom; in Guantánamo, they will watch from behind soundproof glass, which can be screened off, with the sound eliminated, at any time.

"You know why the courtroom has the sealed-off press section, don't you?" Stafford Smith said. "All they care about is the evidence of the accused being tortured. They keep saying that the accused will see all the evidence, but the accused already knows he's been tortured. The point is to make sure that the media and the public don't see the evidence of torture. The key thing that they say is classified is evidence of torture and abuse."

That is not how Hartmann sees it. "The window is there in case the prosecutors want to use classified information, and they have advised that there will be relatively little used," he said. Still, classified information often involves "sources and methods" of intelligence gathering, and details about the interrogations of the detainees are likely to be kept from the public. This, of course, comes in the context of admissions by the government that several of the leading defendants, including Khalid Sheikh Mohammed and Abu Zubaydah, were subjected to waterboarding—the use of near-drowning during questioning. "The statute says that torture is illegal, and statements derived from torture are inadmissible," Hartmann told me. But is waterboarding torture? "These are evidentiary matters to be decided in the courtroom," he said.

To try to forestall trials centered on the alleged torture of the defendants, the prosecutors have assembled "clean teams"—investigators who were not directly involved in the interrogation—to build cases against Mohammed and the others which exclude any evidence that might be tainted. "The clean teams are a joke," Stafford Smith said. "It's impossible to 'unhear' what they said when they were tortured." But it is true that prosecutors in American criminal trials, when confronted with potentially illegally obtained evidence, sometimes devise ways to present the same facts to the jury. Still, the mere possibility that evidence will be aired about the waterboarding of Mohammed and the others suggests the political, not just the legal, dimension of the commission cases.

"We will all deal with the legacy of Abu Ghraib, but that is not the commissions," Hartmann said. "The commissions are not the detention facilities, they are not the C.S.R.T.s"—the review tribunals. "They are not even Guantánamo Bay and Camp X-Ray. The commissions are the commissions, and people are going to see that they are fair."

That claim of fairness suffered a significant blow last fall, when Air Force Colonel Morris D. Davis, the chief prosecutor for the commissions, resigned his post in protest. Davis, who has served as a military lawyer for twenty-four years, took the job in September 2005. He told me that he operated without interference for about a year. The situation changed when Susan Crawford, a protégée of Vice-President Dick Cheney who is close to his counsel and chief of staff, David Addington, was named the "convening authority" of the commissions and Hartmann took over as legal adviser. Crawford was a political appointee, and her position made her a kind of one-person grand jury. Davis came to believe that Hartmann and Crawford were more concerned with the Administration's interests than with the integrity of the process.

"The commissions had such a bad image that it was important from the start to do things as openly and transparently as possible, so I spent a long time trying to get evidence declassified," Davis told me. Crawford and Hartmann, he said, made it clear that they thought that declassifying the evidence was too much trouble and that "we've got to get this moving quickly, even if it means doing it behind closed doors."

Davis went on, "I knew that a few of our likely defendants had been waterboarded, and I just made a decision that we were not going to use any evidence from them that was coerced, and no one challenged that opinion." But Hartmann, Davis says, questioned whether Davis had the authority to judge the admissibility of evidence.

In the end, it was the structure of the commissions, rather than any single decision by his superiors, that prompted Davis to resign. "I thought the whole idea was for Hartmann and Crawford to be the referees, not beholden to the defense or the prosecution," he said. "But if Hartmann is in our office each day, assigning lawyers, deciding which cases to bring, what evidence to use, and then supervising the case—that wasn't right." (Hartmann denied virtually all of Davis's version of events; a Department of Defense investigation determined that there was no wrongdoing on his part. Crawford declined to comment on her role. Davis is retiring from the Air Force this summer.)

It remains to be seen if the first two trials, scheduled to open in May and June, will even begin. One is the Hamdan case; in the other, Omar Khadr, a Canadian national who was fifteen years old when he was captured, is accused of killing an American soldier with a hand grenade. Among the outstanding legal questions in these cases are whether conspiracy is a war crime, and whether the defendants, to prepare their own cases, can interview Khalid Sheikh Mohammed and the other high-value detainees. And there is the issue, also currently unresolved, of whether Khadr should be charged as an adult. Most of the death-penalty defendants, meanwhile, have not yet even been assigned defense attorneys, and their trials are likely months away, at best.

Even if the commissions can somehow begin, the larger question of what to do with the remaining detainees is, for now, unsettled. One response to that quandary is a controversial proposal, by the law professors Neal Katyal and Jack Goldsmith, that is attracting a great deal of attention in the small world of national-security law—and which may offer an electoral lifeline for the Republicans this fall.

Katyal and Goldsmith make unlikely allies. A law professor at Georgetown and former Clinton Administration official, Katyal won widespread renown when he argued and won Salim Hamdan's case before the Supreme Court in 2006. Goldsmith is a former Bush Administration official who, despite leaving the government in 2004, in part over concerns about civil liberties in the war on terror, remains a strong national-security conservative. (He is now a professor at Harvard Law School.) But the two men shared a conviction that both military commissions and ordinary criminal prosecutions would be impractical for a few of those captured on distant battlefields. Together, they came up with an alternative: a national-security court.

According to their proposal, which was recently the subject of a conference sponsored by American University's Washington College of Law and the Brookings Institution, sitting federal judges would preside over proceedings in which prosecutors would make the case that a person should be detained. There would be trials of sorts, and detainees would have lawyers, but they would have fewer rights than in a criminal case. Hearsay evidence may be admissible—so government agents could testify about what informants told them—and there would be no requirement for Miranda warnings before interrogations. Some proceedings would be closed to the public. "It's a new system that's needed only in extreme circumstances," Katyal said. "It's not a default option."

Civil libertarians are, for the most part, aghast. "It's the liberals who support this, the ones who should know better, that are dangerous," Ben Wizner, a staff attorney for the American Civil Liberties Union, who has long dealt with detainee issues, said. "The real problem is that there is an emerging consensus that we need to have some legal authority to detain people without trial, and that's wrong. The government has proved it can criminally prosecute people in terrorism cases—in the African embassy-bombing cases, in the John Walker Lindh case, and others. That's what the government should do—prosecute them, or release them." Katyal says, "Would I love every case to be tried in criminal court? Of course. The reality is, when you're dealing with foreign investigations, particularly concerning events that occurred a long time ago, there are going to be a small handful of cases that you can't try in criminal court." Wizner and others assert that the jurisdiction of any new court would be sure to expand and swallow up more suspects for greater periods of time.

In any case, according to lawyers inside and outside government, the Bush Administration may launch a proposal for a national-security court this summer or fall, after what they presume will be its next loss in the Supreme Court. "It looks like when Boumediene comes down the Court may say to the President and Congress that they need more procedures for the detainees," Goldsmith said. "So, to correct the problem, the President might consider sending something up to Congress this summer or fall. It would help the Republicans in the fall election." The measure would force congressional Democrats to take a stand on the issue in the middle of the campaign—just as Bush did successfully with the Military Commissions Act after the Hamdan defeat. "It worked very well in 2006," Goldsmith said. "The only way the Democrats have to not make it an election issue is to give the President the powers he seeks."

As long as the detainees remain at Guantánamo, the military continues to interrogate them. In this sense, the rationale for the detention center has been unchanged since 2002. Of course, many of the detainees have been talking for five years or more, and it is reasonable to wonder if they have anything left to say.

The head of the Guantánamo Task Force is Admiral Mark Buzby. Moments before he entered a conference room for our interview, an aide brought in the Stars and Stripes and a one-star admiral's flag and set them behind his chair. Buzby is relentlessly on message about the continuing value of the interrogations. "We ask them, 'Tell us how you did that forgery stuff.' That's as timely now as it was back then," he told me. "We are filling in the mosaic." Buzby noted that the detainees' interrogation sessions were sometimes catered by the base's fast-food outlets. "They want those Subway sandwiches!" he said. "Sometimes they just want to talk. Meanwhile, he's chomping on his Subway B.M.T. It's all about that give-and-take and that rapport-building. We still get regular questions in for us to ask from the front in the field. We'll show him a map: 'Thanks a lot, have a Big Mac.'"

It is hard to verify such assertions, because the task force does not allow access to the detainees or to the information they provide. However, many detainees who have been released, and the lawyers for those who remain, contend that the continued interrogations amount to harassment of people who never knew anything of intelligence value in the first place.

Still, the question now, as Buzby acknowledges, is whether Guantánamo, as a symbol and recruiting device for terrorists, endangers more lives than it can possibly save. "It's really for others to weigh whether what we do here is of sufficient value to offset how this place is viewed internationally," Buzby said. For the man in charge on the ground at Guantánamo, the situation with the detainees has devolved into, at best, a lingering standoff. "I don't think any of us envision that they will be here in thirty years, but the question is what to do with them," he said. "The good news is, we got 'em. The bad news is, we got 'em."

McGreevey v. McGreevey

Michael Callahan

from *Philadelphia Magazine*

Everything we didn't really want to know about the former governor and his wife has come out at their ugly divorce trial

"If you had it to do all over again," the girl said, "would you do something else?"

"Nobody has it to do all over again," Craig said.

— *Irwin Shaw,* Evening in Byzantium

SOME 60,000 NEW Jersey couples filed for divorce in 2007, the detritus of their marriages floating through 21 county courthouses—promises of "Till death do us part" that morphed into "Till lawyers do us part." Tucked away in Room 105 of the Union County Courthouse in Elizabeth lies a bulging folder containing the tattered remains of such a union, one that began on a brilliant sunny day in the shadow of the White House and ended on another sunny day inside the New Jersey Statehouse, at a press conference where millions of people watched it crumble, live, behind a podium.

In the beginning, Docket Number FM-20-01166-07G, the Complaint for Divorce between James E. McGreevey, plaintiff, and Dina Matos McGreevey, defendant, showed all sorts of promise, if a divorce proceeding can actually show promise. In his initial filing of February 2, 2007, the disgraced ex-governor of New Jersey was downright cheery. In his motion, he stated that the two parties had mutually agreed to end their marriage and had basically worked out a tentative settlement addressing issues of alimony, custody, child support and parenting time for their five-year-old-daughter, Jacqueline. The document laid out a vision for a very grown-up approach to the split, conjuring the image of two devoted parents committed to dissolving their marriage with dignity and reserve.

A year and a half later, that vision lies in tatters, as anyone following the McGreevey divorce saga can tell you. Read the motions, counter-motions and assorted other legal hand grenades each side has lobbed at the other over that period, and you can almost trace, like a stock chart, the plummeting fortunes of the McGreevey civil discourse. Dina alleged that Jim exposed their daughter to homoerotic art and used her to sell copies of his memoir; she also rolled out a wheelbarrow of past slights, like the accusation that she and Jacqueline were in a car accident and Jim didn't come to the hospital because he was in the middle of his morning workout. Jim returned fire with equal brio, accusing his estranged wife of emotionally manipulating Jacqueline, being a homophobe, and simply morphing into, more or less, "a bitter, vengeful woman."

As the months have ground on, the couple's brawl has devolved into the kind of ludicrous pettiness usually reserved for catfights among sixth-grade girls. The McGreeveys haggled over the drop-off point for Jacqueline's visitations with Jim, down to whether a Barnes & Noble located 9.63 miles from Dina's house (a MapQuest set of directions was actually entered into evidence) was a fair spot. (This bickering alone, which eventually amounted to whether Jacqueline would spend 22 minutes in the car vs. 31 minutes in the car, went on for *two months*.) Last November, Jim went right to court rather than work out a deal with Dina over Jacqueline's American Girl birthday party, a move that caused the aggrieved judge in the case, Karen Cassidy, to declare the whole affair "out of control" and scold both parents, opining that "the hatred you two have for each other overrides everything."

All of which has everybody—everybody, it seems, except Jim and Dina McGreevey—asking a simple question: How? How did the dissolution of the marriage between the affable former governor and his stylish wife dissolve, so quickly and so virulently, into charges of unbridled ambition and Machiavellian emotional manipulation (that's Dina pointing the finger at Jim), Paris Hilton consumerism and scorned-woman revenge (Jim, back at Dina), and, oh yeah, steamy Friday-night threesomes with their studly 20-year-old chauffeur? (More on that shortly.)

Among people who know them, there is an air of recoiling surprise that the McGreevey divorce turned so irrevocably, and unnecessarily, toxic. "I feel sorry for Dina, and I feel sorry for him," says a mutual friend who knew the couple during their days in the governor's mansion. "And I think the fact that neither of them has allowed grace or any sort of redemptive wave to roll over this drama is pathetic."

Finding redemption can be tricky business when two people face a sudden, violent fork in the road and each goes down a different path, one happily skipping, the other staggering. That fork came during the press conference in Trenton at which Jim McGreevey announced he was leaving office and declared publicly, for the first time, "My truth is that I am a gay American." Anyone who has ever come out of the closet will tell you that there ensues a stunning burst of exhilaration, of weight-off-the-shoulders freedom. But for Dina, the moment was exactly the opposite: as her husband took the first steps to a new identity and happily took a sledgehammer to his old one, he also took one to hers, with seemingly no thought given to the fact that *she* had no new life to run to—just an old one now shattered. And so it was in that moment on national television that the perfect storm, set in motion by Jim and Dina McGreevey on the night of his election to the governor's office in 2001, erupted.

IF YOU WERE to spend a few days at the McGreevey divorce trial—and be glad you haven't—what you'd see would be the worst elements of the reality-television culture that we've become. On the right side of the courtroom sits Jim, almost always in an ill-fitting navy suit, a red tie and bad rubber-soled shoes. He bounds into court each day with an aw-shucks enthusiasm that is almost jarring, as if the coach has just called him off the bench. He regularly chats up the jaded press corps, and if he notices their open disdain for both him and these proceedings, he never shows it. He then invariably grabs his leather-bound Bible—his prop of choice since announcing plans last year to become an Episcopal priest—adjusts his glasses, and drops into his role as novice divinity student at the plaintiff's table.

His wife is quite another story. Circumspect and aloof, she almost invariably arrives in court after McGreevey, and unless it's Oprah or Larry King, she doesn't utter a word to the press. With a helmet of anchorwoman hair the color of a school bus and a penchant for tailored suits of the Nancy Reagan era, she has spent most days at the trial with her head down, looking alternately bored and peeved.

Rounding out the drama are the supporting cast: John Post, Dina's patrician, white-haired, mannerly counsel; the theatrical Stephen Haller, the third attorney who has handled McGreevey's case (Jim parted ways with the first two) and a man who, in the words of one courthouse regular, "can be found in any room where there's a camera"; and the aforementioned Judge Cassidy, whose general demeanor suggests a ninth-grade social studies teacher continually exasperated by her students' failure to hand in their book reports on time. Post and Haller have known one another professionally for years. At times, the matchup has taken on the vague air of a vaudeville act. One morning before testimony began, Haller declared his love for Post, and they hugged. "If you hadn't said you had a cold, I'd have kissed you," Haller said as they broke apart. "That's what I was afraid of," Post replied drolly. (Ba-dum-bum.) Another day, Haller slipped his hand onto Post's right thigh. Post almost leapt out of his skin. "Better look out, John," McGreevey smirked from his seat. "It's catching."

Of course, not everyone finds the sideshow so appealing. "It's all just totally unbelievable," says Arlene Lauer, whose job it is to organize civil cases filed in the courthouse every year. Arlene is one of several gossipy, pillowy women I've come to dub The Girls of Civil Procedure during my days wading through the morass that is *McGreevey v. McGreevey*. Since the case began, more than 18 months ago, the Girls have seen the courthouse turned upside down by the circus playing out inside the courtroom on the ninth floor. At one point the Girls had a pool going over how long the trial would last, but in the end there was no winner: none of them had imagined the freak show would still be running.

"I don't know," Arlene remarks to me one day, sitting in her cramped corner cube, reading glasses perched atop her copper-colored bob. "I mean, don't you think this is all ridiculous?" She shakes her head as she reaches for her ringing phone. "Some people," she's saying as she picks up the receiver, "just haven't got any *sense*."

Perhaps not. But what both Jim McGreevey and Dina Matos did have, from the beginning of their unorthodox courtship—he asked her out by having an aide call her to schedule a date—was ambition. And that may help explain how this mess got so, well, messy.

Jim was—and in many ways still is—the kid who wants everyone to like him, and who uses that "Hey, buddy" aura to insinuate himself into the cool kids' club, no matter what the moral cost. "An ambitious politician quickly learns, as I did, to countenance and even sponsor fundamentally corrupt behavior while insulating himself, for as long as he can, behind a buffer of deniability," he writes in *The Confession*, his 2006 autobiography that landed him on Oprah's couch and put a good number of readers to sleep. (An entire section details the history and demographics of Woodbridge, New Jersey.) People wanted shovels of dirt and got teaspoons. The book, like McGreevey himself, is affable, slightly maddening, and often disingenuous.

Perhaps it was this quixotic brew that attracted Dina Matos when she first met him in October 1995, at a meeting of a Portuguese civic group. He was 38; she was 28. She later recalled thinking "he was handsome, in a Tom Hanks kind of way." Dina was and still appears reserved, somewhat entitled and a tad icy, which hasn't served her well through the trial. But as a Portuguese immigrant who came to this country at the age of eight not speaking a whit of English, she always felt somewhat off-center, out of the mix—which may help explain why she so easily mistook the faux intimacy offered by the winsome Jim McGreevey for the real thing. Why, by her own admission, she "missed the signs."

Their courtship was banal and ordinary, mainly conducted at chicken dinners for New Jersey politicians. Jim was the mayor of Woodbridge and an up-and-coming face in the hurly-burly world of New Jersey politics; Dina was a community organizer and an adept fund-raiser for a hospital in Newark. But even without the guidance of hindsight, their romance seems oddly detached, lacking in the tender, tiny, just-the-two-of-us moments that forge genuine love affairs. One of the most telling anecdotes both relay in their respective memoirs is of a romantic getaway they took to Montreal, only to hit a stretch of black ice on a highway en route and spend the night in an off-the-beaten-path motel. (Interestingly, each claims to have taken the wheel as the car spun out of control.) Once inside the room, Jim—according to Dina—began climbing into the opposite single bed from hers, until she convinced him to come snuggle with her.

McGreevey had lost, barely, his initial run for governor against incumbent Christine Todd Whitman in 1997. He was certain he could come out on top in 2001, when he would eventually face conservative firebrand Bret Schundler. And having a Laura Bush Lite wife would surely help. He hoped, he writes in his book, "that living with Dina would help me enforce the boundaries I'd been trying to maintain for years. If I stayed single, with no structural safeguard, there was no telling what sort of volatile situation I might get into."

Their wedding, in October 2000, had all the trappings of an ambitious politician and his equally ambitious wife. Though neither was from the Washington, D.C., area, they got married at the Hay-Adams Hotel, and their wedding photo shows them standing in front of the backdrop of the White House. ("In my mind, it was kind of a campaign stop," Jim wrote later.) In the picture, Jim is in a tux, Dina in Vera Wang—"the dress of my dreams," she said. Dina later hung a poster-size portrait of herself in the dress in her bedroom.

With his new blond wife in tow, McGreevey set out to win the governor's mansion, and this time he did. And one can track back to the exact moment the course of Jim and Dina McGreevey was set—the one that has led them to one of the most hideous divorces ever recorded. It was November 7, 2001, when Jim stood at the podium of the Hilton hotel in East Brunswick and declared victory.

Because it was on this night that Jim McGreevey would discover, all too quickly, that his ambition, stoked for years as he poked about in the muck of New Jersey politics, carried a price. He had spent a lot of political capital getting elected governor, and a lot of people were expecting payback. He had also begun an affair with an aide named Golan Cipel, whom he'd met in Israel, and for the first time the revulsion he felt about his latent homosexuality, carried around like a sack of coal inside his heart for years, gave way to a naive teenager's fantasy of forbidden romance.

The idea of being first lady held enormous appeal for Dina: In her memoir, she refers to herself as the "first lady-elect." (The term "first lady" appears 10 times on page 132 alone.) Seeing herself as a modern-day Jackie Kennedy (a comparison also made in her book), she eventually redecorated Drumthwacket, the governor's mansion, and tried to be the kind of elegant hostess required of the wife of a head of state—even if the state was New Jersey. On the night of Jim's inaugural, a state trooper was "assigned the role of Protector of the Gown," Dina writes. He followed her around with his arms outstretched, to make sure no one stepped on her train.

And so the makings of that perfect storm had gathered: a politician who checked his ethics at the door, whose administration would quickly be riddled by scandal, and who had begun living a high-risk, full-fledged double life that could destroy him at any moment; his wife, who so desperately yearned for the trappings that come from being the governor's spouse that she had an official portrait taken and business cards that read DINA MATOS McGREEVEY, FIRST LADY printed, complete with the official state seal, while by her own admission she ignored the clouds brewing over her marriage; and their daughter, without whom the whole sordid, sad saga of Jim and Dina McGreevey might have quietly died, as it so obviously should have, in a file cabinet drawer in Room 105 of the Union County Courthouse.

"I think he knew in his heart of hearts at the time—he needed to get a wife, and he went and got one. And I think he really used her," says a former friend of the couple. "But I don't think she was an unwitting partner. She probably knew something was up with this guy."

SCANDAL IS THE fuel that feeds our 24-hour news cycle today, and Jim McGreevey's confession that he had a secret gay lover, had hired this lover for a homeland security post he wasn't qualified for, and had been blackmailed by this lover, forcing him to resign his office in August 2004, was the media equivalent of a tractor-trailer of gasoline. Everyone seemed aghast except the governor himself, who proudly declared his gayness as Dina stood by his side in a powder-blue St. John suit, her terrible frozen smile coming off as a sad impersonation of the Joker squaring off against Batman.

Splashes of gasoline have continued to stoke the story, perhaps the biggest being Teddy Pedersen, part of the cabal of good-looking young men who were members of the McGreevey political posse and whom Dina later labeled "The Lost Boys." (Signaling the coming political apocalypse, a month before McGreevey resigned, *The Record* of Bergen County ran an exposé on the Lost Boys: "NJ Governor James E. McGreevey Hires a Dozen 'Pretty Boys'; Big Jobs, No Experience Needed.")

If Teddy is to be believed, he regularly hopped into bed with Jim and Dina for threesomes, assignations they eventually dubbed "Friday-night specials," according to him. In an interview with *The Star-Ledger* in March, Pedersen, now 29 and a real estate developer, claimed the trio would go out to eat at a local TGIFriday's, then retreat to McGreevey's condo for sex. These exploits don't appear in either Jim's or Dina's memoirs, though Pedersen has given a sealed deposition in the divorce case. Dina denies the threesomes ever happened, a view shared by people who know her. "Frankly, I think she's a prude," says one of them. "Look, you can't always tell what someone is like in bed. But it's like some people are good huggers, and others are barely out of the freezer. Dina is a chin-to-chin toucher by way of greeting. Never mind hot—she's not warm. She would be a very odd person to have a threesome."

Which raises one final question: Who cares? In the almost four years since the resignation, as the McGreeveys have squared off—in court, in the media, and, ironically, given their fight over where to drop off Jacqueline, on the shelves of Barnes & Noble—to each get their version of their ridiculous marriage accepted as the official one, the second rule of scandal has surfaced: even in America, there's a point where we've had enough. (Heard from Britney lately? My point exactly.) Jim's book quickly fell off the best-seller list; Dina's never made it there at all.

Dina's seemingly dazed appearance on *Larry King Live* following the Eliot Spitzer sexcapade in March (Silda Spitzer having had her own awful turn at the podium with *her* husband) seemed to somehow put an exclamation point on all the McGreevey fatigue. Speaking in her flat mouthful-of-mashed-potatoes voice, Dina reiterated the Dina canon: Jim married me for political gain, Jim never loved me, Jim's resignation was "as if he were making another political speech during a campaign season."

Jim found himself a hunky, wealthy boyfriend (Australian financier Mark O'Donnell), moved into a baronial mansion in Plainfield, and announced his plans to serve in the Episcopal Church. (While McGreevey is taking classes at the General Theological Seminary in New York, a school spokesman says he isn't currently enrolled in a divinity degree program.) All of which has only served to feed Dina's stewing, brewing anger further, as she sits in her modest *Brady Bunch*-style house and wonders about What Might Have Been If My Husband Hadn't Come Out of the Closet. "Jim seemed to have no sense that this was a catastrophe looming in my life and Jacqueline's as well as his own," she writes in her book, wryly titled *Silent Partner*. "There was no compassion, only self-absorption. I had given so much and worked so hard for Jim, and for goals I believed in as much as he did. Nevertheless, soon I would have no home, no husband, no marriage. And throughout all of this, Jim had never once told me he was sorry."

Today, both of them are unemployed. Both are broke and deep in six-figure legal debt. And both are still dug in, bracing for a possible third phase of their seemingly never-ending divorce trial, this one dealing with Dina's fraud charge, alleging that Jim tricked her into marrying him. If it proceeds to trial—and Dina wants a jury if it does—Teddy Pedersen will, in all likelihood, be called to testify, setting up yet another wince-inducing stretch for The Girls of Civil Procedure and all the rest of us burned out by and fed up with Jim and Dina McGreevey.

"There's a rule: Never pick a fight with someone who's got nothing to lose," McGreevey's attorney, Stephen Haller, says. "Jim's got nothing to lose. He can't be knocked down further, he can't be made fun of more, he can't be denigrated to a lower degree. He has really suffered whatever there is to suffer as a result of this whole business."

Some of Dina's friends feel she's gotten short shrift in media coverage, in large measure because Jim is so much more seasoned in dealing with the press. They also feel that some of Jim's timing during the case—such as announcing his intention to study for the priesthood the day after Dina's memoir was published—has been ruthlessly tactical. "The thing about Jim that nobody gets is that Jim acts like if you say it, it's true," says one Dina pal who didn't want to be identified speaking about her. "So at the same time he's pursuing this incredible vendetta against her, and is passive-aggressive, he will come out and say, 'We're all trying to work this out. We all want what's best,' when he's behaving like a prick. The public sees what he's *saying*, but not what he's *doing*."

I ask Haller when he thinks all of this will be over, when Jim and Dina will finally let go of their hatred, move on. He doesn't hesitate. "I think it will be 12 more years," he says. "Then, Jacqueline will be 18."

A History of Music Torture in the War on Terror

Andy Worthington

from *CounterPunch*

THERE'S AN AMBIGUOUS undercurrent to the catchy pop smash that introduced a pig-tailed Britney Spears to the world in 1999 – so much so that Jive Records changed the song's title to "… Baby One More Time" after executives feared that it would be perceived as condoning domestic violence.

It's a safe bet, however, that neither Britney nor songwriter Max Martin ever anticipated that this undercurrent would be picked up on by U.S. military personnel, when they were ordered to keep prisoners awake by blasting earsplitting music at them —for days, weeks or even months on end—at prisons in Iraq, Afghanistan and Guantánamo Bay.

The message, as released Guantánamo prisoner Ruhal Ahmed explained in an interview earlier this year, was less significant than the relentless, inescapable noise. Describing how he experienced music torture on many occasions, Ahmed said, "I can bear being beaten up, it's not a problem. Once you accept that you're going to go into the interrogation room and be beaten up, it's fine. You can prepare yourself mentally. But when you're being psychologically tortured, you can't." He added, however, that "from the end of 2003 they introduced the music, and it became even worse. Before that, you could try and focus on something else. It makes you feel like you are going mad. You lose the plot, and it's very scary to think that you might go crazy because of all the music, because of the loud noise, and because after a while you don't hear the lyrics at all, all you hear is heavy banging."

Despite this, the soldiers, who were largely left to their own devices when choosing what to play, frequently selected songs with blunt messages—"Fuck Your God" by Deicide, for example, which is actually an anti-Christian rant, but one whose title would presumably cause consternation to believers in any religion—even though, for prisoners not used to Western rock and rap music, the music itself was enough to cause them serious distress. When CIA operatives spoke to ABC News in November 2005, as part of a groundbreaking report into the use of waterboarding and other torture techniques on "high-value detainees" held in secret prisons, they reported that, when prisoners were forced to listen to Eminem's Slim Shady album, "The music was so foreign to them it made them frantic." And in May 2003, when the story broke that music was being used by U.S. psyops teams in Iraq, Sgt. Mark Hadsell, whose favored songs were said to be "Bodies" by Drowning Pool and "Enter the Sandman" by Metallica, told Newsweek, "These people haven't heard heavy metal. They can't take it."

Approval for the Use of Music Torture in the War on Terror

Depending on people's musical tastes, responses to reports that music has been used to torture prisoners often produces flippant comments along the lines of, "If I had to listen to David Gray's 'Babylon'/the theme tune from Barney (the purple dinosaur)/ Christina Aguilera, I'd be crying 'torture' too." But the truth, sadly, is far darker, as Hadsell explained after noting that prisoners in Iraq had a problem with heavy metal music.

"If you play it for 24 hours," Hadsell said, "your brain and body functions start to slide, your train of thought slows down, and your will is broken. That's when we come in and talk to them."

Hadsell, like senior figures in the administration, was blithely unconcerned that "breaking" prisoners, rather than finding ways of encouraging them to cooperate, was not to best way to secure information that was in any way reliable, but the psyops teams were not alone. In September 2003, Lt. Gen. Ricardo Sanchez, the U.S. military commander in Iraq, approved the use of music as part of a package of measures for use on captured prisoners "to create fear, disorient . . . and prolong capture shock," and as is spelled out in an explosive new report by the Senate Armed Services Committee into the torture and abuse of prisoners in U.S. custody (PDF), the use of music was an essential part of the reverse engineering of techniques, known as survival, evasion, resistance, escape (SERE), which are taught in U.S. military schools to train personnel to resist interrogation. The report explains:

During the resistance phase of SERE training, U.S. military personnel are exposed to physical and psychological pressures ... designed to simulate conditions to which they might be subject if taken prisoner by enemies that did not abide by the Geneva Conventions. As one . . . instructor explained, SERE training is "based on illegal exploitation (under the rules listed in the 1949 Geneva Convention Relative to the Treatment of Prisoners of War) of prisoners over the last 50 years." The techniques used in SERE school, based, in part, on Chinese Communist techniques used during the Korean War to elicit false confessions, include stripping detainees of their clothing, placing them in stress positions, putting hoods over their heads, disrupting their sleep, treating them like animals, subjecting them to loud music and flashing lights, and exposing them to extreme temperatures. It can also include face and body slaps, and until recently, for some who attended the Navy's SERE school, it included waterboarding.

The Senate Committee's report, which lays the blame for the implementation of these policies on senior officials, including President George W. Bush, former Defense Secretary Donald Rumsfeld, Vice President Dick Cheney's former legal counsel (and now chief of staff) David Addington, and former Pentagon General Counsel William J. Haynes II, makes it clear not only that the use of music is part of a package of illegal techniques, but also that at least part of its rationale, according to the Chinese authorities who implemented it, was that it secured false confessions, rather than the "actionable intelligence" that the U.S. administration was seeking.

The Experiences of Binyam Mohamed and Donald Vance

In case any doubt remains as to the pernicious effects of music torture, consider the comments by Binyam Mohamed, a British resident still held in Guantánamo, who was tortured in Morocco for 18 months on behalf of the CIA, and was then tortured for four months in the CIA's "Dark Prison" in Kabul, and Donald Vance, a U.S. military contractor in Iraq, who was subjected to music torture for 76 days in 2006.

Speaking to his lawyer, Clive Stafford Smith, the director of the legal action charity Reprieve, Mohamed, like Ruhal Ahmed, explained how psychological torture was worse than the physical torture he endured in Morocco, where the CIA's proxy torturers regularly cut his penis with a razorblade.

"Imagine you are given a choice," he said. "Lose your sight or lose your mind."

In Morocco, music formed only a small part of Mohamed's torture. Toward the end of his 18-month ordeal, he recalled that his captors "cuffed me and put earphones on my head. They played hip hop and rock music, very loud. I remember they played Meatloaf and Aerosmith over and over. I hated that. They also played 2Pac, "All Eyez On Me," all night and all day. … A couple of days later, they did the same thing. Same music. I could not take the headphones off, as I was cuffed. I had to sleep with the music on and even pray with it."

At the Dark Prison, however, which was otherwise a plausible re-creation of a medieval dungeon, in which prisoners were held in complete darkness and were often chained to the walls by their wrists, the use of music was relentless. As Mohamed explained:

It was pitch black, and no lights on in the rooms for most of the time … They hung me up for two days. My legs had swollen. My wrists and hands had gone numb. . . . There was loud music, *Slim Shady* and Dr. Dre for 20 days. I heard this nonstop, over and over. I memorized the music, all of it, when they changed the sounds to horrible ghost laughter and Halloween sounds. It got really spooky in this black hole. . . . Interrogation was right from the start, and went on until the day I left there. The CIA worked on people, including me, day and night. Plenty lost their minds. I could hear people knocking their heads against the walls and the doors, screaming their heads off. . . . Throughout my time, I had all kinds of music and irritating sounds, mentally disturbing. I call it brainwashing.

Vance's story demonstrates not only that the practice of using music as torture was being used as recently as 2006, but also that it was used on Americans. When his story broke in December 2006, *The New York Times* reported that he "wound up as a whistle-blower, passing information to the FBI about suspicious activities at the Iraqi security firm where he worked, including what he said was possible illegal weapons trading," but that "when American soldiers raided the company at his urging, Mr. Vance and another American who worked there were detained as suspects by the military, which was unaware that Mr. Vance was an informer."

Vance, who was held at Camp Cropper in Baghdad, explained that he was routinely subjected to sleep deprivation, taken for interrogation in the middle of the night and held in a cell that was permanently lit with fluorescent lights. He added, "At most hours, heavy metal or country music blared in the corridor." Speaking to the Associated Press last week, he said that the use of music as torture "can make innocent men go mad," and added more about the use of music during his imprisonment, stating that he was "locked in an overcooled 9-foot-by-9-foot cell that had a speaker with a metal grate over it. Two large speakers stood in the hallway outside." The music, he said, "was almost constant, mostly hard rock. There was a lot of Nine Inch Nails, including 'March of the Pigs.' I couldn't tell you how many times I heard Queen's 'We Will Rock You.' " He said the experience "sort of removes you from you. You can no longer formulate your own thoughts when you're in an environment like that."

After his release, Vance said he planned to sue Rumsfeld on the basis that his constitutional rights had been violated, and he noted, "Saddam Hussein had more legal counsel than I ever had." He added that he had written a letter to the camp's commander "stating that the same democratic ideals we are trying to instill in the fledgling democratic country of Iraq, from simple due process to the Magna Carta, we are absolutely, positively refusing to follow ourselves."

Musicians Take Action

Last week, Reprieve launched a new initiative, Zero dB (Against Music Torture), aimed at encouraging musicians to take a stand against the use of their music as torture instruments. This is not the first time that musicians have been encouraged to speak out. In June, Clive Stafford Smith raised the issue in the *Guardian*, and when, in an accompanying article, the *Guardian* noted that David Gray's song "Babylon" had become associated with the torture debate after Haj Ali, the hooded man in the notorious Abu Ghraib photographs, told of being stripped, handcuffed and forced to listen to a looped sample of the song, at a volume so high he feared that his head would burst, Gray openly condemned the practice. "The moral niceties of whether they're using my song or not are totally irrelevant," he said. "We are thinking below the level of the people we're supposed to oppose, and it goes against our entire history and everything we claim to represent. It's disgusting, really. Anything that draws attention to the scale of the horror and how low we've sunk is a good thing."

In a subsequent interview with the BBC, Gray complained that the only part of the torture music story that got noticed was its "novelty aspect"—which he compared to *Guantánamo['s] Greatest Hits*—and then delivered another powerful indictment of the misappropriation of his and other artists' music.

"What we're talking about here is people in a darkened room, physically inhibited by handcuffs, bags over their heads and music blaring at them for 24 hours a day, seven days a week," he said. "That is torture. That is nothing but torture. It doesn't matter what the music is—it could be Tchaikovsky's finest or it could be *Barney the Dinosaur*. It really doesn't matter, it's going to drive you completely nuts.

"No-one wants to even think about it or discuss the fact that we've gone above and beyond all legal process and we're torturing people."

Not every musician shared Gray's revulsion. Bob Singleton, who wrote the theme tune to Barney, which has been used extensively in the War on Terror, acknowledged in an op-ed for the *Los Angeles Times* in July that "if you blare the music loud enough for long enough, I guess it can become unbearable," but refused to accept either that songwriters can legitimately have any say about how their music is used, or that there were any circumstances under which playing music relentlessly at prisoners could be considered torture.

"It's absolutely ludicrous," he wrote. "A song that was designed to make little children feel safe and loved was somehow going to threaten the mental state of adults and drive them to the emotional breaking point?

"The idea that repeating a song will drive someone over the brink of emotional stability, or cause them to act counter to their own nature, makes music into something like voodoo, which it is not."

Singleton was not the only artist to misunderstand how the use of music could indeed constitute torture—especially when used as part of a package of techniques designed to break prisoners.

Steve Asheim, Deicide's drummer, said: "These guys are not a bunch of high school kids. They are warriors, and they're trained to resist torture. They're expecting to be burned with torches and beaten and have their bones broken. If I was a prisoner at Guantánamo Bay and they blasted a load of music at me, I'd be like, 'Is this all you got? Come on.' I certainly don't believe in torturing people, but I don't believe that playing loud music is torture either."

Furthermore, other musicians have been positively enthusiastic about the use of their music. Stevie Benton of Drowning Pool, which has played to U.S. troops in Iraq, told *Spin* magazine, "People assume we should be offended that somebody in the military thinks our song is annoying enough that played over and over it can psychologically break someone down. I take it as an honor to think that perhaps our song could be used to quell another 9/11 attack or something like that."

Fortunately, for those who understand that using music as part of a system of torture techniques is no laughing matter, the Zero dB initiative provides the most noticeable attempt to date to call a halt to its continued use. Christopher Cerf, who wrote the music for *Sesame Street*, was horrified to learn that the show's theme tune had been used in interrogations. "I wouldn't want my music to be a party to that," he said.

Tom Morello of Rage Against the Machine has been particularly outspoken in denouncing the use of music for torture. In 2006, he said to *Spin* magazine: "The fact that our music has been co-opted in this barbaric way is really disgusting. If you're at all familiar with ideological teachings of the band and its support for human rights, that's really hard to stand." On this year's world tour, Rage Against the Machine regularly turned up on stage wearing hoods and orange jumpsuits, and during a recent concert in San Francisco, Morello proposed taking revenge on President Bush: "I suggest that they level Guantánamo Bay, but they keep one small cell, and they put Bush in there . . . and they blast some Rage Against the Machine."

And on Dec. 11, just after the Zero dB initiative was announced, Trent Reznor of Nine Inch Nails posted the following message on his blog:

> *It's difficult for me to imagine anything more profoundly insulting, demeaning and enraging than discovering music you've put your heart and soul into creating has been used for purposes of torture. If there are any legal options that can be realistically taken they will be aggressively pursued, with any potential monetary gains donated to human rights charities. Thank GOD this country has appeared to side with reason, and we can put the Bush administration's reign of power, greed, lawlessness and madness behind us.*

Even James Hetfield of Metallica, who has generally been portrayed as a defender of the U.S. military's use of his band's music, has expressed reservations. In a radio interview in November 2004, he said that he was "proud" that the military had used his music (even though they "hadn't asked his permission or paid him royalties"). "For me, the lyrics are a form of expression, a freedom to express my insanity," he explained, adding, "If the Iraqis aren't used to freedom, then I'm glad to be part of their exposure." Hetfield laughed off claims that music could be used for torture, saying, "We've been punishing our parents, our wives, our loved ones with this music forever. Why should the Iraqis be any different?"

However, he also acknowledged the reason that the military was using his music: "It's the relentlessness of the music. It's completely relentless. If I listened to a death metal band for 12 hours in a row, I'd go insane, too. I'd tell you anything you wanted to know."

While these musicians have at least spoken out, others—including Eminem, AC/DC, Aerosmith, the Bee Gees, Christina Aguilera, Prince and the Red Hot Chili Peppers—remain silent about the use of their work. Britney Spears' views are also unknown, but if her comments to CNN in September 2003 are anything to go by, it's unlikely that she would find fault with it. When Tucker Carlson said to her, "A lot of entertainers have come out against the war in Iraq. Have you?" Britney replied, "Honestly, I think we should just trust our president in every decision he makes and should just support that, you know, and be faithful in what happens." Perhaps she should speak to Pamela Anderson, who recently posted a simple message to Barack Obama on her blog: "Please Shut down Guantánamo Bay—figure it out—make amends/stop torture—it's time for peaceful solutions."

A Moment's Notice

Ben Hallman

from *The American Lawyer*

Weil, Gotshal put together the largest bankruptcy in U.S. history in record time. It was a fitting tribute to the firm's biggest institutional client.

By THE SECOND week of September, investors had all but given up on Lehman Brothers Holings Inc. Creditors wanted the 158-year-old investment bank to put up additional collateral to cover its bets in the derivatives market. Customers were scrambling to close accounts. Traders couldn't move the firm's commercial paper, or settle trades. In its most visible sign of distress, Lehman's share price tumbled in those last days like a sick pigeon from the sky.

These grim facts of life weren't lost on four senior partners from Weil, Gotshal & Manges. On Sunday, September 14, they sat in a taxi, stuck in traffic in lower Manhattan. They were headed to the Federal Reserve Bank of New York. The Weil lawyers knew that without a buyer or a government bailout, a Lehman bankruptcy was possible-hell, even likely. After all, the firm had spent the previous few days planning for that very possibility.

What Stephen Dannhauser, Thomas Roberts, Harvey Miller, and Lori Fife didn't know was that their opinion about whether and when Lehman should file for bankruptcy protection-they had planned to advise the company to wait, to continue to look for a buyer-didn't really matter anymore. That decision had already been made for them.

As the cab crawled south toward lower Manhattan, Roberts, a 62-year-old M&A lawyer with a Dallas twang, got a phone call from a banking client. Then a second one called. Both clients had been at the Fed that afternoon as government officials made a final plea to the banking community to save Lehman. The clients said essentially the same thing, "We've been told by the Fed that Lehman's going to file tonight."

The Weil lawyers were floored. The two bankruptcy attorneys in the group, Miller and Fife, along with Dannhauser, the firm chairman, had met briefly with Fed officials the day before. The lawyers had told the Fed that they were preparing for a possible bankruptcy, but that the planning had barely begun. It was a short meeting, and the Weil partners walked away with the impression that bankruptcy was not in the cards. "It was treated as a hypothetical," Fife recalls. "We gave no indication that we were ready to file."

The lawyers finally arrived at the Federal Reserve's fortress-like headquarters near Wall Street almost an hour after they had left their midtown office. The attorneys persuaded a nervous cabbie to drive them past the news cameras and armed guards into the Fed's parking garage. The quartet entered the building as Vikram Pandit-the Citigroup Inc. chief executive and one of the many bankers the government wanted to enlist in helping Lehman-walked out. The Weil lawyers were escorted to a crowded conference room. As they walked in, Herbert "Bart" McDade, Lehman's chief operating officer, was making an impassioned plea to government officials to save his bank. "You don't understand the consequences," McDade said, according to several onlookers. "You don't understand what will happen."

Fed officials, the Weil lawyers quickly learned, would not sponsor a buyer for the troubled bank, nor would the government back the bank while it explored other options. Furthermore, federal officials were encouraging Lehman's parent company to file for bankruptcy immediately. Before midnight that day, if possible, to limit the damage to the Asian stock markets.

The Weil lawyers, with Miller leading the way, made their best arguments to the government representatives. They weren't ready to file. A precipitous bankruptcy filing would mean Armageddon for the financial sector. It would lead to a meltdown in equity markets around the world.

The federal officials, including Thomas Baxter, the general counsel of the Federal Reserve, called a recess. (There were also representatives from the U.S. Department of the Treasury and the Securities and Exchange Commission in the overcrowded room. The federal agencies didn't respond to requests to comment for this story.) The government officials left for nearly an hour. When they returned, their message hadn't changed. The officials strongly urged Lehman to file for bankruptcy protection that night. "They said it was 'a critical part of a program they wanted to roll out,' " says Miller, who at 75 is the éminence grise of the bankruptcy bar. They didn't explain what that program entailed, he says. It felt, Miller says, "like we were facing a hanging judge."

LEHMAN BROTHERS ENTERED bankruptcy with assets of $639 billion. This is more than the annual gross domestic product of all but the 17 wealthiest nations. The bank's failure shocked world stock markets and triggered a credit freeze as banks, for a while, simply stopped lending to each other.

In the weeks since, as the world's economy has teetered on the edge of disaster, federal officials have faced a steady drumbeat of recrimination and second-guessing. Why, many have asked, did the federal government allow Lehman to fail? And why did it have to file for bankruptcy so quickly?

Treasury secretary Henry Paulson recently said in an interview with *The New York Times* that he didn't have the authority to bail out Lehman. By law, he said, the Federal Reserve could only make a significant loan to the bank if it had enough healthy assets to serve as collateral, which Paulson said it did not.

Lawyers and bankers involved in the negotiations over the weekend of September 13 say they never heard that explanation. They say that officials negotiating on Paulson's behalf-when they were asked why the government wouldn't back a sale, as it had done with Bear Stearns Companies Inc. in the spring-never mentioned Lehman's bad assets. Instead, Lehman bankers and lawyers heard the "great moral hazard" argument. The federal government didn't want to establish the bad precedent of rescuing failing banks. Without a government guarantee, Lehman was cooked.

What would have happened if Lehman had waited a few days to file, or even a few weeks? One lawyer who participated in the negotiations for a Lehman sale that weekend says there wasn't a good alternative to filing. There were no more potential buyers waiting in the wings, Lehman was broke, and the firm stood to get clobbered when the markets opened Monday morning, September 15, this lawyer says.

But Miller says that rather than pushing for a Chapter 11, the Fed could have provided a financial backstop to the firm while it closed its positions and unwound from the rest of the market in an orderly way. Instead, he and the Weil crew were forced to organize, on a moment's notice, the largest and most complex bankruptcy in history. But their work didn't end there. Over the next five days, the lawyers drove a sale of Lehman Brothers Inc., the brokerage unit, through U.S. Bankruptcy Court. They worked knowing that every minute wasted was a minute that the value of the underlying business diminished, "like a melting ice cube on the dock," as Miller said in court. More than 100 Weil,

Gotshal lawyers would take part-many of them working around the clock to finalize deals that would normally take months to complete.

THE RELATIONSHIP BETWEEN Lehman Brothers and Weil, Gotshal dates to 1983. Dannhauser, then a newly minted corporate partner, approached Lewis Glucksman, then the chief executive officer at Lehman Brothers, and a few other senior executives he had met while they worked on opposite sides on a deal. Dannhauser, young and hungry, asked Glucksman for work. "Someone gave you a chance once," he remembers saying. Glucksman's response was not encouraging. "The list [of legal providers] is a hundred years old," Glucksman answered-meaning, Dannhauser assumed, don't hold your breath. Weil was a much smaller law firm in those days, just 279 lawyers, compared with 1,300 lawyers today. It had restructuring and litigation practices, but wasn't a big player on Wall Street. An institutional relationship with a major bank would be a breakthrough, and would allow the New York-based firm to grow multiple practices at once. Despite Glucksman's brush-off, Lehman Brothers passed along some work. Over the years the relationship grew. When it failed, Lehman was Weil's biggest client, accounting for $40 million to $50 million in fees annually, or about 4 percent of Weil's gross revenue. By the summer of 2008, after months of turmoil and falling stock prices, Lehman's management decided that it needed to sell assets to raise capital. Michael Lubowitz, a Weil M&A partner, was tapped by M&A chief Roberts to explore sale options for a stake in Lehman's investment management division, including its crown jewel, Neuberger Berman, Inc., as well as the bank's private equity group.

This wasn't the only potential deal. Weil was also working on the possible spin-off of Lehman's real estate assets. Simpson Thacher & Bartlett was exploring other deal possibilities, including the sale of some or all of the holding company.

As the summer waned, the pressure to complete a deal-fast-grew. So did the likelihood that a sale of part of Lehman's business wouldn't be enough to stanch the bleeding. On Wednesday, September 10, Lehman released its quarterly earning numbers early with the hope of easing investor fears. The announcement showed that the bank lost $4 billion in the third quarter. The share price continued to fall.

At some point that week-Dannhauser declined to say what day-Steven Berkenfeld, a Lehman managing director, called with a request. He wanted Weil to quietly begin preparing for a bankruptcy. (Berkenfeld, now at Barclays plc, declined to comment.) Dannhauser asked Miller to take the lead, but there wasn't much the bankruptcy partner could do until he got access to Lehman's books and its executives. At this point, Lehman felt that a Chapter 11 filing was a remote possibility, and so it didn't invite the bankruptcy lawyers to its midtown headquarters, out of fear that word of a potential filing would leak and trigger a panic.

On Friday, September 12, Lehman's stock price plunged 90 percent. At about 6 P.M., Fed officials and Treasury secretary Paulson called for an emergency meeting of some of Wall Street's top bankers at the New York Federal Reserve office. They told the bankers that the government would not bail out Lehman, and that it was up to Wall Street to sort out the mess, according to press reports. But it was London that almost saved the day. Barclays, a British bank that had been eyeing various parts of the Lehman business for months, was interested. That evening, Simpson Thacher partners John Finley and Andrew Keller, representing Lehman, delivered a draft of a merger agreement to Barclays.

Lubowitz went home that night figuring his role in the drama was over. "I thought our deal was dead," he recalls. "Even if we could have gotten to a letter of intent for the IMD [investment management division] sale, it wasn't large enough to solve the biggest problems. I thought that there would be a deal struck, at the last minute, for the whole company. I told my guys to stand by over the course of the weekend, but in my own mind I thought the IMD sale was off the table."

When Federal Reserve officials asked Miller later that evening if Lehman was planning for a "contingency," if an offer for most of the bank didn't come through, the question was asked as if it were simply a formality, Miller says.

FOR 32 YEARS, until he left Weil in 2002 to join the investment bank Greenhill & Co. Inc., Miller was arguably the top bankruptcy lawyer in the country. "He's the dean of the restructuring bar," says John Butler, Jr., the head of bankruptcy at Skadden, Arps, Slate, Meagher & Flom. An inimitable presence-tall, quick-witted, with a wardrobe that would outshine most heads of state-Miller presided over many of the major bankruptcies of the era, including that of Drexel Burnham Lambert in 1990. In March 2007, after four (profitable) years away at Greenhill, Miller rejoined his old law firm. His return couldn't have been better timed-for Miller, who missed lawyering, or for Weil, which had lost several prominent bankruptcy partners in recent years.

On Saturday, September 13, Weil ramped up its bankruptcy preparation efforts. A sale still seemed likely-even after word spread that Bank of America Corporation, which had also been in the running to buy Lehman, was instead purchasing Merrill Lynch & Co., Inc. for $50 billion-but the precipitous fall in Lehman's share price the day before, along with all the bank's other problems, convinced the players that something significant was in store. The need to prepare for a bankruptcy now outweighed the desire to keep the preparations secret. Early that afternoon, Miller called for reinforcements. He sent a firmwide email to any "[bankruptcy] partner who can help."

Lori Fife was in Weil's New York office working on a speech she was supposed to give in Las Vegas the following week when she got Miller's email. Fife, 50, a restructuring veteran, co-led the firm's representation of WorldCom, Inc. "I figured [Miller's request] was a short-term kind of thing," Fife says. She replied, saying she was available.

That evening, as Miller worked the phones from Weil, Fife and Shai Waisman, another restructuring partner, went to Lehman headquarters near Times Square for the first time to prepare a Chapter 11 filing. They set up shop in a conference room on the busy thirty-first floor, and spent the next five hours asking midlevel Lehman executives a steady stream of questions. What were Lehman's assets? Who were its creditors? What did its insurance policies look like? How did the bank manage its cash? The executives hadn't prepared for the interviews, and couldn't answer many of the most basic business questions. "Almost nothing was prepared at that time," Fife recalls. "All the people were focused on the [potential Barclays] transaction. No one wanted to take the time to talk about insurance policies."

Meanwhile, Lehman was buzzing with activity. Some time that evening, Barclays delivered a counterproposal to the agreement drafted by Simpson Thacher the day before. Barclays offered to buy all of Lehman's assets, with the exception of its commercial real estate holdings. A deal seemed imminent.

The Weil lawyers were back at work early on Sunday. Waisman began drafting Chapter 11 papers-just in case. Dannhauser, Miller, and Fife met to discuss what to tell the Lehman board, which was scheduled to meet at noon. They agreed to recommend that Lehman continue to push for a sale of the company. But the board meeting never happened.

The Barclays deal fell apart on Sunday morning. Press accounts have suggested that British regulators told Barclays at the last minute that the bank needed shareholder consent for the Lehman deal, or its board members could be held personally responsible for Lehman's liabilities. But this isn't the whole story, say people involved in the negotiations. Lawyers and executives on both sides had been working for three days on an agreement. They knew about the shareholder consent rule. Negotiators thought they could structure a deal that would circumvent it, or failing that, they could talk the regulators into issuing a waiver. Neither happened. By Sunday, the only remaining option was to ask the Fed to guarantee Lehman's obligations. This was strike three. "It was made clear to us that the government was not going to put its credit on the line to save Lehman," says a person involved in the negotiations. Paulson and the others didn't want to set a bad precedent. Barclays walked away, and Lehman was left to die alone.

THE WEIL LAWYERS walked into the Lehman building at about 9:30 P.M. that Sunday night. Employees, afraid that they would be locked out the next morning, were filing out of the build-ing with boxes stuffed with their belongings. Fife says the sight brought tears to her eyes.

On the thirty-first floor, the Lehman board of directors gath-ered for its last meeting. The Weil lawyers and Lehman execu-tives recounted what government officials had told them at the meeting at the New York Fed offices earlier that evening.

Soon after the proceedings began, Lehman chief executive Richard Fuld's secretary interrupted to say that SEC chairman Christopher Cox wanted to address the board about filing for bankruptcy. Even by this weekend's standards, this was highly unusual.

"It's very important you make the right decision tonight," Cox said, according to several participants. (The SEC didn't return calls for comment.) The board, says one observer, "was totally blindsided" and "unnerved that the federal government was telling them what to do."

In the end, the board felt that it had no choice. In a tearful session, they voted to dissolve. At 1 A.M. on Monday morning, Waisman filed papers with the U.S. Bankruptcy Court for the Southern District of New York, asking for Chapter 11 protection for Lehman Brothers Holding Co. The long weekend was over, but for the weary Weil lawyers, the work had just begun.

At 7 A.M. that day, as the world was waking up to the news that one of the remaining four major American investment banks had failed, Weil's Roberts, working on three hours of sleep, returned to Lehman's headquarters. Robert Diamond, the Barclays chief executive officer, had requested a meeting.

Diamond still wanted Lehman. Or a piece of it, anyway.

Lubowitz, the M&A partner who had gone home on Friday anticipating that his role in the Lehman drama was over, was called in, too, as were Miller and Fife. Barclays brought a room full of lawyers from Cleary Gottlieb Steen & Hamilton, including M&A partner Victor Lewkow. (Cleary, which had also represented the Federal Reserve over the previous weekend, wasn't the only law firm to double-dip in the crisis. Sullivan & Cromwell, which had been advising Lehman as it negotiated with federal officials, also joined the Barclays team.) Barclays, Diamond said, wanted to buy Lehman's brokerage operation, Lehman Brothers Inc. How long would it take to put a deal together? Miller suggested 15 days.

One of the Barclays representatives stood up, and said, "In that case, we're not interested." "Perhaps we can do better," Miller said.

Working around the clock, the lawyers crafted an agreement in about 40 hours. Lubowitz, who turned 43 on Tuesday, September 16, says that for the first time in his life, he was awake for all 24 hours of his birthday. "There was an underdog mentality that we are not going to fail," he says. Fife says that "everyone felt motivated to save jobs."

"We did in a few days what normally would take at least a month," says Lewkow, the Cleary lawyer. Antitrust clearance, for example, which usually takes 30 days, got done in two days, he says.

Time was so precious that the lawyers didn't even take the time to incorporate the final changes that had been handwritten in the margins of the sale agreement. They submitted it to Judge James Peck, a relatively new federal bankruptcy judge, after midnight, in the early hours of Wednesday morning, and immediately began work on an amendment to the agreement.

As the lawyers and business executives were racing to save the investment business, the company was coming to grips with the bankruptcy. The Weil lawyers hadn't had any time to prepare the executives, so the atmosphere that first week at Lehman head-quarters was chaotic. Alvarez & Marsal, restructuring consultants that manage companies in distress, was brought in. Dannhauser also called in two veterans of the Enron Corp. bankruptcy, Dallas partners D. Gilbert Friedlander and Glenn West, who set up a crisis center at Lehman headquarters. "Basically I was there to answer immediate questions about what should and shouldn't be done," West recalls. This included, he says, "everything from answering questions from the secretary who wonders if she is going to get a paycheck to substantive business questions."

One of many thorny issues involved the use of the Lehman Brothers credit card. The company had put up dozens of executives and back office people in hotels in New York as part of the Barclays talks. Once news of the bankruptcy got out, the hotels began declining the Lehman credit cards and threatening to evict the employees. West stepped in, eventually charging about $50,000 in hotel stays on his Weil credit card.

The race to complete a sale before the assets melted away played havoc on all the lawyers involved, not just those for Lehman and Barclays. Milbank, Tweed, Hadley & McCloy, led by partner Dennis Dunne, was among four finalists to repre-sent Lehman's unsecured creditors. Milbank lawyers pitched the job at 1:30 P.M. on Wednesday, learned they had won the beauty contest at 3:10 P.M., and were in court for the first hearing at 4 P.M.

Judge Peck set an aggressive schedule, and on Friday, just 48 hours after the first hearing, the lawyers for all the parties, along with a motley collection of creditors, journalists, and hedge funders (including former first daughter Chelsea Clin-ton), packed into the claustrophobic courtroom. At 1 A.M. on

Saturday, September 20, five days from the hour that the parent company had filed for protection in his court, Judge Peck approved a $1.35 billion sale of the brokerage arm to Barclays. "I have to approve this transaction because it is the only available transaction," he said.

The sale required the unusual intervention of the Securities Investor Protection Corporation (SIPC), a government-chartered entity created 37 years ago to protect investor accounts in the event of a brokerage firm failure. Miller asked the SIPC to initiate a liquidation proceeding for the brokerage that would correspond with the bankruptcy hearing. This was necessary to complete a sale because a brokerage can't technically file for Chapter 11 protection under federal bankruptcy law. The timing was important to allow for the seamless transfer of customer accounts from the Lehman to the Barclays platform. "It was ingenious," says Miller, not the modest type, of the legal maneuvering. "It's never been done before." After another long weekend clarifying amendments, the sale closed on Monday, September 22.

The short-term assignment that Fife thought she was accepting has taken over her life. She now coordinates Weil's response to the bankruptcy, as Miller's second-in-command, putting in long hours day after day. In the weeks since the filing she worked on the sale of the Neuberger Berman investment management business for $2.15 billion, and dozens of smaller sales of Lehman entities. Her husband, Fife says, is understanding. "It's your Super Bowl," he told her.

Roberts and Lubowitz, M&A men, have moved on to other deals.

Dannhauser continues to manage the firm. The Lehman bankruptcy was "tragic," he says. "We grew up with these guys." But from a business perspective, his view is mixed. The firm lost a big client, but got a whale of a job. Under one estimate, by Lynn LoPucki, who teaches bankruptcy law at UCLA Law School, the firm stands to bill about $209 million. Miller, who was recently inducted into the inaugural class of the restructuring hall of fame in New Orleans, seems to be enjoying this, perhaps a last moment in the sun. He says the events of the past few months may mean big changes for the way bankruptcy works for financial institutions. He believes that something more akin to a conservatorship, where for 60–90 days the bank comes under control of the federal government, may be a more rational way to deal with failing banks. He has also been increasingly outspoken about the government's inaction as Lehman tumbled and fell. At a court hearing in October, he said it showed "a lack of foresight" that reminded him of "the federal government's reaction to Katrina."

As a bankruptcy lawyer and an investment banker, Miller was perhaps uniquely qualified to predict what would happen if Lehman Brothers filed for bankruptcy. That he was correct-if the filing didn't spawn Armageddon in the financial markets, it came close-now seems obvious. But it didn't take an expert to predict what would happen, Miller says. Just knowledge of simple physics. "When a stone starts rolling downhill, it gathers momentum," he says.

Katrina's Hidden Race War

A.C. Thompson

from *The Nation*

A.C. Thompson's reporting on New Orleans was directed and underwritten by the Investigative Fund at The Nation Institute. ProPublica *provided additional support, as did the* Center for Investigative Reporting *and* New America Media.

THE WAY DONNELL Herrington tells it, there was no warning. One second he was trudging through the heat. The next he was lying prostrate on the pavement, his life spilling out of a hole in his throat, his body racked with pain, his vision blurred and distorted.

It was September 1, 2005, some three days after Hurricane Katrina crashed into New Orleans, and somebody had just blasted Herrington, who is African-American, with a shotgun. "I just hit the ground. I didn't even know what happened," recalls Herrington, a burly 32-year-old with a soft drawl.

The sudden eruption of gunfire horrified Herrington's companions–his cousin Marcel Alexander, then 17, and friend Chris Collins, then 18, who are also black. "I looked at Donnell and he had this big old hole in his neck," Alexander recalls. "I tried to help him up, and they started shooting again." Herrington says he was staggering to his feet when a second shotgun blast struck him from behind; the spray of lead pellets also caught Collins and Alexander. The buckshot peppered Alexander's back, arm and buttocks.

Herrington shouted at the other men to run and turned to face his attackers: three armed white males. Herrington says he hadn't even seen the men or their weapons before the shooting began. As Alexander and Collins fled, Herrington ran in the opposite direction, his hand pressed to the bleeding wound on his throat. Behind him, he says, the gunmen yelled, "Get him! Get that nigger!"

The attack occurred in Algiers Point. The Point, as locals call it, is a neighborhood within a neighborhood, a small cluster of ornate, immaculately maintained 150-year-old houses within the larger Algiers district. A nationally recognized historic area, Algiers Point is largely white, while the rest of Algiers is predominantly black. It's a "white enclave" whose residents have "a kind of siege mentality," says Tulane University historian Lance Hill, noting that some white New Orleanians "think of themselves as an oppressed minority."

A wide street lined with towering trees, Opelousas Avenue marks the dividing line between Algiers Point and greater Algiers, and the difference in wealth between the two areas is immediately noticeable. "On one side of Opelousas it's 'hood, on the other side it's suburbs," says one local. "The two sides are totally opposite, like muddy and clean."

Algiers Point has always been somewhat isolated: it's perched on the west bank of the Mississippi River, linked to the core of the city only by a ferry line and twin gray steel bridges. When the hurricane descended on Louisiana, Algiers Point got off relatively easy. While wide swaths of New Orleans were deluged, the levees ringing Algiers Point withstood the Mississippi's surging currents, preventing flooding; most homes and businesses in the area survived intact. As word spread that the area was dry, desperate people began heading toward the west bank, some walking over bridges, others traveling by boat. The National Guard soon designated the Algiers Point ferry landing an official evacuation site. Rescuers from the Coast Guard and other agencies brought flood victims to the ferry terminal, where soldiers loaded them onto buses headed for Texas.

Facing an influx of refugees, the residents of Algiers Point could have pulled together food, water and medical supplies for the flood victims. Instead, a group of white residents, convinced that crime would arrive with the human exodus, sought to seal off the area, blocking the roads in and out of the neighborhood by dragging lumber and downed trees into the streets. They stockpiled handguns, assault rifles, shotguns and at least one Uzi and began patrolling the streets in pickup trucks and SUVs. The newly formed militia, a loose band of about fifteen to thirty residents, most of them men, all of them white, was looking for thieves, outlaws or, as one member put it, anyone who simply "didn't belong."

The existence of this little army isn't a secret—in 2005 a few newspaper reporters wrote up the group's activities in glowing terms in articles that showed up on an array of pro-gun blogs; one Cox News story called it "the ultimate neighborhood watch." Herrington, for his part, recounted his ordeal in Spike Lee's documentary *When the Levees Broke*. But until now no one has ever seriously scrutinized what happened in Algiers Point during those days, and nobody has asked the obvious questions. Were the gunmen, as they claim, just trying to fend off looters? Or does Herrington's experience point to a different, far uglier truth?

Over the course of an eighteen-month investigation, I tracked down figures on all sides of the gunfire, speaking with the shooters of Algiers Point, gunshot survivors and those who witnessed the bloodshed. I interviewed police officers, forensic pathologists, firefighters, historians, medical doctors and private citizens, and studied more than 800 autopsies and piles of state death records. What emerged was a disturbing picture of New Orleans in the days after the storm, when the city fractured along racial fault lines as its government collapsed.

Herrington, Collins and Alexander's experience fits into a broader pattern of violence in which, evidence indicates, at least eleven people were shot. In each case the targets were African-American men, while the shooters, it appears, were all white.

The new information should reframe our understanding of the catastrophe. Immediately after the storm, the media portrayed African-Americans as looters and thugs—Mayor Ray Nagin, for example, told Oprah Winfrey that "hundreds of gang members" were marauding through the Superdome. Now it's clear that some of the most serious crimes committed during that time were the work of gun-toting white males.

So far, their crimes have gone unpunished. No one was ever arrested for shooting Herrington, Alexander and Collins—in fact, there was never an investigation. I found this story repeated over and over during my days in New Orleans. As a reporter who has spent more than a decade covering crime, I was startled to meet so many people with so much detailed information about potentially serious offenses, none of whom had ever been interviewed by police detectives.

Hill, who runs Tulane's Southern Institute for Education and Research and closely follows the city's racial dynamics, isn't surprised the Algiers Point gunmen have eluded arrest. Because of the widespread notion that blacks engaged in looting and thuggery as the disaster unfolded, Hill believes, many white New Orleanians approved of the vigilante activity that occurred in places like Algiers Point. "By and large, I think the white mentality is that these people are exempt—that even if they committed these crimes, they're really exempt from any kind of legal repercussion," Hill tells me. "It's sad to say, but I think that if any of these cases went to trial, and none of them have, I can't see a white person being convicted of any kind of crime against an African-American during that period."

YOU CAN TRACE the origins of the Algiers Point militia to the misfortune of Vinnie Pervel. A 52-year-old building contractor and real estate entrepreneur with a graying buzz cut and mustache, Pervel says he lost his Ford van in a carjacking the day after Katrina made landfall, when an African-American man attacked him with a hammer. "The kid whacked me," recalls Pervel, who is white. "Hit me on the side of the head." Vowing to prevent further robberies, Pervel and his neighbors began amassing an arsenal. "For a day and a half we were running around getting guns," he says. "We got about forty."

Things quickly got ugly. Pervel remembers aiming a shotgun at a random African-American man walking by his home—even though he knew the man had no connection to the theft of his vehicle. "I don't want you passing by my house!" Pervel says he shouted out.

Pervel tells me he feared goons would kill his mother, who is in her 70s. "We thought we would be dead," he says. "We thought we were doomed." And so Pervel and his comrades set about fortifying the area. One resident gave me video footage of the leafy barricades the men constructed to keep away outsiders. Others told me they created a low-tech alarm system, tying aluminum cans and glass bottles together and stringing them across the roads at ankle height. The bottles and cans would rattle noisily if somebody bumped into them, alerting the militia.

Pervel and his armed neighbors point to the very real chaos that was engulfing the city and claim they had no other choice than to act as they did. They paint themselves as righteous defenders of property, a paramilitary formation protecting their neighborhood from opportunistic thieves. "I'm not a racist," Pervel insists. "I'm a classist. I want to live around people who want the same things as me."

Nathan Roper, another vigilante, says he was unhappy that outsiders were disturbing his corner of New Orleans and that he was annoyed by the National Guard's decision to use the Algiers Point ferry landing as an evacuation zone. "I'm telling you, it was forty, fifty people at a time getting off these boats," says Roper, who is in his 50s and works for ServiceMaster, a house-cleaning company. The storm victims were "hoodlums from the Lower Ninth Ward and that part of the city," he says. "I'm not a prejudiced individual, but you just know the outlaws who are up to no good. You can see it in their eyes."

The militia, according to Roper, was armed with "handguns, rifles [and] shotguns"; he personally carried "a .38 in my waistband" and a "little Uzi." "There was a few people who got shot around here," Roper, a slim man with a weathered face, tells me. "I know of at least three people who got shot. I know one was dead 'cause he was on the side of the road."

DURING THE SUMMER of 2005 Herrington was working as an armored-car driver for the Brink's company and living in a rented duplex about a mile from Algiers Point. Katrina thrashed the place, blowing out windows, pitching a hefty pine tree limb through the roof and dumping rain on Herrington's possessions. On the day of the shooting, Herrington, Alexander and Collins were all trying to escape the stricken city, and set out together on foot for the Algiers Point ferry terminal in the hopes of getting on an evacuation bus.

Those hopes were dashed by a barrage of shotgun pellets. After two shots erupted, Collins and Alexander took off running and ducked into a shed behind a house to hide from the gunmen, Alexander tells me. The armed men, he says, discovered them in the shed and jammed pistols in their faces, yelling, "We got you niggers! We got you niggers!" He continues, "They said they was gonna tie us up, put us in the back of the truck and burn us. They was gonna make us suffer.... I thought I was gonna die. I thought I was gonna leave earth."

Apparently thinking they'd caught some looters, the gunmen interrogated and verbally threatened Collins and Alexander for ten to fifteen minutes, Alexander says, before one of the armed men issued an ultimatum: if Alexander and Collins left Algiers Point and told their friends not to set foot in the area, they'd be allowed to live.

Meanwhile, Herrington was staring at death. "I was bleeding pretty bad from my neck area," he recalls. When two white men drove by in a black pickup truck, he begged them for help. "I said, Help me, help me—I'm shot," Herrington recalls. The response, he tells me, was immediate and hostile. One of the men told Herrington, "Get away from this truck, nigger. We're not gonna help you. We're liable to kill you ourselves." My God, thought Herrington, what's going on out here?

He managed to stumble back to a neighbor's house, collapsing on the front porch. The neighbors, an African-American couple, wrapped him in a sheet and sped him to the nearest hospital, the West Jefferson Medical Center, where, medical records show, he was X-rayed at 3:30 P.M. According to the records, a doctor who reviewed the X-rays found "metallic buckshot" scattered throughout his chest, arms, back and abdomen, as well as "at least seven [pellets] in the right neck." Within minutes, Herrington was wheeled into an operating room for emergency surgery.

"It was a close-range buckshot wound from a shotgun," says Charles Thomas, one of the doctors who operated on Herrington. "If he hadn't gotten to the hospital, he wouldn't have lived. He had a hole in his internal jugular vein, and we were able to find it and fix it."

After three days in the hospital, which lacked running water, air conditioning and functional toilets, Herrington was shuttled to a medical facility in Baton Rouge. When he returned to New Orleans months later, he paid a visit to the Fourth District police station, whose officers patrol the west bank, and learned there was no police report documenting the attack. Herrington, who now has a wide scar stretching the length of his neck, says the officers he spoke with failed to take a report or check out his story, a fact that still bothers him. "If the shoe was on the other foot, if a black guy was willing to go out shooting white guys, the police would be up there real quick," he says. "I feel these guys should definitely be held accountable. These guys had absolutely no right to do what they did."

Herrington, Alexander and Collins are the only victims, so far, to tell their stories. But they certainly weren't the only ones attacked in or around Algiers Point. In interviews, vigilantes and residents—citing the exact locations and types of weapons used—detail a string of violent incidents in which at least eight other people were shot, bringing the total number of shooting victims to at least eleven, some of whom may have died.

Other evidence bolsters this tally. Thomas, the surgeon who treated Herrington, staffed one of the few functioning trauma centers in the area, located just outside the New Orleans city line, not far from Algiers Point, for a full month after the hurricane hit. "We saw a bunch of gunshot wounds," he tells me. "There were a lot of gunshot wounds that went unreported during that time." Though Thomas couldn't get into the specifics of the shooting incidents because of medical privacy laws, he says, "We saw a couple of other shotgun wounds, some handgun shootings and somebody who was shot with a high-velocity missile [an assault-rifle round]." The surgeon remembers handling "five or six nonfatal gunshot wounds" as well as three lethal gunshot cases.

In addition, state death records show that at least four people died in and around Algiers Point, a suspicious number, given that most Katrina fatalities were the result of drowning, and that the community never flooded. Neighborhood residents, black and white, remember seeing corpses lying out in the open that appeared to have been shot.

WHILE THE MILITIA patrolled the streets of Algiers Point, the New Orleans Police Department, which had done little to brace for the storm, was crippled. "There was no leadership, no equipment, no nothing," recalls one high-ranking police official. "We did no more to prepare for a hurricane than we would have for a thunderstorm." Without functioning radios or dispatch systems, officers had no way of knowing what was happening a block away, let alone on the other side of the city. NOPD higher-ups had no way to give direction to unit commanders and other subordinates. As the chain of command disintegrated, the force dissolved into a collection of isolated, quasi-autonomous bands.

Around Algiers Point people say they rarely saw cops during the week after Katrina tore through Louisiana, and in this law enforcement vacuum the militia's unique brand of justice flourished. Most disturbing, one of the vigilantes, Roper, claims on videotape recorded just weeks after the storm that the shootings took place with the knowledge and consent of the police. When we talk he makes the same assertion: "The police said, If they're breaking in your property do what you gotta do and leave them [the bodies] on the side of the road."

As we drive through Algiers Point in a battered white van, Roper tells me he witnessed a fatal shooting. Roper says he was talking on his cellphone to his son in Lafayette one evening when he spied an African-American man trying to get into Daigle's Grocery, a corner market on the eastern edge of the neighborhood, which was shuttered because of the hurricane. Another militia member shot the man from a few feet away, killing him. "He was done," Roper recalls.

During our conversations, Roper never acknowledges firing his weapon, but in 2005 a Danish documentary crew videotaped him talking about his activities. In this footage Roper says, when pressed, that he did indeed shoot somebody.

Fellow militia member Wayne Janak, 60, a carpenter and contractor, is more forthcoming with me. "Three people got shot in just one day!" he tells me, laughing. We're sitting in his home, a boxy beige-and-pink structure on a corner about five blocks from Daigle's Grocery. "Three of them got hit right here in this intersection with a riot gun," he says, motioning toward the streets outside his home. Janak tells me he assumed the shooting victims, who were African-American, were looters because they were carrying sneakers and baseball caps with them. He guessed that the property had been stolen from a nearby shopping mall. According to Janak, a neighbor "unloaded a riot gun"—a shotgun—"on them. We chased them down."

Janak, who was carrying a pistol, says he grabbed one of the suspected looters and considered killing him, but decided to be merciful. "I rolled him over in the grass and saw that he'd been hit in the back with the riot gun," he tells me. "I thought that was good enough. I said, 'Go back to your neighborhood so people will know Algiers Point is not a place you go for a vacation. We're not doing tours right now.'"

He's equally blunt in *Welcome to New Orleans*, an hourlong documentary produced by the Danish video team, who captured Janak, beer in hand, gloating about hunting humans. Surrounded by a crowd of sunburned white Algiers Point locals at a barbeque held not long after the hurricane, he smiles and tells the camera, "It was great! It was like pheasant season in South Dakota. If it moved, you shot it." A native of Chicago, Janak also boasts of becoming a true Southerner, saying, "I am no longer a Yankee. I earned my wings." A white woman standing next to him adds, "He understands the N-word now." In this neighborhood, she continues, "we take care of our own."

Janak, who says he'd been armed with two .38s and a shotgun, brags about keeping the bloody shirt worn by a shooting victim as a trophy. When "looters" showed up in the neighborhood, "they left full of buckshot," he brags, adding, "You know what? Algiers Point is not a pussy community."

Within that community the gunmen enjoyed wide support. In an outtake from the documentary, a group of white Algiers Point residents gathers to celebrate the arrival of military troops sent to police the area. Addressing the crowd, one local praises the vigilantes for holding the neighborhood together until the Army Humvees trundled into town, noting that some of the militia figures are present at the party. "You all know who you are," the man says. "And I'm proud of every one of you all." Cheering and applause erupts from the assembled locals.

Some of the gunmen prowling Algiers Point were out to wage a race war, says one woman whose uncle and two cousins joined the cause. A former New Orleanian, this source spoke to me anonymously because she fears her relatives could be prosecuted for their crimes. "My uncle was very excited that it was a free-for-all—white against black—that he could participate in," says the woman. "For him, the opportunity to hunt black people was a joy."

"They didn't want any of the 'ghetto niggers' coming over" from the east side of the river, she says, adding that her relatives viewed African-Americans who wandered into Algiers Point as "fair game." One of her cousins, a young man in his 20s, sent an email to her and several other family members describing his adventures with the militia. He had attached a photo in which he posed next to an African-American man who'd been fatally shot. The tone of the email, she says, was "gleeful"—her cousin was happy that "they were shooting niggers."

An Algiers Point homeowner who wasn't involved in the shootings describes another attack. "All I can tell you is what I saw," says the white resident, who asked to remain anonymous for fear of reprisals. He witnessed a barrage of gunfire—from a shotgun, an AK-47 and a handgun—directed by militiamen at two African-American men standing on Pelican Street, not too far from Janak's place. The gunfire hit one of them. "I saw blood squirting out of his back," he says. "I'm an EMT. My instinct should've been to rush to him. But I didn't. And if I had, those guys"—the militiamen—"might have opened up on me, too."

The witness shows me a home video he recorded shortly after the storm. On the tape, three white Algiers Point men discuss the incident. One says it might be a bad idea to talk candidly about the crime. Another dismisses the notion, claiming, "No jury would convict."

According to Pervel, one of the shootings occurred just a few feet from his house. "Three young black men were walking down this street and they started moving the barricade," he tells me. The men, he says, wanted to continue walking along the street, but Pervel's neighbor, who was armed, commanded them to keep the barricade in place and leave. A standoff ensued until the neighbor shot one of the men, who then, according to Pervel, "ran a block and died" at the intersection of Alix and Vallette Streets.

Even Pervel is surprised the shootings have generated so little scrutiny. "Aside from you, no one's come around asking questions about this," he says. "I'm surprised. If that was my son, I'd want to know who shot him."

By Pervel's count, four people died violently in Algiers Point in the aftermath of the storm, including a bloody corpse left on Opelousas Avenue. That nameless body came up again and again in interviews, a grisly recurring motif. Who was he? How did he die? Nobody knew—or nobody would tell me.

After hearing all these gruesome stories, I wonder if any of the militia figures I've interviewed were involved in the shooting of Herrington and company. In particular, Pervel's and Janak's anecdotes intrigue me, since both men discussed shooting incidents that sounded a lot like the crime that nearly killed Herrington and wounded Alexander and Collins. Both Pervel and Janak recounted incidents in which vigilantes confronted three black men.

Hoping to solve the mystery, I show Herrington and Alexander video of Pervel, Janak and Roper, all of whom are in their 50s or 60s. No match. The shooters, Herrington and Alexander tell me, were younger men, in their 30s or 40s, sporting prominent tattoos. I have not been able to track them down.

NEW ORLEANS, OF course, is awash in tales of the horrible things that transpired in the wake of the hurricane—and many of these wild stories have turned out to be fictions. In researching the Algiers Point attacks, I relied on the accounts of people who witnessed shooting incidents or were directly involved, either as gunmen or shooting victims.

Seeking to corroborate their stories, I sought out documentary evidence, including police files and autopsy reports. The NOPD, I was told, kept very few records during that period. Orleans Parish coroner Frank Minyard was a different story. The coroner, a flamboyant trumpet-playing doctor who has held the office for more than thirty years, had file cabinets bulging with the autopsies of hundreds of Katrina victims—he just wouldn't let me see them, in defiance of Louisiana public records laws.

After wrangling with the coroner for more than six months, I decided to sue—with a lawyer hired by the Investigative Fund at The Nation Institute—to get access to the autopsies. (We weren't the first to take the coroner to court. CNN and the New Orleans *Times-Picayune* had successfully sued Minyard, seeking particular Katrina-related autopsies.) This past May, Orleans Parish district court judge Kern Reese ruled in our favor, ordering Minyard to allow me to review every autopsy done in the year after the storm. But I soon learned that reconstructing history from the coroner's mess of files was next to impossible, because the paper trail is incomplete. "We carried the records around in our cars, in the trunks of our cars, for four months and, I mean, that— that was the coroner's office," Minyard said in a sworn deposition obtained during the course of our suit. "I'm sure some of the records got lost or misplaced." Even the autopsy files we got were missing key facts, like where the bodies were found, who recovered them, when they were recovered, and so forth.

Many of the manila file folders the coroner eventually turned over were empty, and Minyard said he'd simply chosen not to autopsy some twenty-five to fifty corpses. The coroner also told us he didn't know exactly how many people were shot to death in the days immediately after the storm—"I can't even tell you how many gunshot victims we had"—but figured the number would not "be more than ten."

Under oath Minyard proceeded to say something stunning. The NOPD, he testified, was only investigating three gunshot cases, all of them high-profile—the Danziger Bridge incident, in which police killed two civilians, and the shooting of Danny Brumfield, who was slain by a cop in front of the Convention Center. Minyard's statement buttressed information I'd gotten from NOPD sources who said the force has done little to prosecute people for assaults or murders committed in the wake of the storm.

I contacted the police department repeatedly over many months, providing the NOPD with specific questions about each incident discussed in this story. The department, through spokesman Robert Young, declined to comment on whether officers had investigated any of these crimes and would not discuss any other issues raised by this article.

Sifting through more than 800 autopsy reports and reams of state health department data, I quickly identified five New Orleanians who had died under suspicious circumstances: one, severely burned, was found in a charred abandoned auto; three were shot; and another died of "blunt force trauma to the head." However, it's impossible to tell from the shoddy records whether any of these people died in or around Algiers Point, or even if their bodies were found there.

No one has been arrested in connection with these suspicious deaths. When it comes to the lack of action on the cases, one well-placed NOPD source told me there was plenty of blame to go around. "We had a totally dysfunctional DA's office," he said. "The court system wasn't much better. Everything was in disarray. A lot of stuff didn't get prosecuted. There were a lot of things that were getting squashed. The UCR [uniform crime reports] don't show anything."

In response to detailed queries made over a period of months, New Orleans District Attorney spokesman Dalton Sav-woir declined to say whether prosecutors looked into any of the attacks I uncovered. The office has been through a string of leadership changes since Katrina—Leon Cannizaro is the current DA—and is struggling to deal with crimes that happened yesterday, let alone three years ago, Savwoir told me.

James Traylor, a forensic pathologist with the Louisiana State University Health Center, worked alongside Minyard at the morgue and suspects that homicide victims fell through the cracks. "I know I did cases that were homicides," Traylor says. "They were not suicides." NOPD detectives, the doctor continues, never spoke to him about two cases he labeled homicides, leading him to believe police conducted no investigation into those deaths. "There should be a multi-agency task force—police, sheriffs, coroners—that can put their heads together and figure out what happened to people," Traylor says.

One of the suspicious cases I discovered was that of Willie Lawrence, a 47-year-old African-American male who suffered a "gunshot wound" that caused a "cranio-facial injury" and deposited two chunks of metal in his brain, according to the autopsy report. Minyard never determined whether Lawrence was murdered or committed suicide, choosing to leave the death unclassified. However, the dead man's brother, Herbert Lawrence, who lives in Compton, California, believes his sibling was murdered. Herbert tells me he got a phone call from one of Willie's neighbors shortly after he died. The caller said Willie, whose body, according to state records, was found on the east bank of the Mississippi, was killed by a civilian gunman. "The police didn't do anything," Herbert says, pointing out that NOPD officers didn't create a written report or interview any relatives.

MALIK RAHIM IS one of a handful of African-Americans who live in Algiers Point, and as far as he's concerned, "We are tolerated. We are not accepted." In the days after the storm struck, Rahim says, the vigilantes "would pass by and call us all kind of names, say how they were gonna burn down my house." They thought "all blacks was looting."

As he walked the near-deserted streets in that period, Rahim, 61, a former Black Panther with a mane of dreadlocks, came across several dead bodies of African-American men. Inspecting the bodies, he discovered what he took to be evidence of gunfire. "One guy had about his entire head shot off," says Rahim, who was spurred by the storm to launch Common Ground Relief, a grassroots aid organization. "It's pretty hard to think a person drowned when half their head's been blown off," he says. He thinks some of the gunmen saw Katrina as a "golden opportunity to rid the community of African-Americans."

Sitting at his kitchen table, while a noisy AC unit does its best to neutralize the stifling Louisiana heat, Rahim describes the dead and lists the locations where he found the bodies. He also shows me video footage taken days after the storm. On the tape, Rahim points to the grossly distended corpse of an African-American man lying on the ground.

Rahim introduces me to his neighbor, Reggie Bell, 39, the African-American man Pervel confronted at gunpoint as he walked by Pervel's house. At the time, Bell, a cook, lived just a few blocks down the street from Pervel. In Bell's recollection, Pervel, standing with another gun-toting man, demanded to know what Bell was doing in Algiers Point. "I live here," Bell replied. "I can show you mail."

That answer didn't appease the gunmen, he says. According to Bell, Pervel told him, "Well, we don't want you around here. You loot, we shoot."

Roughly twenty-four hours later, as Bell sat on his front porch grilling food, another batch of armed white men accosted him, intending to drive him from his home at gunpoint, he says.

"Whatcha still doing around here?" they asked, according to Bell. "We don't want you around here. You gotta go."

Bell tells me he was gripped by fear, panicked that he was about to experience ethnic cleansing, Louisiana-style. The armed men eventually left, but Bell remained nervous over the coming days. "I believe it was skin color," he says, that prompted the militia to try to force him out. "That was some really wrong stuff." Bell's then-girlfriend, who was present during the second incident, confirms his story. (In a later interview, Pervel admits he confronted Bell with a shotgun but portrays the incident as a minor misunderstanding, saying he's since apologized to Bell.)

On my final visit to Algiers Point, I stand on Patterson Street, my notebook out, interviewing a pair of residents in the dimming evening light. An older white man, on his way home from a bar, strides up and asks what I'm doing. I reply with a vague explanation, saying I'm working on an article about the "untold stories of Hurricane Katrina."

Without a pause, he says, "Oh. You mean the shootings. Yeah, there were a bunch of shootings."

When I share with Donnell Herrington what the militia men and Algiers Point locals have told me over the course of my investigation, he grows silent. His eyes focus on a point far away. After a moment, he says quietly, "That's pretty disturbing to hear that—I'm not going to lie to you—to hear that these guys are cocky. They feel like they got away with it."

Exhibit A

Emily Maloney

from *Smart Set* from Drexel University

A new D.C. museum celebrates the cloudy pursuit of law and order.

THE NATIONAL MUSEUM of Crime and Punishment opened in Washington, D.C., two weeks ago with McGruff the Crime Dog greeting guests outside the entrance. The museum (which was financed by an Orlando lawyer and produced in conjunction with the Fox TV show *America's Most Wanted*) strives to bring interactivity and entertainment to a museum about crime. I visited on a soft opening day, and then again the next day for the grand opening, the major difference between these days being that on grand opening day, McGruff high-fived me at the door, John Walsh of *America's Most Wanted* was rumored to be in the building, and entrance was free for all law enforcement officers.

Both days, though, were united by the strange tonal shifts one experiences when one engages in silly fun, reads random factoids, and is then admonished occasionally by a but-seriously-people, predators-might-eat-your-children's-heads-if-you-don't-watch-out type of display. The un-Smithsonian-like tone began with McGruff at the door and continued in the queue made of a chain of handcuffs, which lead to ticket sellers dressed in orange prisoner's outfits selling tickets at the un-Smithsonian-like price of $17.95 plus tax.

The first visible wall panel inside the entry gate read, "Every 22.2 seconds a violent crime is committed in the United States." In the stairway leading up to the main floor, flat-screen televisions that hung from the ceiling ran a video montage of real footage mixed with reenactments. Actors robbing a bank cut to a toe tag on a corpse, cut to to O.J. Simpson on trial which cut to the Supreme Court.

The walls were painted black and the steps were metal, and as I climbed to the first floor of the museum, a man with a deep, deeply assured voice announced over the montage, "Sometimes it's overwhelming. It seems we can never stop crime, but fortunately we can always stop criminals. In a nation of laws, we the people do have the right to tell criminals what not to do. There's nothing confusing about it. A crime is what it is: a crime."

By the time I reached the first floor on soft opening day, I understood this was a museum, but one inspired by TV. From the press packet I understood that *America's Most Wanted* was going to be filmed in the basement, but what I didn't know before I arrived and climbed the steps was that the museum itself was going to be curated like TV, selling a simple "us" versus "them" concept of crime.

The first visible artifact at the top of the stairs was a head cage. I read that it was from "ancient times" and used to hold heads still for gauging eyes out and facial branding. A PR woman said, "The museum starts in Europe because that's where we're all from." We being Americans.

In another glass case, in Medieval Times, was a funnel for pouring fetid water down a criminal's throat. A placard read, "Quite often the nostrils of the victim were pinched shut leaving the sufferer no choice but to gasp for air, which only resulted in inhaling more water causing "near drowning"—"near drowning," and not "drowning" being what occurred in dungeons and prisons in the Middle Ages, according to a museum in the capital of a nation debating whether or not to waterboard.

The museum progressed from Medieval Times to Colonial Times, to Pirates, to the Wild West, to the Great Depression Era, to the Mob. Crime relics were mixed seamlessly with Hollywood relics, and in a phrase that sounded practiced in order to confront bad press about mixing real crime relics with Hollywood ones, the PR woman pointed out that Bonnie and Clyde's car was from the movie *Bonnie and Clyde*, but that the bullet holes in the car were real bullet holes. A photo of Faye Dunaway and Warren Beatty hung near the car. Bonnie's poetry and change found in the real car were displayed in a glass case. The PR woman also mentioned that in the Wild West section, the shooting gallery was the only up-sell in the museum and was, "just like a shooting gallery at any carnival.

It was difficult to hold my ground and actually read the material in the Colonial Times section while one voice actor kept repeating that for the crime of drunkenness, he had his nostrils slit, and another repeated that for using the Lord's name in vain, he had his tongue wrought through with a hot iron rung. They were so whiney and repetitious that at the end of my visit I had come to believe that 1) the viewer was not meant to read all the information on the walls in this section, but instead was supposed to take a photo of himself in the stocks and move on, and 2) maybe the voice actors deserved the punishments.

From the Colonial Times section I moved through the Pirate section to the Wild West section. Billy the Kid was described as handsome, which I just can't go down on record as agreeing with. To me his chin looked too large, his eyes uneven and his teeth and ears funky.

On opening day, off-duty police officers came to the museum out of uniform, but certainly not undercover. Their interest in the gun displays gave them away. Also they wore clothes like they usually wore uniforms: shorts when shorts were not really called for, with deeply tucked-in shirts held tight to their waists with belts, and some of them comfortably carrying things like cameras and sunglass attached out of habit to those belts. They had shorter hair and more mustaches than the general public and didn't react out loud to displays, except for the guns. "Look at this," one obvious law enforcement agent on his day off said about a gun near the Bonnie and Clyde exhibit, and another obvious law enforcement officer on his day off said, "Cool, cool."

In the Heist section of the museum, visitors stopped to have their picture taken next to a small photo of Leonardo DiCaprio on a larger photo of the criminal he played in *Catch Me If You Can.* At one point kids tried to uncrack a toy safe called "crack-a-safe" and then gave up when they found out that they had to read directions. I watched an Indian family of three, mother and father flanking the teen daughter who answered, altogether, that: Kid Rock was arrested for assault and battery (in a Waffle House); George Clinton (Dr. Funkenstien) for possession of illegal substances; James Brown (at 70) for assault and battery; Stone Cold Steve Austin for (what else but) assault and battery; and adorable, bumbling Hugh Grant for lewd conduct. The family was doing quite well until they came to Mick Jagger. The daughter looked at her father for guidance, but he didn't know. It was a toughie. They were going to have to guess (answer: assault and battery).

In the Heist room jazz music that sounded like the "Pink Panther Theme" played overhead. I walked over to a wall I had just skimmed the day before and read the Texas A&M shooter's letter of testimony, in which he described shooting his mother because his father treated her like a common slut, and it was the only way he thought he could end her suffering. Something in my stomach sank. The Pink Panthery jazz continued on, and the Indian family was giggling over Lindsay Lohan's DUI arrest and how orange she looked in her mug shot.

I moved on to Serial Killers. A definition on the wall of murderabilia (the collecting of murder memorabilia) included the lines that some collectors "even collect fingernail clippings!" This far into the museum, just feet from John Wayne Gacy's box of clown paints that visitors will have paid $17.95 plus tax to see, I decided that the pronoun on the wall panel should be we. "We the People" are interested in murderabilia.

But even the things that interested visitors, didn't do so for long. I saw several people over the course of two days press a button under an enormous photo of a serial killer and then walk away before the narrator had finished his first sentence. I pressed a button under an overblown black and white photo of the Virginia Tech shooter's face in a row of more traditional serial killer portraits and the voice began, "We all have ways of blowing off steam, but. . . . " I walked away, not exactly out of a disinterest in the details of the horrific, but rather out of exhaustion with overblown delivery and glib writing.

I am ashamed to say that I like TV shows about serial killers when I'm feeling down, and when I walked to a kiosk with a test called *Evil in Our Midst: Serial Killers* I scored a 16/19. The game literally trivialized serial killers, and at one point I saw a woman playing it with a latte in one hand. I think most of us are used to the faces of serial killers in our houses on a little screen, and we listen to their stories while we work on our nonexistent abs or our nutritionally insufficient dinner, and their lives tell us privately that things could always be much, much worse. When I turn off a show on serial killers I feel like my life might have its low points, but at least my brother is not a cannibal, and aren't I lucky. That's a feeling I usually keep kind of private though, and not one I would base a sermon around.

I moved on to a game on a kiosk that asked, "Can you hack it?" in the Silent Criminals section. It was a simulation—I tried to send out spam to get others to write back so I could involve them in some sort of scam. It was a boring and lame game and seemed like an even more boring and lamer crime.

On an opposing wall, there were jokes with cartoons about dumb criminals. The only one I could bring myself to read was about a criminal who grabbed a hotdog from a rotisserie at the convenience store he was robbing and choked on it in the parking lot. It was unclear if he choked to death. I never saw anyone laugh at this wall in the two days I walked by it, and I saw very few law enforcement agents look at it at all. I'm sure they have their own funny and not-so-funny stories about criminals on substances.

In the afternoon of the second day, a family of red-headed kids took over the booking room to get their fingerprints taken. One called out to his mom, "Mom, I'm wanted for contempt of court," which has got to be the happiest way that sentence has ever been uttered. I played around with a display at a child's height that read "Having secrets with people who I have only met online is" a. Risky b. Safe c. Boring. I would have guessed c. Boring, but I knew what the museum's stance on strangers was, so I picked a. Risky.

It was also obvious what the museum's stance on the death penalty was. An electric chair called Old Smokey, in which 125 people had been killed in Tennessee, was set up next to to a fake gas chamber in one room. There were sound effects as gas was released into the chamber, and I got a chill, but not because I was feeling anything other than mild disgust and awe at the lapse in judgment and taste of the people that put this museum together. I looked up. The chill was from a cold air vent blasting air down on me.

While waiting for a turn to drive a police car simulator, I told a little girl and her sister how an infrared video camera worked because the girls were explaining it to each other backwards.

And at first they looked at me as if I was a stranger capable of endangering them in the midst of the museum. Then they realized that I was right, (the PR woman had shown it to me the day before) and the girls started to talk to me. "Look how hot your hands are," one said to me because they showed up on the video screen totally white. "Look how cold your ponytail is," I said because it showed up black. I almost never have bad exchanges with strangers. Often c. Boring ones, but almost never a bad or dangerous exchange.

During the police chase driving game I couldn't get out of the habit of using my signal, and I noticed that the girl with a ponytail was driving more like a cop than I was. In the SWAT team simulation I invaded a suburban house and shot and killed a man and woman in their bedrooms. The woman fell over on her face with a thud and the screen flashed "Scenario Complete!" It was very satisfying, in that way that winning any game is. I passed the gun back to the kid running the simulation who was dressed as a convict, and I wondered why I had never considered going into law enforcement. I seemed like a natural. Then I tried to do two pull-ups, the amount required to become a female police officer, and I failed. Completely. Downstairs I received six out of six on an eye witness memory test, but I would have given away one of those points to be able to do just one pull-up.

I passed through a hallway of CSI information that even I didn't have the patience to read. I heard a man ask a woman, "Do you watch that show?"

On the soft opening day, I asked a museum worker in the morgue, dressed like a convict, why she thought the torso illustrating a bullet entry and exit wound had that round nudey mannequin mound instead of real genitalia and wore underwear. I'm not sure she was used to being held responsible for the content of the museum. "I guess they don't know how old the kids will be that come, so they don't want them to see anything offensive," she said.

On day two in the morgue, I saw a mother lift her child in Crocs (presumably so young that he couldn't tie his own shoes) up to the mannequin corpse so he could press a button and hear about the strangulation wounds, the defensive lacerations, and the gunshot wounds that killed the man. Thank goodness the mannequin corpse was wearing a pair of underwear to protect the boy from anything offensive.

After passing an exhibit on famous unsolved crimes— JonBenet Ramsey, Nicole Brown Simpon, Tupac, and Notorious B.I.G. ("Did you know? Records released after both rappers' deaths continue to sell well into the millions)—I moved into a room devoted to TV crime fighters. The flat-screen TV flashed a compilation: Perry Mason, Charlie's Angels, Zorro, the pregnant cop from *Fargo*. I watched a man take out his phone and snap a photo of a photo of Chuck Norris as Walker, Texas Ranger; his shirt was tucked in deep, but I couldn't quite tell if he was a law enforcement officer or not. Following that, I entered a room that taught about about drinking and driving (briefly), home security, and suggested old people be equipped with a button around their neck so they could call for help.

On the basement set of *America's Most Wanted*, there was a documentary about the series, shown back-to-back with a film of equal length containing the best of *America's Most Wanted* bloopers. When visitors hit a nearby button, a makeup mirror surrounded in lights turned into a video screen and John Walsh answered questions like, "After your son Adam was murdered you became a child advocate. Is that why you started *America's Most Wanted?*" And John Walsh came on screen with less bravado than normal, and in less leather, and gave sincere answers that made him seem likable and his mission— to use TV and publicity to fight violent crime—understandable.

On the afternoon of day two I returned to the beginning of the exhibits and found the real John Walsh in the Pirate section pointing out pirate flags to a friend. I asked if I could take a photo of him, and he suggested we take one together. He put his arm around me. There wasn't time to talk to him about the possible root causes of most crime, like poverty and institutionalized racism, and I could almost hear in the entryway the totally assured male voice repeating, "There's nothing confusing about it. A crime is what it is: a crime."

That's not my experience. My experience with criminals is far less tragic than John Walsh's. I've had a few friends and relatives who have done some time, ultimately because they struggled with addiction and/or mental illness. I have on a few occasions picked out books at Border's to send to them in jail, and I found even that simple task confusing. I tried to pick out books that were entertaining so they could escape for a while, but also ones that might make a person—even a criminal—feel connected to the rest of humanity.

But when John Walsh shook my hand he winked, and I decided I liked him. He looked good in a blue suit jacket, using his normal voice, and it was hard not to like a famous person who winked.

The Fed Who Blew the Whistle

Michael Isikoff

from *Newsweek*

Is he a hero or a criminal?

Thomas M. Tamm was entrusted with some of the government's most important secrets. He had a Sensitive Compartmented Information security clearance, a level above Top Secret. Government agents had probed Tamm's background, his friends and associates, and determined him trustworthy.

It's easy to see why: he comes from a family of high-ranking FBI officials. During his childhood, he played under the desk of J. Edgar Hoover, and as an adult, he enjoyed a long and successful career as a prosecutor. Now gray-haired, 56 and fighting a paunch, Tamm prides himself on his personal rectitude. He has what his 23-year-old son, Terry, calls a "passion for justice." For that reason, there was one secret he says he felt duty-bound to reveal.

In the spring of 2004, Tamm had just finished a yearlong stint at a Justice Department unit handling wiretaps of suspected terrorists and spies—a unit so sensitive that employees are required to put their hands through a biometric scanner to check their fingerprints upon entering. While there, Tamm stumbled upon the existence of a highly classified National Security Agency program that seemed to be eavesdropping on U.S. citizens. The unit had special rules that appeared to be hiding the NSA activities from a panel of federal judges who are required to approve such surveillance. When Tamm started asking questions, his supervisors told him to drop the subject. He says one volunteered that "the program" (as it was commonly called within the office) was "probably illegal."

Tamm agonized over what to do. He tried to raise the issue with a former colleague working for the Senate Judiciary Committee. But the friend, wary of discussing what sounded like government secrets, shut down their conversation. For weeks, Tamm couldn't sleep. The idea of lawlessness at the Justice Department angered him. Finally, one day during his lunch hour, Tamm ducked into a subway station near the U.S. District Courthouse on Pennsylvania Avenue. He headed for a pair of adjoining pay phones partially concealed by large, illuminated Metro maps. Tamm had been eyeing the phone booths on his way to work in the morning. Now, as he slipped through the parade of midday subway riders, his heart was pounding, his body trembling. Tamm felt like a spy. After looking around to make sure nobody was watching, he picked up a phone and called *The New York Times*.

That one call began a series of events that would engulf Washington—and upend Tamm's life. Eighteen months after he first disclosed what he knew, the Times reported that President George W. Bush had secretly authorized the NSA to intercept phone calls and emails of individuals inside the United States without judicial warrants. The drama followed a quiet, separate rebellion within the highest ranks of the Justice Department concerning the same program. (James Comey, then the deputy attorney general, together with FBI head Robert Mueller and several other senior Justice officials, threatened to resign.) President Bush condemned the leak to the Times as a "shameful act." Federal agents launched a criminal investigation to determine the identity of the culprit.

The story of Tamm's phone call is an untold chapter in the history of the secret wars inside the Bush administration. The *New York Times* won a Pulitzer Prize for its story. The two reporters who worked on it each published books. Congress, after extensive debate, last summer passed a major new law to govern the way such surveillance is conducted. But Tamm—who was not the Times's only source, but played the key role in tipping off the paper—has not fared so well. The FBI has pursued him relentlessly for the past two and a half years. Agents have raided his house, hauled away personal possessions and grilled his wife, a teenage daughter and a grown son. More recently, they've been questioning Tamm's friends and associates about nearly every aspect of his life. Tamm has resisted pressure to plead to a felony for divulging classified information. But he is living under a pall, never sure if or when federal agents might arrest him.

Exhausted by the uncertainty clouding his life, Tamm now is telling his story publicly for the first time. "I thought this [secret program] was something the other branches of the government—and the public—ought to know about. So they could decide: do they want this massive spying program to be taking place?" Tamm told *Newsweek*, in one of a series of recent interviews that he granted against the advice of his lawyers. "If somebody were to say, who am I to do that? I would say, 'I had taken an oath to uphold the Constitution.' It's stunning that somebody higher up the chain of command didn't speak up."

Tamm concedes he was also motivated in part by his anger at other Bush-administration policies at the Justice Department, including its aggressive pursuit of death-penalty cases and the legal justifications for "enhanced" interrogation techniques that many believe are tantamount to torture. But, he insists, he divulged no "sources and methods" that might compromise national security when he spoke to the Times. He told reporters Eric Lichtblau and James Risen nothing about the operational details of the NSA program because he didn't know them, he says. He had never been "read into," or briefed, on the details of the program. All he knew was that a domestic surveillance program existed, and it "didn't smell right."

(Justice spokesman Dean Boyd said the department had no comment on any aspect of this story. Lichtblau said, "I don't discuss the identities of confidential sources . . . Nearly a dozen people whom we interviewed agreed to speak with us on the condition of anonymity because of serious concerns about the legality and oversight of the secret program." Risen had no comment.)

Still, Tamm is haunted by the consequences of what he did—and what could yet happen to him. He is no longer employed at Justice and has been struggling to make a living practicing law. He does occasional work for a local public defender's office, handles a few wills and estates—and is more than $30,000 in debt. (To cover legal costs, he recently set up a defense fund.) He says he has suffered from depression. He also realizes he made what he calls "stupid" mistakes along the way, including sending out a seemingly innocuous but fateful email from his Justice Department computer that may have first put the FBI on his scent. Soft-spoken and self-effacing, Tamm has an impish smile and a wry sense of humor. "I guess I'm not a very good criminal," he jokes.

At times during his interviews with *Newsweek*, Tamm would stare into space for minutes, silently wrestling with how to answer questions. One of the most difficult concerned the personal ramifications of his choice. "I didn't think through what this could do to my family," he says.

Tamm's story is in part a cautionary tale about the perils that can face all whistleblowers, especially those involved in national-security programs. Some Americans will view him as a hero who (like Daniel Ellsberg and perhaps Mark Felt, the FBI official since identified as Deep Throat) risked his career and liveli-hood to expose wrongdoing at the highest levels of government. Others—including some of his former colleagues—will deride Tamm as a renegade who took the law into his own hands and violated solemn obligations to protect the nation's secrets. "You can't have runoffs deciding they're going to be the white knight and running to the press," says Frances Fragos Townsend, who once headed the unit where Tamm worked and later served as President Bush's chief counterterrorism adviser. Townsend made clear that she had no knowledge of Tamm's particular case, but added: "There are legal processes in place [for whistle-blowers' complaints]. This is one where I'm a hawk. It offends me, and I find it incredibly dangerous."

Tamm understands that some will see his conduct as "trea-sonous." But still, he says he has few regrets. If he hadn't made his phone call to the *Times*, he believes, it's possible the public would never have learned about the Bush administration's secret wiretapping program. "I don't really need anybody to feel sorry for me," he wrote in a recent email to *Newsweek*. "I chose what I did. I believed in what I did."

If the government were drawing up a profile of a national-security leaker, Tamm would seem one of the least likely sus-pects. He grew up in the shadow of J. Edgar Hoover's FBI. Tamm's uncle, Edward Tamm, was an important figure in the bureau's history. He was once a top aide to Hoover and regularly briefed President Franklin Roosevelt on domestic intelligence matters. He's credited in some bureau histories with inventing (in 1935) not only the bureau's name, but its official motto: Fidelity, Bravery, Integrity. Tamm's father, Quinn Tamm, was also a high-ranking bureau official. He too was an assistant FBI direc-tor under Hoover, and at one time he headed up the bureau's crime lab. Tamm's mother, Ora Belle Tamm, was a secretary at the FBI's identification division.

When Thomas Tamm was a toddler, he crawled around Hoover's desk during FBI ceremonies. (He still remembers his mother fretting that his father might get in trouble for it.) As an 8-year-old, Tamm and his family watched John F. Kennedy's Inaugural parade down Pennsylvania Avenue from the balcony of Hoover's office, then located at the Justice Department.

Tamm's brother also served for years as an FBI agent and later worked as an investigator for the 9/11 Commission. (He now works for a private consulting firm.) Tamm himself, after graduating from Brown University in 1974 and Georgetown Law three years later, chose a different path in law enforcement. He joined the state's attorney's office in Montgomery County, Md. (He was also, for a while, the chairman of the county chapter of the Young Republicans.) Tamm eventually became a senior trial attorney responsible for prosecuting murder, kidnapping and sexual-assault cases. Andrew Sonner, the Democratic state's attorney at the time, says that Tamm was an unusually gifted prosecutor who knew how to connect with juries, in part by "telling tales" that explained his case in a way that ordinary people could understand. "He was about as good before a jury as anybody that ever worked for me," says Sonner, who later served as an appellate judge in Maryland.

In 1998, Tamm landed a job at the Justice Department's Capital Case Unit, a new outfit within the criminal division that handled prosecutions that could bring the federal death penalty. A big part of his job was to review cases forwarded by local U.S. Attorneys' Offices and make recommendations about whether the government should seek execution. Tamm would regularly attend meetings with Attorney General Janet Reno, who was known for asking tough questions about the evidence in such cases—a rigorous approach that Tamm admired. In July 2000, at a gala Justice Department ceremony, Reno awarded Tamm and seven colleagues in his unit the John Marshall Award, one of the department's highest honors.

After John Ashcroft took over as President Bush's attorney general the next year, Tamm became disaffected. The Justice Department began to encourage U.S. attorneys to seek the death penalty in as many cases as possible. Instead of Reno's skepticism about recommendations to seek death, the capital-case committee under Ashcroft approved them with little, if any, challenge. "It became a rubber stamp," Tamm says. This bothered him, though there was nothing underhanded about it. Bush had campaigned as a champion of the death penalty. Ashcroft and the new Republican leadership of the Justice Department advocated its use as a matter of policy.

Tamm's alienation grew in 2002 when he was assigned to assist on one especially high-profile capital case—the prosecution of Zacarias Moussaoui, a Qaeda terrorist arrested in Minnesota who officials initially (and wrongly) believed might have been the "20th hijacker" in the September 11 plot. Tamm's role was to review classified CIA cables about the 9/11 plot to see if there was any exculpatory information that needed to be relinquished to Moussaoui's lawyers. While reviewing the cables, Tamm says, he first spotted reports that referred to the rendition of terror suspects to countries like Egypt and Morocco, where aggressive interrogation practices banned by American law were used. It appeared to Tamm that CIA officers knew "what was going to happen to [the suspects]"—that the government was indirectly participating in abusive interrogations that would be banned under U.S. law.

But still, Tamm says he was fully committed to the prosecution of the war on terror and wanted to play a bigger role in it. So in early 2003, he applied and was accepted for transfer to the Office of Intelligence Policy and Review (OIPR), probably the most sensitive unit within the Justice Department. It is the job of OIPR lawyers to request permission for national-security wiretaps. These requests are made at secret hearings of the Foreign Intelligence Surveillance Court, a body composed of 11 rotating federal judges.

Congress created the FISA court in 1978 because of well-publicized abuses by the intelligence community. It was designed to protect the civil liberties of Americans who might come under suspicion. The court's role was to review domestic national-security wiretaps to make sure there was "probable cause" that the targets were "agents of a foreign power"—either spies or operatives of a foreign terrorist organization. The law creating the court, called the Foreign Intelligence Surveillance Act, made it a federal crime—punishable by up to five years in prison—for any official to engage in such surveillance without following strict rules, including court approval.

But after arriving at OIPR, Tamm learned about an unusual arrangement by which some wiretap requests were handled under special procedures. These requests, which could be signed only by the attorney general, went directly to the chief judge and none other. It was unclear to Tamm what was being hidden from the other 10 judges on the court (as well as the deputy attorney general, who could sign all other FISA warrants). All that Tamm knew was that the "A.G.-only" wiretap requests involved intelligence gleaned from something that was obliquely referred to within OIPR as "the program."

The program was in fact a wide range of covert surveillance activities authorized by President Bush in the aftermath of 9/11. At that time, White House officials, led by Vice President Dick Cheney, had become convinced that FISA court procedures were too cumbersome and time-consuming to permit U.S. intelligence and law-enforcement agencies to quickly identify possible Qaeda terrorists inside the country. (Cheney's chief counsel, David Addington, referred to the FISA court in one meeting as that "obnoxious court," according to former assistant attorney general Jack Goldsmith.) Under a series of secret orders, Bush authorized the NSA for the first time to eavesdrop on phone calls and emails between the United States and a foreign country without any court review. The code name for the NSA collection activities—unknown to all but a tiny number of officials at the White House and in the U.S. intelligence community—was "Stellar Wind."

The NSA identified domestic targets based on leads that were often derived from the seizure of Qaeda computers and cell phones overseas. If, for example, a Qaeda cell phone seized in Pakistan had dialed a phone number in the United States, the NSA would target the U.S. phone number—which would then lead agents to look at other numbers in the United States and abroad called by the targeted phone. Other parts of the program were far more sweeping. The NSA, with the secret cooperation of U.S. telecommunications companies, had begun collecting vast amounts of information about the phone and email records of American citizens. Separately, the NSA was also able to access, for the first time, massive volumes of personal financial records—such as credit-card transactions, wire transfers and bank withdrawals—that were being reported to the Treasury Department by financial institutions. These included millions of "suspicious-activity reports," or SARS, according to two former Treasury officials who declined to be identified talking about sensitive programs. (It was one such report that tipped FBI agents to former New York governor Eliot Spitzer's use of prostitutes.) These records were fed into NSA supercomputers for the purpose of "data mining"—looking for links or patterns that might (or might not) suggest terrorist activity.

But all this created a huge legal quandary. Intelligence gathered by the extralegal phone eavesdropping could never be used in a criminal court. So after the NSA would identify potential targets inside the United States, counterterrorism officials would in some instances try to figure out ways to use that information to get legitimate FISA warrants—giving the cases a judicial stamp of approval.

It's unclear to what extent Tamm's office was aware of the origins of some of the information it was getting. But Tamm was puzzled by the unusual procedures—which sidestepped the normal FISA process—for requesting wiretaps on cases that involved program intelligence. He began pushing his supervisors to explain what was going on. Tamm says he found the whole thing especially curious since there was nothing in the special "program" wiretap requests that seemed any different from all the others. They looked and read the same. It seemed to Tamm there was a reason for this: the intelligence that came from the program was being disguised. He didn't understand why. But whenever Tamm would ask questions about this within OIPR, "nobody wanted to talk about it."

At one point, Tamm says, he approached Lisa Farabee, a senior counsel in OIPR who reviewed his work, and asked her directly, "Do you know what the program is?" According to Tamm, she replied: "Don't even go there," and then added, "I assume what they are doing is illegal." Tamm says his immediate thought was, "I'm a law-enforcement officer and I'm participating in something that is illegal?" A few weeks later Tamm bumped into Mark Bradley, the deputy OIPR counsel, who told him the office had run into trouble with Colleen Kollar-Kotelly, the chief judge on the FISA court. Bradley seemed nervous, Tamm says. Kollar-Kotelly had raised objections to the special program wiretaps, and "the A.G.-only cases are being shut down," Bradley told Tamm. He then added, "This may be [a time] the attorney general gets indicted," according to Tamm. (Told of Tamm's account, Justice spokesman Boyd said that Farabee and Bradley "have no comment for your story.")

One official who was aware of Kollar-Kotelly's objections was U.S. Judge Royce C. Lamberth, a former chief of the FISA court. Lamberth tells *Newsweek* that when the NSA program began in October 2001, he was not informed. But the then chief of OIPR, James Baker, discovered later that year that program intelligence was being used in FISA warrants—and he raised concerns. At that point, Lamberth was called in for a briefing by Ashcroft and Gen. Michael Hayden, the NSA chief at the time. Lamberth made clear to Ashcroft that NSA program intelligence should no longer be allowed in any FISA warrant applications without his knowledge. If it did appear, Lamberth warned, he would be forced to rule on the legality of what the administration was doing, potentially setting off a constitutional clash about the secret program.

Lamberth stepped down as chief FISA judge when his term ended in May 2002, but Kollar-Kotelly asked him to continue as an adviser about matters relating to the program. In early 2004, Kollar-Kotelly thought something was amiss. According to Lamberth, she had concerns that the intelligence community, after collecting information on U.S. citizens without warrants, was again attempting to launder that intelligence through her court—without her knowledge. She "had begun to suspect that they were back-dooring information from the program into" FISA applications, Lamberth tells *Newsweek*. Kollar-Kotelly drew the line and wouldn't permit it. "She was as tough as I was," says Lamberth, who had once barred a top FBI agent from his court when he concluded the bureau hadn't been honest about FISA applications. "She was going to know what she was signing off on before she signed off . . . I was proud of her." (Kollar-Kotelly declined to speak with *Newsweek*.)

Unbeknownst to Tamm, something else was going on at the Justice Department during this period. A new assistant attorney general, a law professor named Jack Goldsmith, had challenged secret legal opinions justifying the NSA surveillance program. (The controversial opinions, written by a young and very conservative legal scholar named John Yoo, had concluded that President Bush had broad executive authority during wartime to override laws passed by Congress and order the surveillance of U.S. citizens.) James Comey, the deputy attorney general, had agreed with Goldsmith and refused to sign off on a renewal of the domestic NSA program in March 2004. Attorney General Ashcroft was in the hospital at the time. The White House first tried to get an extremely ill Ashcroft, drugged and woozy, to overrule Comey, and then, after he refused, President Bush ordered the program to continue anyway. Comey, in turn, drafted a resignation letter. He described the situation he was confronting as "apocalyptic" and then added, "I and the Justice Department have been asked to be part of something that is fundamentally wrong," according to a copy of the letter quoted in "Angler," a book by Washington Post reporter Barton Gellman.

Tamm—who had no knowledge of the separate rebellion within the ranks of the Justice Department—decided independently to get in touch with Sandra Wilkinson, a former colleague of his on the Capital Case Unit who had been detailed to work on the Senate Judiciary Committee. He met with Wilkinson for coffee in the Senate cafeteria, where he laid out his concerns about the program and the unusual procedures within OIPR. "Look, the government is doing something weird here," he recalls saying. "Can you talk to somebody on the intelligence committee and see if they know about this?"

Some weeks passed, and Tamm didn't hear back. So he emailed Wilkinson from his OIPR computer (not a smart move, he would later concede) and asked if they could get together again for coffee. This time, when they got together, Wilkinson was cool, Tamm says. What had she learned about the program? "I can't say," she replied and urged him to drop the subject. "Well, you know, then," he says he replied, "I think my only option is to go to the press." (Wilkinson would not respond to phone calls from *Newsweek*, and her lawyer says she has nothing to say about the matter.)

The next few weeks were excruciating. Tamm says he consulted with an old law-school friend, Gene Karpinski, then the executive director of a public-interest lobbying group. He asked about reporters who might be willing to pursue a story that involved wrongdoing in a national-security program, but didn't tell him any details. (Karpinski, who has been questioned by the FBI and has hired a lawyer, declined to comment.) Tamm says he initially considered contacting Seymour Hersh, the investigative reporter for *The New Yorker*, but didn't know where to reach him. He'd also noticed some strong stories by Eric Lichtblau, the *New York Times* reporter who covered the Justice Department—and with a few Google searches tracked down his phone number.

Tamm at this point had transferred out of OIPR at his own initiative, and moved into a new job at the U.S. Attorney's Office. He says he "hated" the desk work at OIPR and was eager to get back into the courtroom prosecuting cases. His new offices were just above Washington's Judiciary Square Metro stop. When he went to make the call to the *Times*, Tamm said, "My whole body was shaking." Tamm described himself to Lichtblau as a "former" Justice employee and called himself "Mark," his middle name. He said he had some information that was best discussed in person. He and Lichtblau arranged to meet for coffee at Olsson's, a now shuttered bookstore near the Justice Department. After Tamm hung up the phone, he was struck by the consequences of what he had just done. "Oh, my God," he thought. "I can't talk to anybody about this." An even more terrifying question ran through his mind. He thought back to his days at the capital-case squad and wondered if disclosing information about a classified program could earn him the death penalty.

In his book, "Bush's Law: The Remaking of American Justice," Lichtblau writes that he first got a whiff of the NSA surveillance program during the spring of 2004 when he got a cold call from a "walk-in" source who was "agitated about something going on in the intelligence community." Lichtblau wrote that his source was wary at first. The source did not know precisely what was going on—he was, in fact, maddeningly vague, the reporter wrote. But after they got together for a few meetings ("usually at a bookstore or coffee shops in the shadows of Washington's power corridors") his source's "credibility and his bona fides became clear and his angst appeared sincere." The source told him of turmoil within the Justice Department concerning counterterrorism operations and the FISA court. "Whatever is going on, there's even talk Ashcroft could be indicted," the source told Lichtblau, according to his book.

Tamm grew frustrated when the story did not immediately appear. He was hoping, he says, that Lichtblau and his partner Risen (with whom he also met) would figure out on their own what the program was really all about and break it before the 2004 election. He was, by this time, "pissed off" at the Bush administration, he says. He contributed $300 to the Democratic National Committee in September 2004, according to campaign finance records.

It wasn't until more than a year later that the paper's executive editor, Bill Keller, rejecting a personal appeal and warning by President Bush, gave the story a green light. (Bush had warned "there'll be blood on your hands" if another attack were to occur.) BUSH LETS U.S. SPY ON CALLERS WITHOUT COURTS, read the headline in the paper's Dec. 16, 2005, edition. The story—which the *Times* said relied on "nearly a dozen current and former officials"—had immediate repercussions. Democrats, including the then Sen. Barack Obama, denounced the Bush administration for violating the FISA law and demanded hearings. James Robertson, one of the judges on the FISA court, resigned. And on Dec. 30, the Justice Department announced that it was launching a criminal investigation to determine who had leaked to the *Times*.

Not long afterward, Tamm says, he started getting phone calls at his office from Jason Lawless, the hard-charging FBI agent in charge of the case. The calls at first seemed routine. Lawless was simply calling everybody who had worked at OIPR to find out what they knew. But Tamm ducked the calls; he knew that the surest way to get in trouble in such situations was to lie to an FBI agent. Still, he grew increasingly nervous. The calls continued. Finally, one day, Lawless got him on the phone. "This will just take a few minutes," Lawless said, according to Tamm's account. But Tamm told the agent that he didn't want to be interviewed—and he later hired a lawyer. (The FBI said that Lawless would have no comment.)

In the months that followed, Tamm learned he was in even more trouble. He suspected the FBI had accessed his former computer at OIPR and recovered the email he had sent to Wilkinson. The agents tracked her down and questioned her about her conversations with Tamm. By this time, Tamm was in the depths of depression. He says he had trouble concentrating on his work at the U.S. Attorney's Office and ignored some emails from one of his supervisors. He was accused of botching a drug case. By mutual agreement, he resigned in late 2006. He was out of a job and squarely in the sights of the FBI. Nevertheless, he began blogging about the Justice Department for liberal Web sites.

Early on the morning of Aug. 1, 2007, 18 FBI agents—some of them wearing black flak jackets and carrying guns—showed up unannounced at Tamm's redbrick colonial home in Potomac, Md., with a search warrant. While his wife, wearing her pajamas, watched in horror, the agents marched into the house, seized Tamm's desktop computer, his children's laptops, his private papers, some of his books (including one about Deep Throat) and his family Christmas-card list. Terry Tamm, the lawyer's college-age son, was asleep at the time and awoke to find FBI agents entering his bedroom. He was escorted downstairs, where, he says, the agents arranged him, his younger sister and his mother around the kitchen table and questioned them about their father. (Thomas Tamm had left earlier that morning to drive his younger son to summer school and to see a doctor about a shoulder problem.) "They asked me questions like 'Are there any secret rooms or compartments in the house'?" recalls Terry. "Or did we have a safe? They asked us if any *New York Times* reporters had been to the house. We had no idea why any of this was happening." Tamm says he had never told his wife and family about what he had done.

After the raid, Justice Department prosecutors encouraged Tamm to plead guilty to a felony for disclosing classified information—an offer he refused. More recently, Agent Lawless, a former prosecutor from Tennessee, has been methodically tracking down Tamm's friends and former colleagues. The agent and a partner have asked questions about Tamm's associates and political meetings he might have attended, apparently looking for clues about his motivations for going to the press, according to three of those interviewed.

In the meantime, Tamm lives in a perpetual state of limbo, uncertain whether he's going to be arrested at any moment. He could be charged with violating two laws, one concerning the disclosure of information harmful to "the national defense," the other involving "communications intelligence." Both carry penalties of up to 10 years in prison. "This has been devastating to him," says Jeffrey Taylor, an old law-school friend of Tamm's. "It's just been hanging over his head for such a long time . . . . Sometimes Tom will just zone out. It's like he goes off in a special place. He's sort of consumed with this because he doesn't know where it's going."

Taylor got a few clues into what the case was about last September when Agent Lawless and a partner visited him. The FBI agents sat in his office for more than an hour, asking what he knew about Tamm. The agents even asked about Tamm's participation in a political lunch group headed by his former boss, Andrew Sonner, that takes place once a month at a Rockville, Md., restaurant. "What does that have to do with anything?" Taylor asked.

Agent Lawless explained. "This kind of activity"—leaking to the news media—"can be motivated by somebody who is a do-gooder who thinks that something wrong occurred," Lawless said, according to Taylor. "Or it could be politically motivated by somebody who wants to cause harm." If it was the former—if Tamm was a "do-gooder"—the government could face a problem if it tried to bring a case to trial. The jurors might sympathize with

Tamm and "you'd face jury nullification," said Lawless, according to Taylor, referring to a situation in which a jury refuses to convict a defendant regardless of the law.

Just this month, Lawless and another agent questioned Sonner, the retired judge who had served as a mentor to Tamm. The agents wanted to know if Tamm had ever confided in Sonner about leaking to the *Times*. Sonner said he hadn't, but he told the agents what he thought of their probe. "I told them I thought operating outside of the FISA law was one of the biggest injustices of the Bush administration," says Sonner. If Tamm helped blow the whistle, "I'd be proud of him for doing that."

Paul Kemp, one of Tamm's lawyers, says he was recently told by the Justice Department prosecutor in charge of Tamm's case that there will be no decision about whether to prosecute until next year—after the Obama administration takes office. The case could present a dilemma for the new leadership at Justice. During the presidential campaign, Obama condemned the warrantless-wiretapping program. So did Eric Holder, Obama's choice to become attorney general. In a tough speech last June, Holder said that Bush had acted "in direct defiance of federal law" by authorizing the NSA program.

Tamm's lawyers say his case should be judged in that light. "When I looked at this, I was convinced that the action he took was based on his view of a higher responsibility," says Asa Hutchinson, the former U.S. attorney in Little Rock and under secretary of the Department of Homeland Security who is assisting in Tamm's defense. "It reflected a lawyer's responsibility to protect the rule of law." Hutchinson also challenged the idea— argued forcefully by other Bush administration officials at the time—that the *New York Times* story undermined the war on terror by tipping off Qaeda terrorists to surveillance. "Anybody who looks at the overall result of what happened wouldn't conclude there was any harm to the United States," he says. After reviewing all the circumstances, Hutchinson says he hopes the Justice

Department would use its "discretion" and drop the investigation. In judging Tamm's actions—his decision to reveal what little he knew about a secret domestic spying program that still isn't completely known—it can be hard to decipher right from wrong. Sometimes the thinnest of lines separates the criminal from the hero.

Too Weird for *The Wire*

Kevin Carey

from *Washington Monthly*

How black Baltimore drug dealers are using white supremacist legal
theories to confound the Feds.

ON NOVEMBER 16, 2005, Willie "Bo" Mitchell and three co-
defendants—Shelton "Little Rock" Harris, Shelly "Wayne" Martin, and Shawn Earl Gardner— appeared for a hearing in the
modern federal courthouse in downtown Baltimore, Maryland.
The four African American men were facing federal charges of
racketeering, weapons possession, drug dealing, and five counts
of first-degree murder. For nearly two years the prosecutors had
been methodically building their case, with the aim of putting
the defendants to death. In Baltimore, which has a murder rate
eight times higher than that of New York City, such cases are
depressingly commonplace.

A few minutes after 10 A.M., United States District Court
Judge Andre M. Davis took his seat and began his introductory

remarks. Suddenly, the leader of the defendants, Willie Mitchell, a short, unremarkable looking twenty-eight-year old with close-cropped hair, leapt from his chair, grabbed a microphone, and launched into a bizarre soliloquy.

"I am not a defendant," Mitchell declared. "I do not have attorneys." The court "lacks territorial jurisdiction over me," he argued, to the amazement of his lawyers. To support these contentions, he cited decades-old acts of Congress involving the abandonment of the gold standard and the creation of the Federal Reserve. Judge Davis, a Baltimore-born African American in his late fifties, tried to interrupt. "I object," Mitchell repeated robotically. Shelly Martin and Shelton Harris followed Mitchell to the microphone, giving the same speech verbatim. Their attorneys tried to intervene, but when Harris's lawyer leaned over to speak to him, Harris shoved him away.

Judge Davis ordered the three defendants to be removed from the court, and turned to Gardner, who had, until then, remained quiet. But Gardner, too, intoned the same strange speech. "I am Shawn Earl Gardner, live man, flesh and blood," he proclaimed. Every time the judge referred to him as "the defendant" or "Mr. Gardner," Gardner automatically interrupted: "My name is *Shawn Earl Gardner*, sir." Davis tried to explain to Gardner that his behavior was putting his chances of acquittal or leniency at risk. "Don't throw your life away," Davis pleaded. But Gardner wouldn't stop. Judge Davis concluded the hearing, determined to find out what was going on.

As it turned out, he wasn't alone. In the previous year, nearly twenty defendants in other Baltimore cases had begun adopting what lawyers in the federal courthouse came to call "the flesh-and-blood defense." The defense, such as it is, boils down to this: As officers of the court, all defense lawyers are really on the government's side, having sworn an oath to uphold a vast, century-old conspiracy to conceal the fact that most aspects of the federal government are illegitimate, including the courts, which have no constitutional authority to bring people to trial.

The defendants also believed that a legal distinction could be drawn between their name as written on their indictment and their true identity as a "flesh and blood man."

Judge Davis and his law clerk pored over the case files, which led them to a series of strange Web sites. The flesh-and-blood defense, they discovered, came from a place far from Baltimore, from people as different from Willie Mitchell as people could possibly be. Its antecedents stretched back decades, involving religious zealots, gun nuts, tax protestors, and violent separatists driven by theories that had fueled delusions of Aryan supremacy and race war in gun-loaded compounds in the wilds of Montana and Idaho. Although Mitchell and his peers didn't know it, they were inheriting the intellectual legacy of white supremacists who believe that America was irrevocably broken when the 14th Amendment provided equal rights to former slaves. It was the ideology that inspired the Oklahoma City bombing, the biggest act of domestic terrorism in the nation's history, and now, a decade later, it had somehow sprouted in the crime-ridden ghettos of Baltimore.

THE SERIES OF events that led to the prosecution of Willie Mitchell et al are as convoluted, tragic and intermittently absurd as an episode of HBO's acclaimed Baltimore crime drama, *The Wire*. Mitchell and company came of age on the streets of West Baltimore, a few miles and a world away from the rejuvenated inner harbor and the tourist attractions near the federal courthouse. According to prosecutors, the group began selling drugs together as teenagers in the mid-1990s, driving up I-95 to New York City, buying half kilos of cocaine in upper Manhattan and cooking it into crack to sell back home. They added heroin to their repertoire a few years later, as well as robbing and killing other drug dealers. By 2002, they were firmly established in what passes as normal enterprise in a hollowed-out economy like Baltimore, where the drug trade often provides more opportunity than legitimate work and the bedrock institutions of family and school have crumbled. They had children out of wedlock with multiple women. They were occasionally arrested, although they never served much time. It was an insular culture where a ruthless prohibition against "snitching" to the police was often more powerful than any law. Even as cities like New York saw the murder rate decline dramatically, drug killings in Baltimore continued at a steady clip.

According to the indictment, the end began on February 18, 2002, in a downtown Baltimore nightclub called Hammer-jacks, where Mitchell got into a dispute and stabbed a fellow drug dealer in the back, seriously wounding him. If Mitchell had hoped to get away with this attempted murder, he was swiftly and brutally set straight by the drug dealer's associates. When police on patrol found Mitchell later that evening, he was on a side-walk with several men jumping on his head. Mitchell survived the assault, but he remained in serious trouble. The police had issued a warrant for his arrest; more ominously, his enemies had placed a $10,000 contract on his head.

Mitchell probably didn't know exactly what his enemies had in mind, but he was seasoned enough to realize that they wanted him killed. Ten days after the club incident, prosecutors allege, he made a phone call to an associate of the men who had beaten him up. The associate was a drug dealer named Oliver "Woody" McCaffity. Mitchell proposed that the two men meet that evening for a drug deal.

Neither man came to the meeting alone. Mitchell brought a friend, Shelton Harris. McCaffity brought his sometime girl-friend, Lisa Brown. Brown was a pastor's daughter, a computer systems analyst and mother of three. Her parents told report-ers that she had broken up with McCaffity after learning of his involvement with drugs. But when he called and invited her to the movies, she decided to go along.

The two parties drove to the Park Heights section of North-west Baltimore. It was a quick meeting. Mitchell and Harris climbed into the backseat of McCaffity's Infiniti Q-45. Then they shot McCaffity through the head and fired through Brown's raised right hand into her left temple, where police later found a .357 caliber bullet. The bodies of McCaffity and Brown were left in the car, which rolled downhill and rammed into a nearby tree at the dead-end of the street. Police found it two hours later. A palm print on the car window was later matched to Harris, and McCaffity's cell phone records revealed calls that night to Mitchell's phone. Mitchell, suspecting that McCaffity's associates were going to try to kill him, had apparently decided to kill first. The murder would probably not have attracted much attention, except for the fact that McCaffity's Infiniti was owned by Hasim Rahman, the recently dethroned heavyweight boxing champion of the world. McCaffity was a friend and business associate of Rahman, causing the ex-champ to quickly call a press conference denying any involvement in the crimes. (Police have never alleged otherwise.)

If the killing of McCaffity and Brown had been a successful preemptive strike, Mitchell was also prepared to kill for more mundane reasons. On March 24, a few weeks after the McCaffity murder, Mitchell allegedly called a former high school classmate named Darryl Wyche and offered to buy some heroin and cocaine from him. Darryl, excited by the prospect of a big sale, agreed. The two made plans to meet in a nearby industrial park around midnight.

Again, neither party came alone. Wyche brought his younger brother Tony, who had reluctantly agreed to drive. Mitchell brought Harris again, as well as two more friends: Shelly Martin and Shawn Gardner.

The Wyche brothers opened the back door of their Honda to let Mitchell and his men into the back seat. Then each received a bullet in the side of the head. The next morning the police found the bodies, seat belts still on. (Mitchell appears to have seen Wyche as an easy source of drugs and cash.)

But Mitchell's luck was about to end. When Baltimore homicide detectives found the bodies of the Wyche brothers, they assumed they had come across another hard-to-solve drug killing. Then they received an unexpected phone call. It was from Darryl Wyche's mother-in-law, who reported finding a strange message on her phone. Recorded at 12:43 A.M., the message was four and a half minutes of a group of men with names like "Wayne" and "Shorty" saying things like "Bup-bup-bup-bup-bup, yo, they both fucked." The call had come from the cellphone of Darryl Wyche.

Wyche's family and the police soon figured out what had happened: One of the murderers had stolen Darryl Wyche's phone and forgotten to turn it off. While the killers were driving away, one of them had accidentally pressed the phone's speed dial button, calling Darryl's mother-in-law and producing a most unusual piece of evidence: a voicemail confession. With considerable understatement, a lieutenant in the city homicide unit reflected on his good fortune to the *Baltimore Sun*. "We got lucky," he said. Willie Mitchell and Shelly Martin were soon rounded up and put in jail.

What would become the fifth and final murder charge in the case of Willie Mitchell and his cohorts took place two months later. This time, only Mitchell's friend Shawn Gardner was directly involved. It began with a man named Darius Spence, who had found out that his wife, Tanya, was cheating on him with a local drug dealer everyone called "Momma."

Spence decided to have Momma beaten up severely. To accomplish this, he negotiated with another drug dealer named Willie Montgomery. Would Montgomery be willing to beat up Momma in exchange for money? But Montgomery had another proposition altogether. Beating Momma up didn't make sense, Montgomery argued, because then Momma would undoubtedly try to kill Montgomery. It was better just to kill Momma outright, and for five thousand dollars, Montgomery would be glad to do the job. Spence said he'd think it over.

Unfortunately for Darius Spence, Montgomery wasn't interested in waiting around for an answer. Instead, sensing opportunity, Montgomery decided to tell Momma about the hit. If I turn down the deal, Montgomery explained, then Spence will probably just hire someone else to kill you. Therefore, Montgomery reasoned, you should hire me to kill Spence first. Momma was persuaded. (As Montgomery later explained to the prosecutors, "I guess he like that idea better than Darius Spence's idea.")

To execute the hit on Spence, Montgomery recruited two associates, one of whom was Shawn Gardner. For the next two months, the three men staked out Spence's apartment. The plan was for Shawn Gardner and his associate to invade from the basement and carry out the killing, and then run to a nearby getaway car, which was to be driven by Montgomery. Special care was to be taken not to harm Tanya, and they would cover her eyes with duct tape to prevent her from identifying them. Still, Montgomery warned Momma that he couldn't guarantee Tanya's safety. "If it's up to me, she won't be hurt," Montgomery told Momma, "but some things could go wrong." Momma's reply was to the point: "Do what you do."

On June 7, 2002, the three men drove to the Spence apartment, a worn red brick building at the end of a cul-de-sac a few miles from Baltimore city. But the hit didn't go as planned. Darius Spence wasn't in the apartment, and they didn't manage to blindfold Tanya. As children played outside the Spence apartment, Tanya burst through the kitchen door on the third floor, screaming, "No! No!" Lifting one leg over the balcony, she tried to climb down to the floor below but lost her grip and fell fifteen feet to the ground, landing a few feet from the children. Gasping for breath, she motioned for them to run away before crawling under the first floor balcony. Moments later, the two killers emerged from the Spence apartment, ran down the steps and stopped a few feet from Tanya, now lying in the fetal position in the dirt and begging for her life. One pulled out a large caliber revolver and fired two shots into Tanya's chest as the children watched. Then both men ran away.

Unfortunately for the killers, Montgomery wasn't where they thought he'd be. Somehow the meeting place had gotten confused, and the getaway failed. Police quickly apprehended Shawn Gardner and his associate. Eventually, the law caught up to Montgomery, too.

GARDNER WAS TRIED, convicted, and sentenced in state court to life in prison without the possibility of parole for the murder of Tanya Spence. Meanwhile, Willie Mitchell and Shelly Martin were charged by the state with the Wyche brothers' killings and sat in prison for the next year and a half as police and prosecutors assembled their case.

Then, on January 22, 2004—nearly two years after the first four murders—the word came down from the office of U.S. Attorney Thomas DiBiagio: the Willie Mitchell case was going federal, and the government was seeking the death penalty. The Justice Department, DiBiagio explained, was going after "individuals responsible for making life hell in Baltimore."

For Mitchell and company, this was bad news. Instead of jurors selected from the city pool, Mitchell would likely be judged by an all-white panel of citizens from places like Maryland's westernmost rural counties or the far reaches of the Eastern Shore. He would face better-funded prosecutors, and was far more likely to get the death penalty. Maryland has only executed five people in the last thirty years, but in 2005, then-Attorney General John Ashcroft was aggressively seeking death sentences. In fact, the Justice Department was even retrying cases in order to win death penalties for crimes like the Spence murder, for which Shawn Gardner was already serving life without parole.

DiBiagio's office also added a raft of conspiracy charges to the indictment, filed under the federal Racketeering Influenced and Corrupt Organizations (RICO) Act. By alleging that the defendants were part of an organized conspiracy—the so-called "Willie Mitchell organization"—prosecutors could hold all four defendants responsible for any of the crimes the others had committed. That's why Shelton Harris, who wasn't originally arrested for the Wyche or the McCaffity and Brown murders, was pulled off the street and charged with the full slate of crimes. It's also why Mitchell and Harris were charged with the Spence murder, although they were already in jail when Shawn Gardner committed it. RICO is normally applied to members of the mafia and organized crime, and its use sent a clear message: the government was coming at Mitchell and company with everything it had.

The prosecutors bolstered the conspiracy argument by noting that, unlike most Baltimore drug dealers, Mitchell and company had incorporated a legal entity for which they all worked and allegedly funneled proceeds of their drug business into: "Shake Down Entertainment, Ltd." The group promoted rap CDs and concerts through the company, which even had its own record label, "Shystyville." Soon, Shystyville CDs with titles like "Pure Shit" became evidence of not just the conspiracy but the crimes themselves, with prosecutors entering into the record lyrics like these:

> *I watch ya brains fly all over on the bitch next to you*
> *Homeboy it's up to you I could put this pup to you*
> *Then to pumpin' you up like a innertube*
> *Send shots that'll pump up the end of you*
> *Leave you all fat and bloated you know I keep*
> *the Mac loaded then I like ta clack rollin'*
> *That's why Bo and Weez on lock now and every day on lock down*
> *Niggas getting shot down for runnin' they mouth clown*
> *Tell me how it feels with a gun in ya mouth now*

Prosecutors alleged that the "bitch next to you" was Lisa Brown, who was sitting beside Oliver McCaffity when he was shot through the head, that a "pup" is slang for the largecaliber revolver used in the killing, that the "Bo" on "lock now" was the imprisoned Willie "Bo" Mitchell, and that the reference to "Niggas getting shot for runnin' they mouth" amounted to witness intimidation. Faced with the prospect of an all-white jury hearing this music in the courtroom, the defense lawyers objected on the grounds that lots of songs have lyrics that "proudly refer to violent retaliation," offering by way of example country star Toby Keith's "Courtesy of the Red, White and Blue (The Angry American)."

Nearly two years passed. The wheels of justice were turning, slowly but surely. Then came the memorable hearing in which the defendants debuted the flesh-and-blood defense. After that, everything changed.

A MONTH AFTER the hearing, Judge Davis took the unusual step of issuing a written opinion denying all of the defendant's "unusual—if not bizarre" arguments. "Perhaps they would even be humorous," Davis wrote, "were the stakes not so high ... It is truly ironic that four African- American defendants here apparently rely on an ideology derived from a famously discredited notion: the illegitimacy of the Fourteenth Amendment." One can understand his incredulity that four Baltimore drug dealers might invoke a racist argument that dates back to the nineteenth century. But as it turns out, that's when the seeds of the flesh-and-blood defense were sown.

In 1878, southern Democrats pushed legislation through Congress limiting the ability of the federal government to marshal troops on U.S. soil. Known as Posse Comitatus, (Latin for "power of the county") the law's authors hoped to constrain the government's ability to protect black southerners from violence and discrimination. The act symbolically marked the end of Reconstruction and the beginning of Jim Crow.

For the next eight decades, black Americans lived under the yoke of institutional racism. But by the late 1950s, the civil rights movement was growing in strength. In 1957, President Eisenhower sent 1,200 troops from the 101st Airborne Division to Little Rock, Arkansas, so that nine black students could safely enter a previously all-white high school. The landmark Civil Rights Act followed in 1964.

These developments horrified one William Gale, a World War II veteran, insurance salesman, self-styled minister of racist Christian Identity theology, and raving anti-Semite. In 1971, he launched a movement whose impact would reverberate through the radical fringes of American society for decades to come. He called it Posse Comitatus, named for the 1878 law he believed Eisenhower had violated by sending the troops to Little Rock. In a series of tapes and self-published pamphlets, Gale explained that county sheriffs were the supreme legal law enforcement officers in the land, and that county residents had the right to form a posse to enforce the Constitution—however they, as "sovereign citizens," chose to interpret it. Public officials who interfered, instructed Gale, should be "hung by the neck" at high noon.

Gale's racist beliefs were hardly unique. His singular innovation was to devise a "legal" philosophy that was enormously appealing to disaffected, alienated citizens. It was a promise of power, a means of asserting that *they* were the true inheritors of the founding fathers' ideal, a dream they believed had been corrupted by a vast conspiracy that only they could see. Gale's ideas gave people on the paranoid edge of society a collective identity. It told them what they desperately wanted to hear: that the federal government was illegitimate, and that the legal weapons the state used to oppress them could be turned against the state.

Soon, Posses were sprouting across the country, attracting veterans of the 1960s-era tax protest movement, Second Amendment absolutists, Christian Identity adherents, and ardent anticommunists who had abandoned the John Birch Society because they felt the organization wasn't extreme enough. Local groups would meet to share literature, listen to tapes of Gale's sermons, and discuss preparations for the approaching End Times. This extremist stew produced exotic amalgamations of paranoia, such as when Posse members would explain the need for local militias to stockpile weapons in order to defend white Christians from blacks in the coming race war sparked by the inevitable economic collapse caused by the income tax and a cabal of international Jewish bankers bent on global dominance through one world government, for Satan.

While local Posses would periodically confront law enforcement officials in the 1970s, (usually in property disputes), they were often incompetent, and few people were hurt. But things took a serious turn in 1978, when thousands of farmers rallied in Washington D.C. seeking relief from low commodity prices, high interest rates, and farm debt. When Congressional relief attempts failed, some farmers became susceptible to peddlers of the Posse ideology, which preached that the farm crisis had been brought on by the international Jewish banking conspiracy, abandonment of the gold standard and a malevolent Federal Reserve.

By 1982, Bill Gale had flown to Kansas to conduct paramilitary training and indoctrination for splinter groups of disaffected farmers. At night, a country music station in Dodge City broadcast tapes of Gale's sermons. "You're either going to get back to the Constitution of the United States in your government," he intoned, "or officials are gonna hang by the neck until they're dead ... Arise and fight! If a Jew comes near you, run a sword through him." As Posse ideology rippled across the distressed farm belt, violence followed. Several deadly confrontations between Posse adherents and law enforcement made national headlines; Geraldo Rivera descended on Nebraska to document the "Seeds of Hate" in America's heartland. By 1987, Gale's rhetoric had escalated further. He told his followers that "You've got an enemy government running around . . . its source and its location is Washington, D.C., and the federal buildings they've built with your tax money all over the cities in this land."

Hucksters and charlatans prowled the Midwest as the farm crisis deepened, selling desperate farmers expensive seminars and prepackaged legal defenses "guaranteed" to cancel debts and forestall foreclosure. Since the gold standard had been abandoned in 1933, they argued, money had no inherent value, and so neither did their debts. All they had to do, farmers were told, was opt out of the system by sending a letter to the appropriate authorities renouncing their driver's license, birth certificate, and social security number. That number was allegedly tied to a secret government account held in a secure subterranean facility in lower Manhattan, where citizens are used as collateral against international debts issued by the Fed and everyone's name is on a master list, spelled in capital letters—the very same capital letters used in the official court documents detailing foreclosure and other actions against them. The capital letter name was nothing but an artificial construct, they were told, a legal "straw man." It wasn't *them*—natural, live, flesh and blood men.

Bill Gale died on April 28, 1988, three months after being sentenced in federal court for conspiracy, tax crimes, and mailing death threats to the Internal Revenue Service. By that time, the farm crisis had begun to recede. Posse ideology simmered for the next few years, morphing into the "Christian Patriot" movement, which sanded down some of the roughest racist and anti-Semitic edges while retaining the core beliefs of Constitutional fundamentalism. The patriots saw themselves as "sovereign citizens," unlike the "federal citizens" who had been created by the 14th Amendment's guarantee of equal protection under the law.

The deadly confrontations between federal agents and extremists at Ruby Ridge in 1992 and Waco, Texas in 1993 brought latent anger with the federal government back to a boil. The militia movement of the 1990s built on Posse tenets of county- based, self-organized paramilitary groups led by citizens expressing their basic Constitutional rights. Most groups stuck with conducting survivalist training camps and filing bogus liens against houses owned by local judges. But a few did much more.

In 1993, a Michigan farmer and survivalist named James Nichols was pulled over for speeding. Instead of simply paying the fine, he argued in court that his "sovereign citizen" status made him immune to prosecution. That same year, James' brother Terry tried to pay off a $17,000 debt with a fake check issued by a radical "family farm preservation" group run by Posse adherents. Two years later, Terry Nichols helped to bring the Posse's anti-government hatred to its ultimate fruition. On April 18, 1995, he and a friend named Timothy McVeigh loaded 108 fifty-pound bags of ammonium nitrate fertilizer into a Ryder truck. The next day, McVeigh bombed the Murrah federal building in Oklahoma City, killing 168 people on the second anniversary of Waco.

After the attack, the Feds began cracking down on white supremacist groups, including one called the "Montana Free-men," who were, in the words of hate-group expert Daniel Levi-tas, "the direct ideological descendants of the Posse Comitatus." (Levitas' book, *The Terrorist Next Door*, contains the definitive account of Bill Gale and the Posse.) The Freemen were arrested in their isolated compound after a threemonth standoff with the FBI. At trial, they filed an array of bizarre documents citing the Fed, the gold standard, the 14th Amendment, and the Uniform Commercial Code, but to no avail. They were sent to the maxi-mum security "Supermax" federal prison in Florence, Colorado, where they remain today.

But the appeal of their anti-government dogma didn't disap-pear. The Freemen continued to attract sympathizers outside Supermax walls. Some collected the documents the Freemen filed during their trial and began offering them for sale via adver tisements in "America's Bulletin," a newsletter espousing Posse- style anti-government theories that is widely distributed throughout the prison system by white supremacists.

In October 2004, a prisoner named Michael Burpee arrived at the Maryland Correctional Adjustment Center in downtown Baltimore. Burpee had recently been convicted in Florida of trafficking PCP to Maryland. Hoping for leniency, he pled guilty, only to receive a twenty seven-year prison sentence dictated by harsh federal sentencing guidelines. Desperate for a way out, he began listening to someone—presumably a fellow prisoner—who explained how the charges were all part of a secret government conspiracy against him. Then Burpee was brought up on new federal drug charges in Maryland, and shipped north. He carried with him a pile of documents that were remarkably similar to those that had been filed by the Montana Freemen.

In Baltimore, Burpee found a group of inmates at the margins of society, people like Willie Mitchell and company who were staring at the full force of the federal government. As one defense attorney representing a flesh-and-blood defendant put it, they "saw a freight train coming and felt three feet tall." Soon the unorthodox legal filings and courtroom outbursts began to multiply. It was, one public defender later explained, "like an infection that was invading our client population of pre-trial detainees." Burpee appears to have been patient zero in the epidemic. For over a year, he harangued his lawyers and judge about the conspiracy and spread the word in the Baltimore lockup. Then, in a stroke of bad luck for the public defender's office, the U.S. Attorney's office decided to drop the charges against Burpee—perhaps reasoning that he wasn't worth the hassle considering that he had already been sentenced to twenty-seven years. For Burpee's peers, the decision imbued the flesh-and-blood defense with legitimacy and the hope of freedom.

Before long, the relatives of the defendants were scanning Web sites like www.redemptionservice.com, which offers maps showing how Satanic runes were secretly incorporated into the street plan of Washington, D.C., and a deluxe package of instructions for renouncing one's social security number for only $3,900, payable by check or money order.

Like the Midwestern farmers before them, the Baltimore inmates were susceptible to the notion that the federal government was engaged in a massive, historic plot to deprive them of life, liberty, and property. Such suspicions are prevalent in certain pockets of the black community—that year, a study from the Rand Corporation found that over 25 percent of African Americans surveyed believed the AIDS virus was developed by the government, and 12 percent thought it was released into the population by the CIA. And black separatist groups like the Nation of Islam—also fond of conspiracy theories—have long cultivated members through the prison system; some of these groups have explicitly adopted the language of constitutional fundamentalists. Given these developments, Levitas told me, "I'm surprised this didn't happen sooner."

This, then, was how Willie Mitchell came to draw on the accumulated layers of three decades of right-wing paranoia and demand that his case be dismissed "in accord with ... House Joint Resolution 192, and Public Law 73–10"—laws that involved the abandonment of the gold standard and the Federal Reserve. And it explained why Shawn Gardner kept insisting that he be addressed as "Shawn-Earl: Gardner," rather than the capital-letter SHAWN GARDNER printed on the indictment: he thought that if he could convince the court to call him by his "natural" name, it would be tantamount to admitting that the charges had been filed against someone else.

On the morning of January 10, 2006, two months after the first flesh-and-blood hearing, Gardner returned to Judge Davis's courtroom. Moments after Davis arrived, Gardner stood up. "I object," he said, over and over, until Judge Davis had finally had enough. "Do you know what you're doing?" he asked Gardner. "You are committing suicide in broad daylight. There are public suicides in this country far too often. People jump off the Golden Gate Bridge, the Brooklyn Bridge. People walk into their workplaces with a gun and put the gun up to their head and pull the trigger. People slash their wrists. I don't want you to join that community, but that's what you're doing, sir."

Gardner tried to argue that the court had no power over him under "common law." "At common law," Judge Davis replied, "you were property. You were bought and sold just like those Timberlands on your feet today can be bought and sold. That's what your ancestors were, some of them, and that is what my ancestors were, some of them."

"You have invoked ideas formulated and advanced by people who think less of you than they think of dirt," Davis continued. "The extremists who have concocted these ideas that you are now advancing in this courtroom are laughing their heads off. You are giving them everything they ever wished for. They should be paying you to do what you are doing. They are going to make you the poster child for their movement. When you complete this suicide, they will honor you because you are doing their work, better and more effectively than any of them ever dreamed they could do. Some of them—" "I object," said Gardner, interrupting. "The government wants to do the same thing anyway. So what's the difference?"

Gardner, unrepentant, was escorted from the courtroom. And so the tenets of Posse Comitatus continued their long, strange journey, from the racist, hate-filled mind of William Gale to four black defendants on trial for their life in Baltimore federal court.

A LITTLE MORE than a year after the November 2005 hearing, the flesh-and-blood phenomenon took another twist. A key part of the conspiracy indictment against Mitchell et al was the allegation that the defendants acted *together* in pursuit of criminal goals. The seemingly choreographed speeches and the identical filings, all submitted on the same day and mailed by the same person, suggested that the four defendants were going to great lengths to coordinate their actions, despite being housed in separate prison facilities and having no obvious means of communication. Ergo, evidence that the conspiracy was continuing in jail. The U.S. Attorney's office also added new charges of felony obstruction of justice, citing the disruptive nature of the fleshand- blood defense. The prosecutors weren't just rejecting the defense as an argument for innocence. They were saying that it was, itself, a crime.

Undaunted, Mitchell and company continued making courtroom speeches and filing more nonsensical motions. One, for instance, claimed that Judge Davis' court only had jurisdiction over crimes committed in federally owned "forts, magazines, arsenals, dockyards, and enclaves."

None of these arguments had a prayer of overturning the charges. But they had an impact nonetheless. They made a long, complex trial longer and more complex still. Seeking the death penalty is rightfully arduous—it requires legal justifications for the penalty itself, enhanced scrutiny over jury selection, an additional penalty phase after a conviction, and so on. Conspiracy charges create further legal burdens. And the way Mitchell et al chose to deal with their attorneys— not dismissing them outright, but asking them to sign a peculiar "contract" that would essentially prohibit them from mounting a defense—created more problems. If the defendants weren't dealt with carefully, they might be able to appeal by claiming that they had been inadequately represented. The last thing Judge Davis wanted was for an appellate court to throw out a verdict and send the case back to Baltimore to start all over again. According to a source close to the court, dealing with the flesh and blood defense has been "one of the greatest challenges Davis has faced in twenty years as a judge, by far."

By mid-2007, the federal prosecutors were starting to run low on a vital resource: time. As years go by, memories fade, police officers retire or transfer, informants change their mind, and juries wonder, why, if the case is so straightforward, it took so long to make. On September 6, 2007, prosecutors withdrew the death penalty for all four defendants.

Nobody in the Baltimore federal courthouse is willing to state, or even speculate on the record, that Mitchell and his cohorts may have averted death with the flesh-and-blood defense. There are other possibilities involving evidence, witnesses, and

Justice Department policy. But the elaborate processes of federal capital cases weren't built to accommodate farcical *pro se* filings and challenges. Traffic offenses, tax cases—even farm foreclosures—are one thing. When the end goal is execution, even the most ludicrous defenses are taken seriously.

ON JANUARY 8, 2008, the case of *United States of America v. Willie Mitchell et al* convened once again in the main courtroom of the federal courthouse. The lawyers arrived first, chatting in the manner of people who had spent nearly four years and counting on the odyssey of this case. The defendants came next. While Shawn Gardner wore the blue work shirt of a lifer in state prison, Willie Mitchell sported comfortable baggy jeans and a stylish black shirt. Mitchell sauntered to his table, and spied the lone spectator in the courtroom's auditorium-style gallery of one hundred- plus seats, a slender black woman who looked to be in her late twenties. His eyes lit up as he smiled and mouthed "How are you?" "I'm good, I'm good" she murmured. "Your new lawyer—get his card!"

Judge Davis arrived last, emerging from a wooden door behind the bench, beneath oil portraits of judges from days gone by. The hearing will be short, he said; the purpose is to establish a schedule for future motions, and ultimately the trial. Davis and the lawyers spent the next twenty minutes trying find eight weeks of available courtroom time for ten busy lawyers plus the judge. Then, apropos of nothing, Shelton Harris stood up. "Good morning your honor," he began. Davis saw where this was going and cut him off. "I haven't recognized you yet, Mr. Harris. You'll have time to talk later," he said. "I accept your offer," Harris replied softly, and sat down.

The scheduling discussion continued; Mitchell rested his head in his arms as though bored. Finally, Judge Davis allowed Harris to speak. Harris launched into the now familiar oration—"I request you, the judge, close the accounts . . . ." He spoke rapidly in a low, gravelly voice, as if he'd worked hard to memorize the speech and didn't want to leave anything out.

Harris finished, sat, and Judge Davis turned to the defendants. The speech you just gave has no legal meaning whatsoever, he said sternly. They were words in the English language, but they have no meaning as a matter of law. If, in future proceedings, you persist—even politely—in making these speeches, you face a severe risk of being expelled from the courtroom. The court also may conclude that you are waiving your right to appointed counsel, in which case you would have to represent yourself. That would be a sad day. "We are in recess," Davis said. He turned back toward the door to leave.

Then several things happened at once. Shawn Gardner, handcuffed, slumped in the arms of the federal marshals, who seized him beneath his armpits and dragged him across the courtroom toward the door. Willie Mitchell raised his right hand to speak, intent on giving his version of Harris' speech, but the marshals grabbed his arm and forced it down behind his back toward his left wrist, which was already cuffed. Mitchell struggled and yelled at his lawyer, "They got my arm in a chicken wing!" The marshals forcibly moved Martin and Harris toward the door. Judge Davis watched with consternation as they were dragged from his court.

Willie Mitchell and company won't go on trial until September, if then, and they won't face the death penalty, even though they probably deserve it if anyone does. But they will probably be convicted and spend the rest of their lives in federal prison, never to be heard from again, because in the end, the flesh-and-blood defense is no defense at all. The 14th Amendment didn't revoke Shawn Gardner's natural citizenship—it gave him protection under the law, and paved the way for another black man to judge his case. There's no international cabal of Jewish bankers conspiring against him—one of his lawyers, a professor at Howard University Law School, is Jewish. The secret histories and grand conspiracies that have fueled decades of right-wing paranoia, morphing to accommodate one doomed cause after another until finding an unlikely temporary home in a Baltimore lockup, are lies and nothing more.

As the marshals shoved the four men toward the courtroom door, back to the prison they'll never leave, they shook their heads and looked at each other smiling, as if to say right, right, isn't it always just like this? One of them let out a chuckle that rose above the din. Judge Davis turned to the court reporter. "Let the record show," he said, "that Mr. Harris is laughing."

The Truth About Jena

Amy Waldman

from *The Atlantic*

Why America's black-and-white narratives about race don't reflect reality

In the fall of 2006, Mychal Bell was a football hero, and his hometown, Jena, Louisiana, loved him for it. As his high-school team posted its best season in six years, Bell scored 21 touchdowns, rushed for 1,006 yards, and was named player of the week three times by *The Jena Times*. The paper celebrated his triumphs in articles and photographs, including a dramatic one in which Bell, who's black, stiff-arms a white defender by clutching his face guard. But within weeks after the season's end, Bell was transformed into a villain, accused of knocking out a white student, Justin Barker, who was then beaten by a group of black students. The parish's white district attorney charged Bell and five others with attempted second-degree murder. Six months later—after the DA had reduced the charges against Bell—a white jury convicted him, as an adult, of aggravated second-degree battery, a crime that carried a possible 22-year prison sentence. By then, he, along with his co-defendants, had been transformed yet again: together, they'd been dubbed the Jena Six and had become icons of a 21st-century civil-rights movement.

That movement swelled through an electronic underground of blogs and black radio and Web sites, then burst into the national spotlight. On September 20, 2007, it culminated in a protest march that drew some 20,000 people to Jena, a town of roughly 3,000. The movement's grievance wasn't just the severe treatment of the Jena Six, but the light treatment of white youths who'd been in fights or hung nooses on a school tree—the "white tree"—after a black student asked if he could sit under it. Together, the galvanizing facts tapped into a larger ache: the record incarceration of African American males—the shift "from plantations to penitentiaries," as the Reverend Al Sharpton put it at the protest. All of the frustration at the disproportionate imprisonment of black men seemed to find its way to Jena, as if here, at last, in a small town's idea of justice, was an explanation. At home and around the world, the media found answers in the black-and-white clarity of *Race Hate in America*, as the British Broadcasting Corporation called an early documentary.

But soon the simple narrative began to fray. For every fact, a countervailing one emerged. Blacks had sometimes sat under the "white tree." Justin Barker had not been involved in the noose-hanging or in the interracial fights that had occurred over the weekend before he was attacked. Mychal Bell, described in news reports as an "honor student," turned out to have racked up, along with good grades, at least four previous juvenile offenses. He was said to be living with a white friend, suggesting that black-white relations in Jena were more complex than people assumed, and so on. Skeptics seized on each such revelation to argue that the case was more about black criminality than white racism—a manufactured racial drama à la Tawana Brawley (with Sharpton once again playing a role) or the Duke rape case.

Neither version was correct—and both were. The reality was complex enough that people could assemble a story line, buffet-style, to suit their outlook. The proliferation of media outlets made this even easier. New "facts" popped up everywhere. The Nationalist Movement, a white-supremacist ("pro-majority") group, ran interviews on its Web site with the victim and the town mayor, providing ammunition for those seeking to prove the town's racism. On MySpace, a picture appeared of one of the Jena Six posing with $100 bills coming out of his mouth, providing ammunition for those who said the families were milking the cause for money. Anonymous readers posted the arrest record of Mychal Bell's mother, and other allegations about the family, in an online forum of *The Town Talk*, a daily newspaper based in nearby Alexandria. It was Wikinews with no mechanism for achieving consensus on the truth—making it maybe the truest version of all.

Even as events refused to cohere into a sensible whole, activists, reporters, and participants kept trying to package them into a recognizable story line. Bell was used to affirm white racism or black thuggery, as two-dimensional as a Kara Walker silhouette but without the artist's irony. J. Reed Walters, the white district attorney, devolved into caricature, as did Jena itself. The pieces didn't add up to real people or a real place, and that argued for checking the math.

Along with football, church, and hunting, the most popular pastimes among young Jena residents include "looping"—driving up and back the length of the town, which sprawls along Highway 84 in central Louisiana. After a day or two in Jena, where I went a month after the marchers and other reporters had left, I took to looping myself, past Maw and Paw's and the Caboose Café, past Blade-N-Barrel and the town hall, past Papa Ron's Drive-Thru convenience store and Gracie's Hair and Tanning Salon, past church after church after church. As I did, I noticed that most of the areas where blacks live are outside the official town limits. As it turned out, all of the Jena Six lived outside of Jena.

I found Melissa Bell, the 38-year-old mother of Mychal Bell, in one such black neighborhood, "The Quarters," in the trailer she and her children have called home for the past four years. On an unseasonably cold day, she lay huddled beneath a blanket on her couch, with a space heater plugged in, the oven on and open, and four gas burners flaming blue into the darkness.

Until her son's arrest, Melissa Bell's life had been both prosaic and emblematic. Her father was imprisoned when she was 16. She graduated from Jena High and at 20, after half a year of college, gave birth to Mychal. She had a daughter and another son and by 23 was largely on her own with three children, working nights and relying on her mother's help. She and Mychal's father, Marcus Jones, were never a couple, Jones told me; and when Mychal was little, she took Jones to court for child support. In 2000, when Mychal was 10, Jones decamped for Dallas, returning only for intermittent visits until 2007, when he came to free the son he'd left behind. "He has not been there," said Anthony Jackson, a teacher at Jena High who is related to Marcus Jones. "The mother has had the responsibility of raising Mychal."

Melissa Bell worked a series of low-wage jobs—at a hospital, Burger Barn, Procter and Gamble—and had her own run-ins with the law, including a stream of bounced checks, for amounts as small as $4, in 2005. To her son, she was more friend than limit-setter, according to Mychal's best friend, John McPherson. And she was often at work. At 16, Bell was coming into manhood on his own. By the first semester of his junior year, he was spending most of his time with McPherson and his wife in their nearby trailer. McPherson, an oil-field worker, is white—a fact that defenders of the town have made much of—but for him, race was irrelevant. He bonded with Mychal over football and became a mentor to him. "I just knew he needed somebody to give him a break," says McPherson, who is now 20.

Given the poverty of Bell's background, the odds were against him: black men in Louisiana are five times as likely to go to prison as to college; in LaSalle Parish, they are incarcerated at twice their proportion in the population. But Bell's athletic gift gave him a shot at a college scholarship. He combined a knack for the game with the work ethic to make it look easy. After the team watched a game film together, Mychal would borrow it to study more. When opponents lined up, he knew exactly what they were going to run, Mack Fowler, his former coach, says: "He was like a coach on the field"—a leader. As a junior, Bell was already one of the 10 best players Fowler had seen in a 34-year career.

The erratic, and occasionally embarrassing, performance of Jena High's football team has never diminished the town's devotion. Schools love to play Jena because of its "gates"—so many townspeople turn out. The Wal-Mart Supercenter sells Jena Giants clothing, and local businesses sponsor the player of the week and plaster the playing field with ads, making the games profitable for the school, too. Bell was a draw, which helps explain why, when he began to get in trouble—to be trouble—so many adults looked the other way. Or as his father put it, "He couldn't have been too bad—I mean, y'all didn't prosecute him all this time here."

In the year leading up to the attack on Barker, Bell had punched a girl, physically assaulted a man, and committed two acts of vandalism—four offenses he was found guilty of in juvenile court. (His father called it "kid stuff" and complained about "Uncle Toms" running to whites at the courthouse.) Fowler, a jowly white man of 56 who says he was "like a granddaddy" to his players, told me of other incidents that he had heard about involving the crowd Bell ran with, which included some of the Jena Six. In the summer of 2006, for example, that crowd had attacked a black ex-convict who had himself once been feared in the neighborhood.

As a child, Bell was "scared of everything," his mother says—fire engines, police sirens. But as he grew up, his temper began to scare others. "He was hotheaded a lot—that was his only flaw, I believe," McPherson says, along with "hanging out with the wrong people." Bell also had a father who believed that no slight should go unanswered—that if you were in the right, as Jones put it, "you have the right to be a man."

Bell's volatility became evident in dramatic fashion when he assaulted a female student, LaTara Hart, on Christmas Day, 2005. She got in the middle of Bell's long-running dispute with her cousin, and ended up at the hospital with injuries—to her eye, jaw, and chest—that her family describes as more serious than Justin Barker's.

Like John McPherson, LaTara Hart has become ammunition in the information wars, used, in her case, by those seeking to prove that Bell was violent. She has no interest in playing that role, she said when I found her at her family's comfortable brick house on a weekend back from college. (While Hart had been anonymously, and inaccurately, described in Web accounts, this was the first time she had spoken on the record.) In a community so small that, as Marcus Jones puts it, "if you burp you can hear it all over town" (perhaps on the police scanners that many residents have in their homes), the families are connected: Jones was best man at LaTara's parents' wedding. Partly for that reason, the Harts did not press for anything more serious than probation and an apology. LaTara and her mother forgave Bell, although her father has not. (His initial reaction to Bell's arrest in the Barker case was "They ought to lock him up forever.") Anlynne Hart, like her daughter, joined the protests against the charging of the Jena Six, but she also believes the whole drama need never have come to pass. "The boy had a history of getting in trouble," she says, and it should have been reckoned with. At the time he punched LaTara, he seemed to be going through something, "just butting heads" with everyone. The coaches and school officials had to know, she says, because other players told them: "They wanted the child to bring them their touchdowns—and that's not fair."

Bell's legal troubles never cost him a game. Nor did the problems he began to have in school during the fall of 2006, when his grade-point average, which had been above 3.0, slipped substantially. According to Fowler, Bell and another member of the Jena Six were written up so often that school officials asked the school board whether there was a policy on excessive infractions. There wasn't. The coach said that if necessary, Bell should be sent to an alternative school. He wasn't. The assistant principal was "sports-minded, you know, so he didn't want to disrupt," Fowler says. "And we finished 7 and 3 and barely missed the playoffs. But you look back and wonder—well. But [Bell] was never nothing but 'Yes sir, no sir' around us." Still, Fowler knew enough to warn Bell that if he didn't watch out, the streets would "whup" him and he would end up with nothing.

That Bell failed to heed that warning is perhaps understandable. As a football star, he seemed to have found the loophole in his father's lesson that a black man can't get a break. No wonder he didn't see that punching a white boy at school could change the rules. "This is Jena," Anlynne Hart says. "You had the judge and DA at those ball games Friday night, clapping them on—you see what I'm saying? And all this is going through the courts while they're clapping him on, running up and down the football field, and then the minute this happened to the white boy—it's like, uh-oh—click-click—he going to jail."

The district attorney, J. Reed Walters, does not know whether he ever saw Bell play, since he and his wife (who works for the school system) took a break from games after their sons graduated from Jena High. Nearly four decades earlier, Walters had played high-school football himself, in the nearby town of Olla, but he was no Mychal Bell. His aspirations lay elsewhere, in becoming a lawyer. He loves being a small-town prosecutor, and having never craved the spotlight, he feels only "puzzlement" at the global storm he generated. But thanks to the legal discretion that Louisiana grants its district attorneys, it is Walters's character, not any "Jim Crow" statute, that has shaped the course of Bell's case. That character, in turn, reflects in no small measure the character of his community.

Raised in Olla by a schoolteacher mother and a father who worked in the timber industry, Walters has spent most of his life in LaSalle Parish. As he entered adolescence, the parish, like many places across the South, was fighting a rear-guard action against school desegregation, a battle chronicled with unabashed bias in its newspaper. The first blacks didn't enter Jena High until 1969, 15 years after *Brown v. Board of Education*. The following year, the first black faces appeared in the football team photo; from what I could see, those players also integrated the pages of *The Jena Times*, which was owned and edited then, as now, by Sammy Franklin. A 1971 photo of Olla's high-school football team included Walters, then in 10th grade, and one black player. In that same issue, a columnist argued that just because "a Black man cannot work as well as can a White with ideas, symbols, numbers and the like," he was not inferior—just different.

Over the next decades, Jena settled into its post-segregation identity. Blacks could walk in the front door of the Burger Barn, instead of going to a side window. Relations were cordial, barring a few incidents of white-on-black violence recounted with the horror of legend and occasional school fights stemming from interracial dating. Gas-and-oil exploration joined timber as a stalwart of the economy. Walters settled in Jena in 1981, after law school at Louisiana State University, and has never left. He raised his sons in a large house with a swimming pool on "Snob Hill," as Jena's wealthier section is called. He handled the routine cases of a small-town lawyer, and was also drafted into defending the poor. In fact, Walters's sense that he was winning too many cases for his indigent clients helped inspire his run for district attorney. "Walters Elected D.A., LaSalle Goes for Duke," reported *The Jena Times* on October 10, 1990. Sixty-eight percent of voters in LaSalle Parish had turned out, and 63 percent of them had voted for David Duke, the ex-Klansman, for U.S. senator, giving him one of his highest margins in the state. Walters won 51.6 percent of the vote—3,212 votes. By the time Mychal Bell turned 16, Walters had been reelected twice. By statute, he also advises the police jury (akin to a parish council), the school board, and the hospital. The lifelong son of the parish has become a town father.

A number of those town fathers—the police chief; Sammy Franklin of *The Jena Times*; Walters himself—attend the same church, Midway Baptist, which sits on Highway 84. Midway is among Jena's larger and more prosperous churches, and Walters is among its pillars. A licensed minister who pinch-hits for the preacher, he also sings (off-key, by his own admission) in the choir, heads its pastor-search committee, and teaches Bible study twice a week. Along with the small-town culture in which he was raised, Walters's Southern Baptist creed—his certainty of the path to eternal salvation—helps to explain him: in matters of faith, or law, he has the confidence of his convictions.

On the October Sunday morning when I visited, he began Bible study by taking attendance (six adults, including his wife) then turned to the Sermon on the Mount, explaining why Jesus had come to reconcile man to the law of God. Human beings who kept trying to bend the law to their convenience and desires needed an "attitude adjustment," he said, offering a modern example of bending the law: even though the speed limit is 55, we interpret it as 64 because that's what will trigger a ticket.

Walters believes time is "critically short" before the Second Coming, when everyone will have to stand before Jesus, and all must perfect themselves for that moment. He strives for that perfection—taking Jesus' injunction against tearing asunder "what God has joined" so literally, for example, that he frets about the prospect of ever having to pronounce divorces. He actually tries to drive 55. When I asked if he had ever made a mistake, he thought for a moment, then cited a 25-year-old case in which he had misread a report and failed to file a lawsuit in time.

Walters remained convinced that everything he did in the case of the Jena Six was "absolutely 100 percent correct—without question." Never mind that even some of Walters's white friends say he charged too severely, not least because the victim was able to attend a school function that night. Walters believed his decision to charge Bell as an adult with attempted murder reflects both the facts of the case, including Bell's history, and the values that his community holds dear—"conservative," "help-oriented," and "Christian." (I spotted a photocopy of the Ten Commandments hanging on the courthouse bulletin board, next to the bail-bondsman and paternity-testing ads.)

Walters says he does not look at race in his prosecutions. But that does not mean the racial boundaries of his community do not influence him. Whites outnumber blacks by 7-to-1 in the parish; beyond one black member apiece on the 10-member school board and on the 10-member police jury—both from a racially gerrymandered ward—no black has a position of power. There are four black teachers on a parish staff of 196. Black-owned businesses? Sammy Franklin could think of two: a car-detailer and a funeral home.

As for Walters himself, his world—like that of many white Americans—is white, as is most of his neighborhood. The restaurants he frequents rarely have black employees or black patrons. The worshippers at his church are white, as are the small-town-elite circles in which he moves. In 17 years, he says, he has never had a black employee, beyond some who helped him "privately." He offered as evidence of Jena's "perfect" race relations that the high school's white quarterback throws to both black and white players. The white kids who hung the nooses were of Walters's world—indeed, one of their families attends his church. Mychal Bell was, in essence, a stranger.

That reality was not lost on Jena's black residents, including Mychal Bell's mother. She told me a story about going to pick up

Mychal's grades in 2006, before he "got locked up." Mychal had been failing math, and the teacher was regularly sending him to the principal's office for clowning around and sleeping. As Bell stood in line, she says, she watched the teacher, who was white, embrace and smile at Jena's better-off whites, even as she greeted black and lower-class white parents much less warmly. Bell confronted her: "I said, 'You ain't got no business being around black kids, because you don't even want to teach them. You just showed your cards right here: everyone you knew—everyone you knew who got money—they was all good with you.'"

The teacher, Kim Franklin, happens to be married to Craig Franklin, the assistant editor and heir apparent of *The Jena Times*, which has presented uncritically Walters's account of the events. (In an op-ed for *The Christian Science Monitor*, Craig Franklin dismissed the entire affair as journalistic malfeasance, calling Jena a place "where friends are friends regardless of race.") Kim Franklin says she has always treated all of her students the same, and she and Melissa Bell clearly don't like each other. But their polarized perceptions, as much as the legal encounter between Walters and Bell, seemed to capture the competing truths of the Jena saga: Bell's denial of her son's responsibility, and the town's denial of its racial cliquishness. The white residents' loving solicitousness toward their own was subtler than crude racism—which Jena also had—but no less powerful. It reflected a conception of "separate but equal" communities that ultimately weren't equal at all. Witness the town's selectively fluid geography: even as black areas have remained unincorporated—unable to vote for mayor or police chief, ineligible for town services like garbage collection—in 2005 Jena annexed a new subdivision to the north of "Snob Hill."

On September 20, for a span of hours, Jena's demography inverted: suddenly, the protesters against the status quo outnumbered its defenders by at least 6-to-1. But although the protesters passed right over the town lines, they didn't take up the cause of moving them. For all its noise, the Jena Six movement lacked a clear sense of where to apply its force. It probably helped reduce the charges against the boys, although Walters denies that public pressure swayed him. Vigorous defense lawyering got Bell's conviction as an adult overturned earlier that month. And it's unlikely that, at least in Jena, public officials will treat noose-hanging lightly in the future. But so much else was left untouched. The protesters didn't press to improve the parish's indigent-defense system, poor even by the standards of Louisiana; didn't ask why two schools in the southern part of the parish are still effectively segregated, providing an escape valve for white Jena parents who wish to avoid sending their children to integrated schools; and didn't talk about the habitual-offender law Walters used to send a peer of Bell's father to the Louisiana State Penitentiary at Angola for life for three nonviolent offenses. "We will not stop marching until justice runs down like waters," Jesse Jackson said. But the Jena Six movement seemed like a mighty flood that left bent and broken twigs in its wake—and the contours of the riverbanks unchanged.

Less surprising is that the movement avoided the other side of Mychal Bell's story: his own choices, for starters, or the link between the generational disintegration of black families and black incarceration. The lip service about not excusing Bell's past or the boys' attack on Barker didn't diminish the hagiography, which climaxed in a standing ovation for two of the Jena Six when they appeared as presenters at the Black Entertainment Television awards (dressed in hip-hop gear, which coach Fowler says they never wore in Jena).

Anlynne Hart, the mother of Bell's earlier victim, says his parents should have acknowledged his history up front and declared that he deserved help in spite of it. But would such a movement have grown around an icon with a tragic flaw? There is a reason we tell these stories as we do. On Melissa Bell's wall hung a commendatory plaque from the Southern Christian Leadership Conference, the organization Martin Luther King Jr. co-founded and led. Simply by mothering Mychal and standing by him, she became a heroine of this civil-rights movement, an elevation that perhaps spoke more to its character than to hers.

On the gray day when I met Melissa Bell, her mood was as dismal as the weather. Her son's future seemed unpredictable. His conviction in the Justin Barker case had been overturned on the grounds that he shouldn't have been tried as an adult, but he faced retrial as a juvenile. He had come home in September after more than nine months in prison—then been returned to custody two weeks later because of his previous juvenile offenses. He had missed Christmas and his birthday and at least one U.S. Army National Combine game, a national forum where high-school players show their stuff. He was, even at that moment, missing his senior season of football, and all the promise that had portended.

One weekend last year, Marcus Jones drove north from Jena to visit his son in prison. He was excited: a recruitment letter for Bell had come from LSU, whose football team is revered here.

"Now *this* is the college," he told Mychal, handing him the letter. He realized his mistake only with his son's rueful reaction: "Oh Lord, that was a dream right there."

Instead of a bright future, as Jones had initially thought, the letter evidenced only how much Bell had thrown away—or had had taken from him, depending on whose version you believed. From then on, Jones said, when Bell asked whether other letters had come, his mother lied and said no.

But in December, Bell's forecast changed. Days before his trial was scheduled to start, he and Walters made a deal: Bell pleaded guilty to second-degree battery, a misdemeanor; acknowledged in open court that he had punched Barker; and agreed to testify against his co-defendants should they go to trial. He was sentenced to 18 months, including time served, which means he should be out by summer. Even as both sides claimed victory of a sort, it was hard to escape the sense that they had fought to an exhausted draw.

Under the terms of the deal, Bell will be admitted into a high school yet to be determined, which means he could be playing football again by fall. He now has a second chance at that LSU scholarship—to the extent, that is, that he ever had a chance at all.

As it turns out, Fowler, Bell's former coach, didn't think Bell would make it to LSU, as he told me when we met in October. The rain was beating through the pine thicket around his home, and dark had fallen early. His cat, Fancy, nestled on his belly. Fowler, who spent his life in sports and education, had retired prematurely at the end of the school year, his spirit broken in part by the jailing of Bell and two other players who were part of the Jena Six. He struck me as wanting to unburden himself— even if doing so exposed his own clay feet.

As talented and versatile as Bell was, Fowler said, at 5 feet 9 inches or so, and maybe 190 pounds, he probably wasn't big enough for LSU, and likely could have played only for a Division II or a small Division I school. Those prized recruitment letters? Fowler, like every other coach, put his best players' names out; the schools then blanketed prospects with pro forma letters of interest. "I'm gonna tell you, these colleges, they send 1,000 a day," Fowler said. Until the college recruiters look at game film, they can't say whether they're truly interested or not.

Bell and the other players didn't know that, and Fowler and the other coaches didn't tell them. During the offseason, the letters helped propel the kids through the tedium of running and lifting weights—keeping them working, so their high-school teams could keep on winning.

Not Your Dad's Divorce

Susanna Schrobsdorff

from *Newsweek*

How changes in child-support laws, and a push by fathers for equal time, are transforming the way this generation of ex-spouses raise their children.

MOST PARENTS WILL never forget the details of the day their children were born. For those who divorce, there's another day—equally vivid, totally different—that etches into memory: when they have to tell their children their mother and father are splitting up. What I remember is pacing through our apartment the night before, watching my girls sleep. The older one was 8 and still slept as she had when she was a newborn, arms thrown high above her head. The little one, just 4, was curled at the top of her bed, leaving two thirds of it empty.

Their dad and I had read the divorce books and rehearsed our speech about how none of this was their fault, that we loved them. All of this was true, but it seemed insufficient. He and I made a big calendar, as advised, with mom days in red and dad days in purple. In the half-light of that sad morning, I opened the calendar and realized that this crazy quilt would be a map for our lives from now on.

In the morning, we sat the girls on the sofa and told them. They cried, and were confused, but they didn't ask the big questions we thought they would. They wanted to know where they'd live, and whether they would still have the same last name. When we showed them the calendar, our older girl turned it a few pages ahead to her birthday month, which we hadn't colored in yet. She panicked. "But Mom, is my birthday red or purple?" Her dad and I looked at each other and said, "Both. We'll both be there." She would not rest until we filled the day in with red and purple. And with that, our new family life was born.

Birthdays had been part of the initial conversations my exhusband, Jorgen, and I had had about how the schedule would work. When his parents divorced in the 1970s, they adopted the standard every-other-weekend-with-dad setup. He remembered missing his father tremendously and didn't want that for our kids. We talked about sharing time with them more equally—legally it's called joint physical custody, as opposed to the more common joint legal custody, where the child may live primarily with one parent, butboth parents make big decisions, like which school the child goes to, together.

Joint custody meant that the girls would be spending several nights a week with their dad. Switching would require collaboration and communication about homework and school projects and the thousand other things that kids need from day to day. To make it work, we'd have to live near each other for the next 13 years, until the youngest girl was off to college. It was a commitment not unlike marriage, and, given that feelings were still raw post-divorce, neither of us thought it would be easy.

No child custody schedule is. It can involve long commutes and budgets strained by the costs of maintaining two households. The traditional dad-gets-every-other-weekend formula is logistically easier than what Jorgen and I planned. But ours is an increasingly common arrangement. "It's not like it was 20 years ago," says Leslie Drozd, editor of the Journal of Child Custody. "There's no longer the same presumption that young children must be with their mother."

Courts are changing as well; in the small percentage (5 percent) of custody cases that do go to litigation, judges are now more inclined to disregard gender and look at who's the better parent, says Gary Nickelson, president of the American Academy of Matrimonial Lawyers. "Now they look at parenting skills. Who took care of the children before the divorce?" Most often, children still end up living primarily with the mother; according to the most recent census, moms are the official primary residential parent after a divorce in 5 out of 6 cases, a number that hasn't changed much since the mid-'90s.

Nationwide, the proportion of divorced spouses who opt for joint physical custody, where kids spend anywhere between 33 and 50 percent of their time with one parent and the rest with the other, are still small—about 5 percent, according to an analysis of data from the '90's on post-divorce living arrangements by clinical psychologist Joan B. Kelly in the journal Family Process in 2007. But in California and Arizona, where statutes permitting joint physical custody were adopted in the '80s, a decade earlier than in most states, the joint-physical-custody rates were higher, ranging from 12 to 27 percent.

Formal custody assignments don't tell the whole story of increased involvement by divorced fathers. Research to be published in the journal Family Relations in 2009 shows that there have been significant increases in how much nonresident dads (those who don't have primary custody) are seeing their kids. In 1976, only 18 percent of these dads saw their children (ages 6–12) at least once a week. By 2002, that number had risen to 31 percent.

"It's likely that more fathers are seeing their children midweek for dinner or an overnight. It's a change that really started in the 1990s," says Robert Emery, one of the coauthors of the

2009 Family Relations study (along with Paul R. Amato and Catherine E. Myers). "There's been a cultural shift—a father's involvement with their children is seen as important and positive," says Emery who is also the author of "The Truth About Children and Divorce" (*Viking Penguin*, 2004).

The laws governing child support have also evolved and affected child-custody arrangements. In the last 15 years or so, most states have passed legislation that ties child-support payments to how much time a child spends with the nonresident parent paying the support. So if a father spends more than a given threshold of nights with his kids, he can have his child support adjusted according to formulas that vary by state.

The change in support law has been applauded by fathers' rights groups. But Jocelyn Elise Crowley, author of "The Politics of Child Support in America" (*Cambridge*, 2003) and "Defiant Dads" (*Cornell University*, 2008), notes that women generally suffer more economic hardship after a divorce; even an incremental reduction in child-support payments could knock their standard of living down significantly. As it is, 27.7 percent of custodial mothers live below the poverty line, compared to only 11.1 percent of custodial fathers. And she notes that much child support goes unpaid. More than $30 billion in child-support payments was due to custodial parents last year. Only $19 billion was paid. Still, that's better than it was for women in the '60s. Before the 1984 federal Child Support Enforcement Amendments, there was virtually no enforcement of support awards or comprehensive tracking of unpaid support.

Crowley says the problem with linking support payments and time spent with kids is that in some cases it can create a "less than pure incentive for fathers to ask for more time with their children." Gary Nickelson of the AAML says men have come into his office sayingthey want custody of their kids half the time so that they can pay half the support. "I tell them to find another lawyer," he says. "If that's why you're in it, you're not going to win." Most men, though, he says, "just want a fair shake. They want to be involved with their kids."

Fathers and Families is just one of many organizations for fathers who believe that they're not getting a fair shake. Dr. Ned Holstein, a public health physician who heads the 4,500-member group, says it represents men who want more time for the right reasons. He attributes the fact that statistics still show that about 85 percent of primary physical custody goes to women, to the variety of factors leading fathers to cede custody to mothers.

Some dads do jump right into the single life, leaving the bulk of the child-raising to the mothers. But Holstein believes they regret it: "They enter into divorce with the fantasy that they can buy a sports car, go to singles bars and spend their time dating and still have a close relationship with their kids, only seeing them every other weekend, but it doesn't work." And it's a bit of bravado, says Holstein. "You take them to a bar, and they'll start crying because they know they've essentially lost their kids, that their relationship has dwindled. There are legions of men for whom this is a really painful thing."

Why don't the men who are unhappy with the arrangements they have fight for more time? (Currently about seven percent of sole custodial parents are men.) Holstein says the legal system deters them. "The lawyers are telling them, 'You can't fight this, you won't get it, and it will cost you a lot of money and heartache.'" While the numbers show that men who do fight for primary custody win as much as women do, Holstein says those cases are self-selecting: "They've been told in advance they have a chance at winning because they were Mr. Mom before the divorce—or there's an obvious problem with the mother."

Nickelson of the AAML disagrees. He says that mother bias has largely gone by the wayside. "Thirty-five years ago, when I started practicing, there was gender bias. Mom got the kids unless there was something really wrong with mom, but now most states have provisions that say gender can't be the determining factor in deciding who is going to be the primary custodial parent."

To be sure, the minority of cases that do end up in family court can quickly get ugly—and expensive. The battle over who's the better parent often ends up as a mud fight where the goal is to prove that the other parent is unfit. Couples who do get this far have likely already exhausted various methods of alternative conflict resolution—some states even mandate pre-court mediation—and are at each other's throats.

OFTEN, BOTH SIDES hire expensive psychologists. Charges of abuse, both child and spousal, can fly. And now, exes have a whole new array of weapons thanks to computers. Surveys from the AAML this year and last found that more than two thirds of their members have seen an increase in digital evidence (often gathered by spyware) brought into court—from browser histories to cell phone records.

Deedra Hunter, coauthor of "Winning Custody" (*St. Martin's Griffin*, 2001), coaches women who are embroiled in these kinds of battles. She warns clients that everything they do could be brought into court, from their emails to their antidepressant prescriptions to the case of wine they bought online for a party. "I say you're no longer living a life, you're living a case." She says women should keep meticulous records to prove that they're using their child-support money for the kids, and use a camera with a date stamp to prove that the children's father is getting access to the kids as ordered. The experience is traumatic and can go on for years if one partner is unable to let go, she warns. In one extreme case, she recalls, a child died and the parents went to court to fight over the ashes.

Now there's a new charge: parental alienation, more often aimed at mothers than fathers, whereby one parent accuses the other of turning the children against them. Experts say there's a certain amount of bad-mouthing of the other spouse in any divorce and Dr. Jonathan W. Gould an author and partner in Child Custody Consultants, a North Carolina-based group that provides expert testimony in custody cases, explains that this behavior can be very damaging to kids. It happens when a parent loses perspective and can't separate his or her own feelings about the ex from the child's needs. "They truly believe they're protecting the child by filtering access to the other parent." But absent cases of abuse, kids do best, he explains, when they have unfettered access to the other parent—when they feel they can call when they need to talk, or email, without repercussions from the other parent.

"Children build internal working models of mommy and daddy, and it's important that these structures are as strong as possible. If you don't have access to dad, then the structure is going to be robust for mom, but not dad," says Gould. From a child's point of view, what matters is that the child knows that both parents can care for him equally, no matter what the exact time split. Gould, who does custody evaluations for the court system, adds: "If they don't have a room or don't know the neighbors where their father lives, it can feel like they're visiting an uncle."

Holstein of Fathers and Families argues that making kids feel at home at dad's house is difficult when support payments can eat up as much as 40 percent of his after-tax income. They may have to leave the neighborhood for smaller quarters, leaving the children's friends behind. To change that, and to give dads more time and an adjustment in child support according to the new laws, Holstein feels the courts should start with a presumption that there will be joint physical custody. Much of the research on the subject shows that a majority of kids who have grown up in joint physical custody arrangements report that they are satisfied with the way it worked, while kids who grew up in an "every other weekend arrangement" were more likely to be dissatisfied and want more contact with their fathers.

Still, joint custody may not be for every family. Paul Amato, a leading researcher on the subject and a professor of sociology at Penn State, argues that because joint custody is generally granted to parents who request it and are cooperative with each other, it's unclear whether it would work for every couple. Forcing uncooperative couples into a joint arrangement could end up creating more parental conflict, which most experts agree is the most damaging part of a divorce for kids. "I do not think it's a good idea to impose joint physical custody on unwilling parents," he says. "This strategy is likely to do more harm than good."

The willingness of both parents to cooperate is the key factor in how kids adjust to a divorce. Nickelson reminds parents that they should start creating a collaborative relationship with an ex-spouse early on. "You're not going to sign the child-custody agreement, whatever it is, and be done with your wife or husband. I tell my clients, if you're lucky, you'll be sitting next to them for graduations and marriages and all kinds of achievements, so learn to get along."

It's not easy to tame the natural resentments that flare up. My family has had to learn a new way to be together. But after three years of separation and divorce, we've celebrated one middle-school graduation, a first day of kindergarten, several Halloweens and six birthday parties. It's starting to feel close to normal. Sure, those first few birthday parties had some brutal moments, but now, with one girl only a few years away from leaving for college, nobody in our odd group is in any rush for that day to arrive when we're not together for big events.

The Campus Rape Myth

Heather MacDonald

from *City Journal*

The reality: bogus statistics, feminist victimology, and university-approved sex toys

IT'S A LONELY job, working the phones at a college rape crisis center. Day after day, you wait for the casualties to show up from the alleged campus rape epidemic—but no one calls. Could this mean that the crisis is overblown? No: it means, according to the campus sexual-assault industry, that the abuse of coeds is worse than anyone had ever imagined. It means that consultants and counselors need more funding to persuade student rape victims to break the silence of their suffering.

The campus rape movement highlights the current condition of radical feminism, from its self-indulgent bathos to its embrace of ever more vulnerable female victimhood. But the movement is an even more important barometer of academia itself. In a delicious historical irony, the baby boomers who dismantled the university's intellectual architecture in favor of unbridled sex and protest have now bureaucratized both. While women's studies professors bang pots and blow whistles at antirape rallies, in the dorm next door, freshman counselors and deans pass out tips for better orgasms and the use of sex toys. The academic bureaucracy is roomy enough to sponsor both the dour antimale feminism of the college rape movement and the promiscuous hookup culture of student life. The only thing that doesn't fit into the university's new commitments is serious scholarly purpose.

The campus rape industry's central tenet is that one-quarter of all college girls will be raped or be the targets of attempted rape by the end of their college years (completed rapes outnumbering attempted rapes by a ratio of about three to two). The girls' assailants are not terrifying strangers grabbing them in dark alleys but the guys sitting next to them in class or at the cafeteria.

This claim, first published in *Ms* magazine in 1987, took the universities by storm. By the early 1990s, campus rape centers and 24-hour hotlines were opening across the country, aided by tens of millions of dollars of federal funding. Victimhood rituals sprang up: first the Take Back the Night rallies, in which alleged rape victims reveal their stories to gathered crowds of candle-holding supporters; then the Clothesline Project, in which T-shirts made by self-proclaimed rape survivors are strung on campus, while recorded sounds of gongs and drums mark minute-by-minute casualties of the "rape culture." A special rhetoric emerged: victims' family and friends were "co-survivors"; "survivors" existed in a larger "community of survivors."

An army of salesmen took to the road, selling advice to administrators on how to structure sexual-assault procedures, and lecturing freshmen on the "undetected rapists" in their midst. Rape bureaucrats exchanged notes at such gatherings as the Inter Ivy Sexual Assault Conferences and the New England College Sexual Assault Network. Organizations like One in Four and Men Can Stop Rape tried to persuade college boys to redefine their masculinity away from the "rape culture." The college rape infrastructure shows no signs of a slowdown. In 2006, for example, Yale created a new Sexual Harassment and Assault Resources and Education Center, despite numerous resources for rape victims already on campus.

If the one-in-four statistic is correct—it is sometimes modified to "one-in-five to one-in-four"—campus rape represents a crime wave of unprecedented proportions. No crime, much less one as serious as rape, has a victimization rate remotely approaching 20 or 25 percent, even over many years. The 2006 violent crime rate in Detroit, one of the most violent cities in America, was 2,400 murders, rapes, robberies, and aggravated assaults per 100,000 inhabitants—a rate of 2.4 percent. The one-in-four statistic would mean that every year, millions of young women graduate who have suffered the most terrifying assault, short of murder, that a woman can experience. Such a crime wave would require nothing less than a state of emergency—Take Back the Night rallies and 24-hour hotlines would hardly be adequate to counter this tsunami of sexual violence. Admissions policies letting in tens of thousands of vicious criminals would require a complete revision, perhaps banning boys entirely. The nation's nearly 10 million female undergrads would need to take the most stringent safety precautions. Certainly, they would have to alter their sexual behavior radically to avoid falling prey to the rape epidemic.

None of this crisis response occurs, of course—because the crisis doesn't exist. During the 1980s, feminist researchers committed to the rape-culture theory had discovered that asking women directly if they had been raped yielded disappointing results—very few women said that they had been. So *Ms.* commissioned University of Arizona public health professor Mary Koss to develop a different way of measuring the prevalence of rape. Rather than asking female students about rape per se, Koss asked them if they had experienced actions that she then classified as rape. Koss's method produced the 25 percent rate, which *Ms.* then published.

Koss's study had serious flaws. Her survey instrument was highly ambiguous, as University of California at Berkeley social-welfare professor Neil Gilbert has pointed out. But the most powerful refutation of Koss's research came from her own subjects: 73 percent of the women whom she characterized as rape victims said that they hadn't been raped. Further—though it is inconceivable that a raped woman would voluntarily have sex again with the fiend who attacked her—42 percent of Koss's supposed victims had intercourse again with their alleged assailants.

All subsequent feminist rape studies have resulted in this discrepancy between the researchers' conclusions and the subjects' own views. A survey of sorority girls at the University of Virginia found that only 23 percent of the subjects whom the survey characterized as rape victims felt that they had been raped—a result that the university's director of Sexual and Domestic Violence Services calls "discouraging." Equally damning was a 2000 campus rape study conducted under the aegis of the Department of Justice. Sixty-five percent of what the feminist researchers called "completed rape" victims and three-quarters of "attempted rape" victims said that they did not think that their experiences were "serious enough to report." The "victims" in the study, moreover, "generally did not state that their victimization resulted in physical or emotional injuries," report the researchers.

Just as a reality check, consider an actual student-related rape: in 2006, Labrente Robinson and Jacoby Robinson broke into the Philadelphia home of a Temple University student and a Temple graduate, and anally, vaginally, and orally penetrated the women, including with a gun. The chance that the victims would not consider this event "serious enough to report," or physically and emotionally injurious, is exactly nil. In short, believing in the campus rape epidemic depends on ignoring women's own interpretations of their experiences—supposedly the most grievous sin in the feminist political code.

None of the obvious weaknesses in the research has had the slightest drag on the campus rape movement, because the movement is political, not empirical. In a rape culture, which "condones physical and emotional terrorism against women as a norm," sexual assault will wind up underreported, argued the director of Yale's Sexual Harassment and Assault Resources and Education Center in a March 2007 newsletter. You don't need evidence for the rape culture; you simply know that it exists. But if you do need evidence, the underreporting of rape is the best proof there is.

Campus rape researchers may feel that they know better than female students themselves about the students' sexual experiences, but the students are voting with their feet and staying away in droves from the massive rape apparatus built up since the *Ms.* article. Referring to rape hotlines, rape consultant Brett Sokolow laments: "The problem is, on so many of our campuses, very few people ever call. And mostly, we've resigned ourselves to the under-utilization of these resources."

Federal law requires colleges to publish reported crimes affecting their students. The numbers of reported sexual assaults—the law does not require their confirmation—usually run under half a dozen a year on private campuses and maybe two to three times that at large public universities. You might think that having so few reports of sexual assault a year would be a point of pride; in fact, it's a source of gall for students and administrators alike. Yale's associate general counsel and vice president were clearly on the defensive when asked by the Yale alumni magazine in 2004 about Harvard's higher numbers of reported assaults; the reporter might as well have been needling them about a Harvard-Yale football rout. "Harvard must have double-counted or included incidents not required by federal law," groused the officials. The University of Virginia does not publish the number of its sexual-assault hearings because it is so low. "We're reticent to publicize it when we have such a small 'n' number," says Nicole Eramu, Virginia's associate dean of students.

Campuses do everything they can to get their numbers of reported and adjudicated sexual assaults up—adding new categories of lesser offenses, lowering the burden of proof, and devising hearing procedures that will elicit more assault charges. At Yale, it is the accuser who decides whether the accused may confront her—a sacrifice of one of the great Anglo-Saxon truth-finding procedures. "You don't want them to not come to the board and report, do you?" asks physics professor Peter Parker, convener of the university's Sexual Harassment Grievance Board.

The scarcity of reported sexual assaults means that the women who do report them must be treated like rare treasures. New York University's Wellness Exchange counsels people to "believe unconditionally" in sexual-assault charges because "only 2 percent of reported rapes are false reports" (a ubiquitous claim that dates from radical feminist Susan Brownmiller's 1975 tract *Against Our Will*). As Stuart Taylor and K. C. Johnson point out in their book *Until Proven Innocent*, however, the rate of false reports is at least 9 percent and probably closer to 50 percent. Just how powerful is the "believe unconditionally" credo? David Lisak, a University of Massachusetts psychology professor who lectures constantly on the antirape college circuit, acknowledged to a hall of Rutgers students this November that the "Duke case," in which a black stripper falsely accused three white Duke lacrosse players of rape in 2006, "has raised the issue of false allegations." But Lisak didn't want to talk about the Duke case, he said. "I don't know what happened at Duke. No one knows." Actually, we do know what happened at Duke: the prosecutor ignored clearly exculpatory evidence and alibis that cleared the defendants, and was later disbarred for his misconduct. But to the campus rape industry, a lying plaintiff remains a victim of the patriarchy, and the accused remain forever under suspicion.

So what reality does lie behind the campus rape industry? A booze-fueled hookup culture of one-night, or sometimes just partial-night, stands. Students in the sixties demanded that college administrators stop setting rules for fraternization. "We're adults," the students shouted. "We can manage our own lives. If we want to have members of the opposite sex in our rooms at any hour of the day or night, that's our right." The colleges meekly complied and opened a Pandora's box of boorish, sluttish behavior that gets cruder each year. Do the boys, riding the testosterone wave, act thuggishly toward the girls? You bet! Do the girls try to match their insensitivity? Indisputably.

College girls drink themselves into near or actual oblivion before and during parties. That drinking is often goal-oriented, suggests University of Virginia graduate Karin Agness: it frees the drinker from responsibility and "provides an excuse for engaging in behavior that she ordinarily wouldn't." A Columbia University security official marvels at the scene at homecomings: "The women are shit-faced, saying, 'Let's get as drunk as we can,' while the men are hovering over them." As anticipated, the night can include a meaningless sexual encounter with a guy whom the girl may not even know. This less-than-romantic denouement produces the "roll and scream: you roll over the next morning so horrified at what you find next to you that you scream," a Duke coed reports in Laura Sessions Stepp's recent book *Unhooked*. To the extent that they're remembered at all, these are the couplings that are occasionally transformed into "rape"—though far less often than the campus rape industry wishes.

The magazine *Saturday Night: Untold Stories of Sexual Assault at Harvard*, produced by Harvard's Office of Sexual Assault Prevention and Response, provides a first-person account of such a coupling:

> What can I tell you about being raped? Very little. I remember drinking with some girlfriends and then heading to a party in the house that some seniors were throwing. I'm told that I walked in and within 5 minutes was making out with one of the guys who lived there, who I'd talked to some in the dining hall but never really hung out with. I may have initiated it. I don't remember arriving at the party; I dimly remember waking up at some point in the early morning in this guy's room. I remember him walking me back to my room. I couldn't have made it alone; I still had too much alcohol in my system to even stand up straight. I made myself vulnerable and even now it's hard to think that

someone here who I have talked and laughed with could be
cold-hearted enough to take advantage of that vulnerability.
I'd rather, sometimes, take half the blame than believe that
a profound evil can exist in mankind. But it's easy for me
to say, that, of the two of us, I'm the only one who still has
nightmares, found myself panicking and detaching during
sex for many months afterwards, and spent more time look-
ing into the abyss than any one person should.

The inequalities of the consequences of the night,
the actions taken unintentionally or not, have changed
the course of only one of our lives, irrevocably and
profoundly.

Now perhaps the male willfully exploited the narrator's
self-inflicted incapacitation; if so, he deserves censure for taking advantage of a female in distress. But to hold the narrator
completely without responsibility requires stripping women of
volition and moral agency. Though the Harvard victim does not
remember her actions, it's highly unlikely that she passed out
upon arriving at the party and was dragged away like roadkill
while other students looked on. Rather, she probably participated voluntarily in the usual prelude to intercourse, and probably even in intercourse itself, however woozily.

Even if the Harvard victim's drunkenness cancels any responsibility that she might share for the interaction's finale, is she
equally without responsibility for all of her behavior up to that
point, including getting so drunk that she can't remember anything? Campus rape ideology holds that inebriation strips women
of responsibility for their actions but preserves male responsibility
not only for their own actions but for their partners' as well. Thus
do men again become the guardians of female well-being.

As for the story's maudlin melodrama, perhaps the narrator's life really has been "irrevocably" changed, for which one
sympathizes. One can't help observing, however, that the effect
of this "profound evil" on at least her sex life appears to have

been minimal—she "detached" during sex for "many months afterwards," but sex she most certainly had. Real rape victims, however, can fear physical intimacy for years, along with suffering a host of other terrors. We don't know if the narrator's "look into the abyss" led her to reconsider getting plastered before parties and initiating sexual contact with casual acquaintances. But if a Harvard student doesn't understand that getting very drunk and becoming physically involved with a boy at a hookup party carries a serious probability of intercourse, she's at the wrong university, if she should be at college at all.

A large number of complicating factors make the *Saturday Night* story a far more problematic case than the term "rape" usually implies. Unlike the campus rape industry, most students are well aware of those complicating factors, which is why there are so few rape charges brought for college sex. But if the rape industrialists are so sure that foreseeable and seemingly cooperative drunken sex amounts to rape, there are some obvious steps that they could take to prevent it. Above all, they could persuade girls not to put themselves into situations whose likely outcome is intercourse. Specifically: don't get drunk, don't get into bed with a guy, and don't take off your clothes or allow them to be removed. Once you're in that situation, the rape activists could say, it's going to be hard to halt the proceedings, for lots of complex emotional reasons. Were this advice heeded, the campus "rape" epidemic would be wiped out overnight.

But suggest to a rape bureaucrat that female students should behave with greater sexual restraint as a preventive measure, and you might as well be saying that the girls should enter a convent or don the burka. "I am uncomfortable with the idea," e-mailed Hillary Wing-Richards, the associate director of the Office of Sexual Assault Prevention and Women's Resource Center at James Madison University in Virginia. "This indicates that if [female students] are raped it could be their fault—it is never their fault—and how one dresses does not invite rape or violence. . . . I would never allow my staff or myself to send the message it is the victim's fault due to their dress or lack of restraint in any way." Putting on a tight tank top doesn't, of course, lead to what the bureaucrats call "rape." But taking *off* that tank top does increase the risk of sexual intercourse that will be later regretted, especially when the tank-topper has been intently mainlining rum and Cokes all evening.

The baby boomers who demanded the dismantling of all campus rules governing the relations between the sexes now sit in dean's offices and student-counseling services. They cannot turn around and argue for reregulating sex, even on pragmatic grounds. Instead, they have responded to the fallout of the college sexual revolution with bizarre and anachronistic legalism. Campuses have created a judicial infrastructure for responding to postcoital second thoughts more complex than that required to adjudicate maritime commerce claims in Renaissance Venice.

University of Virginia students, for example, have at least three different procedural channels open to them following carnal knowledge: they may demand a formal adjudication before the Sexual Assault Board; they can request a "Structured Meeting" with the Office of the Dean of Students by filing a formal complaint; or they can seek voluntary mediation. The Structured Meetings are presided over by the chair of the Sexual Assault Board, with assistance from another board member or senior staff of the Office of the Dean of Students. The Structured Meeting, according to the university, is an "opportunity for the complainant to confront the accused and communicate their feelings and perceptions regarding the incident, the impact of the incident and their wishes and expectations regarding protection in the future." Mediation, on the other hand, "allows both you and the accused to discuss your respective understandings of the assault with the guidance of a trained professional," says the school's sexual-assault center.

Rarely have primal lust and carousing been more weirdly paired with their opposites. Out in the real world, people who regret a sexual coupling must work it out on their own; no counterpart exists outside academia for this superstructure of hearings, mediations, and negotiated settlements. If you've actually been raped, you go to criminal court—but the overwhelming majority of campus "rape" cases that take up administration time and resources would get thrown out of court in a twinkling, which is why they're almost never prosecuted. Indeed, if the campus rape industry really believes that these hookup encounters are rape, it is unconscionable to leave them to flimsy academic procedures. "Universities are equipped to handle plagiarism, not rape," observes University of Pennsylvania history professor Alan Charles Kors. "Sexual-assault charges, if true, are so serious as to belong only in the criminal system."

Risk-management consultants travel the country to help colleges craft legal rules for student sexual congress. These rules presume that an activity originating in inchoate desire, whose nuances have taxed the expressive powers of poets, artists, and philosophers for centuries, can be reduced to a species of commercial code. The process of crafting these rules combines a voyeuristic prurience and a seeming cluelessness about sex. "It is fun," writes Alan D. Berkowitz, a popular campus rape lecturer and consultant, "to ask students how they know if someone is sexually interested in them." (Fun for whom? one must ask.) Continues Berkowitz: "Many of the responses rely on guesswork and inference to determine sexual intent." Such signaling mechanisms, dating from the dawn of the human race, are no longer acceptable on the rape-sensitized campus. "In fact," explains our consultant, "sexual intent can only be determined by clear and unambiguous communication about what is desired." So much for seduction and romance; bring in the MBAs and lawyers.

The campus sex-management industry locks in its livelihood by introducing a specious clarity to what is inherently mysterious and an equally specious complexity to what is straightforward. Both the pseudo-clarity and pseudo-complexity work in a woman's favor, of course. "If one partner puts a condom on the other, does that signify that they are consenting to intercourse?" asks

Berkowitz. Short of guiding the thus-sheathed instrumentality to port, it's hard to imagine a clearer signal of consent. But perhaps a girl who has just so outfitted her partner will decide after the fact that she has been "raped"—so better to declare the action, as Berkowitz does, "inherently ambiguous." He recommends instead that colleges require "clear verbal consent" for sex, a policy that the recently disbanded Antioch College introduced in the early 1990s to universal derision.

The university is sneaking back in its *in loco parentis* oversight of student sexual relations, but it has replaced the moral content of that regulation with supposedly neutral legal procedure. The generation that got rid of parietal rules has re-created a form of bedroom oversight as pervasive as Bentham's Panopticon.

But the post-1960s university is nothing if not capacious. It has institutionalized every strand of adolescent-inspired rebellion familiar since student sit-in days. The campus rape industry may decry ubiquitous male predation, but a campus sex industry puts bureaucratic clout behind the message that students should have recreational sex at every opportunity.

In late October, for example, New York University's professional "sexpert" set up her wares in the light-filled atrium of the Kimmel Student Center. Along with the usual baskets of lubricated condoms, female condoms, and dental dams (a lesbian-inspired latex innovation for "safe" oral sex), Alyssa La Fosse, looking thoroughly professional in a neatly coiffed bun, also provided brightly colored instructional sheets on such important topics as "How to Female Ejaculate" ("First take some time to get aroused. Lube up your fingers and let them do the walking") and "Masturbation Tips for Girls" ("Draw a circle around your clitoris with your index finger"). In a heroic effort at inclusiveness, she also provided a pamphlet called "Exploring Your Options: Abstinence," but a reader could be forgiven for thinking that he had mistakenly grabbed the menu of activities at a West Village bathhouse. NYU's officially approved "abstinence options" include "outercourse, mutual masturbation, pornography, and sex toys such as vibrators, dildos, and a paddle." Ever the responsible parent-surrogate, NYU recommends that "abstinence" practitioners cover their sex toys "with a condom if they are to be inserted in the mouth, anus, or vagina."

The students passing La Fosse's table showed a greater interest in the free Hershey's Kisses than in the latex accessories and informational sheets; very occasionally, someone would grab a condom. No one brought "questions about sexuality or sexual health" to La Fosse, despite the university's official invitation to do so. NYU is not about to be daunted in its mission of promoting better sex, however. So it also offers workshops on orgasms— "how to achieve that (sometimes elusive) state"—and "Sex Toys for Safer Sex" ("an evening with rubber, silicone, and vibrating toys") in residence halls and various student clubs.

Similarly, Brown University's Student Services helps students answer the compelling question: "How can I bring sex toys into my relationship?" Brown categorizes sex toys by function ("Some sex toys are meant to be used more gently, while others are used for sexual acts involving dominance and submission . . . such as restraints, blindfolds, and whips") and offers the usual safe-sex caveats ("If sharing sex toys, such as dildos, butt plugs, or vibrators, use condoms and dental dams"). UCLA's Arthur Ashe Student Health and Wellness Center advises on how a man might "increase the amount of time before he ejaculates"; Tufts University's 2006 Sex Fair featured a "Dildo Ring Toss" and dental-dam slingshots; and Barnard College suggests that participants in sadomasochistic sex, "where 'no, please don't' . . . can be a part of the fun," agree on a "safeword" that "will stop all play immediately." A Princeton student who thinks that a "docking sleeve" may be some kind of maritime hardware, or a "suction device" something used for plumbing, had better bone up, so to speak, before playing the school's official "Safer Sex Jeopardy" game, because these objects are in the "grab bag" categories of penile toys and nipple toys, respectively. Encyclopedic knowledge is advisable: game developers list six types of vibrators, including the "rabbit vibrator," and eight kinds of penile toys, including the "pocket pussy."

By now, universities have traveled so far from their original task of immersing students in the greatest intellectual and artistic creations of humanity that criticizing any particular detour seems arbitrary. Still, the question presents itself: Why, exactly, are the schools offering workshops on orgasms and sex toys instead of on Michelangelo's Campidoglio or Pushkin's *Eugene Onegin*? Are students already so saturated with knowledge of Renaissance humanism or the evolution of constitutional democracy, say, that colleges can happily reroute resources to matters readily available on porn websites?

Strange Bedfellows at William and Mary

Anyone who still thinks of sorority girls as cashmere-clad innocents, giggling as they wait by the phone for that special someone to call, won't understand much of the campus "date rape" scene. A few incidents at the College of William and Mary, a pioneer in sexual-assault awareness, may correct lingering misconceptions.

In October 2005, at a Delta Delta Delta formal, drunken sorority girls careened through the host's house, vomiting, falling, and breaking furnishings. One girl ran naked through a hallway; another was found half-naked with a male on the bed in the master suite. A third had intercourse with her escort in a different bedroom. On the bus back from the formal, she was seen kissing her escort; once she arrived home, she had sex with a different male. Later, she accused her escort of rape. The district attorney declined to prosecute the girl's rape charges. William and Mary, however, had already forced the defendant to leave school and, even after the D.A.'s decision, wouldn't let him return until his accuser graduated. The defendant sued his accuser for $5.5 million for defamation; the parties settled out of court.

The incident wasn't as unusual as it sounds. A year earlier, a William and Mary student had charged rape after having provided a condom to her partner for intercourse. The boy had cofounded the national antirape organization One in Four; the school suspended him for a year, anyway. In an earlier incident, a drunken sorority girl was filmed giving oral sex to seven men. She cried rape when her boyfriend found out. William and Mary found one of the recipients, who had taped the event, guilty of assault and suspended him.

But in the fall semester of 2005, rape charges spread through William and Mary like witchcraft accusations in a medieval village. In short succession after the Delta Delta Delta bacchanal, three more students accused acquaintances of rape. Only one of these three additional victims pressed charges in court, however, and she quickly dropped the case.

A fifth rape incident around the same time followed a different pattern. In November 2005, a William and Mary student woke up in the middle of the night with a knife at her throat. A 23-year-old stranger with a prior conviction for peeping at her apartment complex had broken into her apartment; he raped her, threatened her roommate at knifepoint, and left with two stolen cell phones and cash. The rapist was caught, convicted, and sentenced to 57 years in prison.

Guess which incident got the most attention at William and Mary? The Delta Delta Delta formal "rape." Like many *stranger* rapists on campus, the knifepoint assailant was black, and thus an unattractive target for politically correct protest. (The 2006 Duke stripper case, by contrast, seemingly provided the ideal and, for the industry, sadly rare configuration: white rapists and a black victim.)

Stranger rapes also provide less opportunity for bureaucratic expansion. After the spate of "date rapes," William and Mary's vice president for student affairs announced that the school would hire a full-time sexual-assault educator, in addition to its existing sexual-assault services and counseling staff and numerous sexual-assault awareness organizations. Freshmen would now have to attend a gender-specific sexual-assault awareness program. None of this new apparatus—for instance, the "Equality Wheel," which explains the "dynamics of a healthy relationship"—has the slightest relevance to stranger rapes.

However, the cross-currents of campus political correctness are so intense that they produce some surprising twists. William and Mary's sexual-assault resources webpage invites visitors to "listen to what people affected by sexual assault are sharing." It then offers ten audio accounts of sexual assaults, exactly half of which are male. "My experience came very close to killing me," one man reports. One would need the skills of a Kremlinologist to interpret this gender lineup, and the site doesn't explain who exactly these voices are—but it's hard to escape the impression that William and Mary has admitted either a *huge* gay community or some very beefy women. Diversity politics, gay politics, and the sexual-assault movement produce strange bedfellows.

Columbia University's *Go Ask Alice* website illustrates the dilemma posed by a college's simultaneous advocacy of "healthy sexuality" and of the "rape is everywhere" ideology. *Go Ask Alice* is run by Columbia's Health Services; it answers both nonsexual health queries and such burning questions as: "Sex with four friends—Mutual?" and "Will it ever be good for me?" (from a virgin). In one post, titled "I'm sure I was drunk, but I'm not sure if I had sex," Alice takes up the classic hookup scenario: a girl who has no recollection of whether she had intercourse during a drunken encounter and now wonders if she's pregnant. Alice's initial reaction is pure hip-to-free-love toleration: "Depending upon your relationship with your partner, you may want to ask what happened. Understandably, this might feel awkward and embarrassing, but the conversation might . . . help you to understand what happened and what steps you might decide to take." Absent that pesky worry about insemination, there would presumably be no compelling reason to engage in something as "awkward and embarrassing" as a post-roll-in-the-hay conversation.

But then a shadow passes over the horizon: the date-rape threat. "On a darker note," continues Alice, "it's possible your experience may have been non-consensual, considering that you were drunk and don't remember exactly what happened." Alice recommends a call to Columbia's Rape Crisis/Anti-Violence Support Center (officially dedicated to "speaking our truths about sexual violence"). Alice's advice shows the incoherence of the contemporary university's multiple stances toward college sex. It's hard to speak your truths about sexual violence when your involvement with your potential date-rapist is so tenuous that it's awkward to speak to *him*. And the support center can't know whether the encounter was consensual. But Alice declines to condemn the behavior that both got the girl into her predicament and erased her memory of it.

The only lesson that Alice offers is that the girl might—purely as an optional matter—want to think about how alcohol affected her. As for rethinking whether she should be getting into bed with someone whom, Alice presumes, she would be reluctant to contact the next day, well, that never comes up. Members of the multifaceted campus sex bureaucracy never seem to consider the possibility that the libertinism that one administrative branch champions, and the sex that another branch portrays as rape, may be inextricably linked.

Modern feminists defined the right to be promiscuous as a cornerstone of female equality. Understandably, they now hesitate to acknowledge that sex is a more complicated force than was foreseen. Rather than recognizing that no-consequences sex may be a contradiction in terms, however, the campus rape industry claims that what it calls campus rape is about not sex but rather politics—the male desire to subordinate women. The University of Virginia Women's Center intones that "rape or sexual assault is not an act of sex or lust—it's about aggression, power, and humiliation, using sex as the weapon. The rapist's goal is domination."

This characterization may or may not describe the psychopathic violence of stranger rape. But it is an absurd description of the barnyard rutting that undergraduate men, happily released from older constraints, seek. The guys who push themselves on women at keggers are after one thing only, and it's not a reinstatement of the patriarchy. Each would be perfectly content if his partner for the evening becomes president of the United States one day, so long as she lets him take off her panties tonight.

One group on campus isn't buying the politics of the campus "rape" movement, however: students. To the despair of rape industrialists everywhere, students have held on to the view that women usually have considerable power to determine whether a campus social event ends with intercourse.

Rutgers University Sexual Assault Services surveyed student athletes about violence against women in the 2001–02 academic year. The female teams were more "direct," the survey reported, in "expressing the idea that women who are raped sometimes put themselves in those situations." A female athlete told interviewers: "When we go out to parties, and I see girls and the way they dress and the way they act . . . and just the way they are, under the influence and um, then they like accuse them of like, oh yeah, my boyfriend did this to me or whatever, I honestly always think it's their fault." Another brainwashed victim of the rape culture.

Equally maddening must be the reaction that sometimes greets performers in *Sex Signals*, an improvisational show on date rape whose venues include Harvard, Yale, and schools throughout the Midwest. "Sometimes we get women who are advocates for men," the show's founders told a Chicago public radio station this October, barely concealing their disbelief. "They blame the victim and try to find out what the victim did so they won't do it." Such worrisome self-help efforts could shut down the campus rape industry.

"Promiscuity" is a word that you will never see in the pages of a campus rape center publication; it is equally repugnant to the sexual liberationist strand of feminism and to the Catherine Mac-Kinnonite "all-sex-is-rape" strand. But it's an idea that won't go away among the student Lumpenproletariat. Students refer to "sororistutes"—those wild and crazy Greek women so often featured in *Girls Gone Wild* videos. And they persist in seeing a connection between promiscuity and the alleged campus rape epidemic. A Rutgers University freshman says that he knows women who claim to have been sexually assaulted, but adds: "They don't have the best reputation. Sometimes it's hard to believe that kind of stuff."

Rape consultant David Lisak faced a similar problem this November: an auditorium of Rutgers students who kept treating women as moral agents. He might have sensed the trouble ahead when in response to a photo array of what Lisak calls "undetected rapists," a girl asked: "Why are there only white men? Am I blind?" It went downhill from there. Lisak did his best to send a tremor of fear through the audience with the news that "rape happens with terrifying frequency. I'm not talking of someone who comes onto campus but students, Rutgers students, who prowl for victims in bars, parties, wherever alcohol is being consumed." He then played a dramatized interview with a student "rapist" at a fraternity that had deliberately set aside a room for raping girls during parties, according to Lisak. The students weren't buying it. "I don't understand why these parties don't become infamous among girls," wondered one. Another asked: "Are you saying that the frat brothers decided that this room would be used for committing sexual assault, or was it just: 'Maybe I'll get lucky, and if I do, I'll go there'?" And then someone asked the most dangerous question of all: "Shouldn't the victim have had a little bit of education beforehand? We all know the dangers of parties. The victim had miscalculations on her part; alcohol can lead to things."

In a column this November in the University of Virginia's student newspaper, third-year student Katelyn Kiley gave the real scoop on frat parties: They're filled with boys hoping to have sex. She did not call these boys "rapists." She did not demonize their sex drive. She merely offered some practical wisdom to the "scantily clad" freshman girls trooping off to Virginia's fraternity row: "That frat boy really is just trying to get into your pants." Most disturbingly, she advised the girls to exercise sexual control: "So dance with that good-looking guy. If he offers, you can even go up to his room to get a mixed drink. . . . Flirt. But it's probably a good idea to keep your clothes on, and at the end of the night, to go home to your own bed. Interestingly enough, that's how you get them to keep asking you back."

You can read thousands of pages of rape crisis center hysteria without coming across such bracing common sense. Amazingly, Kiley hasn't received any of the millions of dollars that feminists in the federal government have showered on campuses to prevent what they call rape.

Some student rebels are going one step further: organizing in favor of sexual restraint. Such newly created campus groups as the Love and Fidelity Network and the True Love Revolution advocate an alternative to the rampant regret sex of the hookup scene: wait until marriage. Their message would do more to return a modicum of manners to campus male—and female—behavior than endless harangues about the rape culture ever could.

Maybe these young iconoclasts can take up another discredited idea: college is for learning. The adults in charge have gone deaf to the siren call of beauty that for centuries lured people to the classics. But fighting male dominance or catering to the libidinal impulses released in the 1960s are sorry substitutes for the pursuit of knowledge. The campus rape and sex industries are signs of how hollow the university has become.

"Justifiable Homicides" Are on the Rise: Have Self-Defense Laws Gone Too Far?

Liliana Segura

from *AlterNet*

ONE YEAR AGO today, a 61-year old Texan named Joe Horn looked out his window in Pasadena, just outside of Houston, and saw a pair of black men on his neighbor's property. It appeared to be a burglary in action, so he called 911. But as he described what he saw to the emergency dispatcher, he began to get agitated. The police would take too long to get there, he decided. Instead, he'd stop the crime himself.

"I've got a shotgun," Horn told the 911 dispatcher. "You want me to stop him?"

The dispatcher tried to talk him down. "Nope, don't do that," he told Horn. "Ain't no property worth shooting somebody over, OK?"

It was not OK with Horn. With the dispatcher still on the phone, he grabbed his gun, went outside, yelled, "Move, you're dead!"—and shot the two men in the back.

The victims turned out to be two undocumented immigrants from Colombia, Diego Ortiz and Miguel de Jesus. Both died on the scene.

The killings sparked instant controversy nationwide, with some labeling it a deplorable act of vigilante justice, and others calling Horn a hero for defending his neighbor's property. Because the victims were in the country illegally, the controversy was further fueled by the ugly, ongoing fight over immigration. Protesters who arrived on Horn's block to call for justice for his victims were met with counterprotesters waving signs in support of their neighbor. "Once again, our chaotic immigration system has led to death," Bill O'Reilly fumed on Dec. 6, 2007.

This summer, Horn was officially cleared of wrongdoing, when a grand jury failed to indict him on any charges. The decision was met with dismay by the families of Ortiz and de Jesus. Diamond Morgan, Ortiz's widow, will now raise their infant son without him. "It's horrible," she said about the 911 recording. "(Horn) was so eager, so eager to shoot." "This man took the law into his own hands," Stephanie Storey, de Jesus' fiancee, told reporters. "He shot two individuals in the back after having been told over and over to stay inside. It was his choice to go outside and his choice to take two lives."

But Horn and his attorney claimed that in addition to protecting his neighbor's home, he was acting in self-defense. "He was afraid for his life," his lawyer, Tom Lambright argued. " . . . I don't think Joe had time to make a conscious decision. I think he only had time to react to what was going on. Short answer is, he was defending his life. "

But the 9/11 recording tells a different story:

Horn: He's coming out the window right now, I gotta go, buddy. I'm sorry, but he's coming out the window.

Dispatcher: Don't, don't—don't go out the door. Mr. Horn? Mr. Horn?

Horn: They just stole something. I'm going after them, I'm sorry.

Dispatcher: Don't go outside.

Horn: I ain't letting them get away with this shit. They stole something. They got a bag of something.

Dispatcher: Don't go outside the house.

Horn: I'm doing this.

Dispatcher: Mr. Horn, do not go outside the house.

Horn: I'm sorry. This ain't right, buddy.

Dispatcher: You're going to get yourself shot if you go outside that house with a gun, I don't care what you think.

Horn: You want to make a bet?

Dispatcher: OK? Stay in the house.

Horn: They're getting away!

Dispatcher: That's all right. Property's not worth killing someone over, OK?

Horn: (curses)

Dispatcher: Don't go out the house. Don't be shooting nobody. I know you're pissed and you're frustrated, but don't do it.

Horn: They got a bag of loot.

Dispatcher: OK. How big is the bag? . . . Which way are they going?

Horn: I'm going outside. I'll find out.

Dispatcher: I don't want you going outside, Mr. Horn.

Horn: Well, here it goes, buddy. You hear the shotgun clicking and I'm going.

Dispatcher: Don't go outside.

Horn: (yelling) Move, you're dead!

(Sound of shots being fired)

Besides being a disturbing recording, the tape is also notable for what it reveals about the moments before Horn saw Ortiz and de Jesus emerge from the window. "I have a right to protect myself too, sir," Horn argued with the dispatcher. "... And the laws have been changed in this country since September the first, and you know it and I know it."

Horn was referring to Texas's newly enacted Castle Law, signed by Gov. Rick Perry on March 27, 2007, and which had gone into effect that fall. The law, as described by the governor, "allows Texans to not only protect themselves from criminals, but to receive the protection of state law when circumstances dictate that they use deadly force." Its benefit, Perry said, is that "it protects law-abiding citizens from unfair litigation and further clarifies their right to self-defense."

It may seem like a stretch to say Horn was acting out of self-defense. As CNN legal analyst Jeffrey Toobin observed after listening to the tape, "He does not appear to be someone who's in a panic. It's a very cool and rather chilling determination to go out and use his gun, against the instructions of the 911 operator." Nevertheless, the new statute ultimately saved Horn from prosecution. Whether or not the law was designed to protect private property as much as human life, rather than "clarifying" the right to self-defense, as Perry claims, the practical effect of Texas' Castle Law appears to be a broadening of the definition to an unprecedented—and deadly—degree.

"Stand Your Ground" Laws

The Castle Law is not some wild Texas invention. In fact, the "castle doctrine" is a concept that dates back to English Common Law. As Ohio State law professor and criminal justice expert Joshua Dressler explains, the castle doctrine basically dictates "that your home is your castle; it's the one place where you should be able to be free from intrusion." This idea has provided the legal basis for self-defense legislation across the country for years—legislation that traditionally has also acknowledged a person's "duty to retreat" in the face of a threatening situation. "The law has always taken the view for self-defense that someone can use deadly force to respond to what the person reasonably believes is a threat," explains Dressler. But, he adds, "the old law tended to be that people ought not to use deadly force until absolutely necessary. They tended to require people to find non-deadly solutions."

Recent decades have seen some exceptions. One precursor to the new Texas law is a 1985 Colorado law, nicknamed the "Make My Day" law, that treats property crimes as legitimate grounds for the use of force. The law came under national scrutiny in 1990, when an 18-year-old named Laureano Jacobo Grieigo Jr. was shot in the head by a 69-year-old-man as he fled his the man's home in an unsuccessful robbery attempt. No charges were filed, and an article published in the *New York Times* at the time called the law an "unusual" statute "that protects people from any criminal charge or civil suit if they use force—including deadly force—against an invader of the home." (The same article quoted a criminologist at Florida International University, Dr. William Wilbanks, who warned that the law was ripe for abuse. "The danger is not that this kind of law will be abandoned, but that it will be extended even more," he said. ''The public sentiment is clearly behind this kind of law.")

Almost two decades later, Texas' Castle Law is part of a wave of similar legislation passed by states throughout the country, building upon the castle doctrine and broadening the right of civilians to use lethal force under the auspices of self-defense. The new laws are particularly expansive in that they go beyond the boundaries of private homes to include cars, workplaces or anywhere else a person may feel threatened. In this sense, says Dressler, "what is happening is that the castle doctrine is becoming less important."

Leading the pack was Florida. In 2005, Gov. Jeb Bush signed a law that, as written, "authorizes (a) person to use force, including deadly force, against (an) intruder or attacker in (a) dwelling, residence, or vehicle under specified circumstances." The law "provides that person is justified in using deadly force under certain circumstances," and "provides immunity from criminal prosecution or civil action for using deadly force." Formally called the "Protection of Persons/Use of Force" law, it became known as the "Stand Your Ground" law.

Heavily backed by the National Rifle Association, Florida's new law alarmed more than just gun control advocates. Many people were appalled at the fact that it could apply in public spaces. As the *Christian Science Monitor* reported at the time:

"Most significantly, (the law) now extends that right to public places, too, meaning that a person no longer has a duty to retreat from what they perceive to be a threatening situation before they are entitled to pull the trigger. Members of the public may now stand their ground and "meet force with force," it states, without fear of criminal prosecution or civil litigation. "It's common sense to allow people to defend themselves," said Gov. Jeb Bush (R) as he signed the new law."

Only 20 state legislators opposed the law. One Democratic critic worried that it could "turn Florida into the OK Corral," but other Democratic politicians "admitted that they did not want to appear soft on crime by voting against it." It helped that one of the driving forces behind the law was Marion Hammer, a lobbyist who argued that the law would protect women against abuse and assault. She "characterized herself as a feminist," recalls Dressler, "but ... more relevantly, was a former president of the NRA."

Mere months after the passage of Florida's "Stand Your Ground" law, similar legislation was being proposed in more than 20 states. The NRA was happy to take the credit. "Today, the NRA is feeding the firebox of Castle Doctrine legislation in states throughout the country," an article posted on the NRA's Institute for Legislative Action Web site boasted, crediting itself with "reuniting Americans with the right to protect themselves and loved ones from danger."

"Justifiable Homicides" on the Rise

Today, there are similar new laws in at least 15 states across the country, and while it may be too early to know the effects, in Texas, the newly passed Castle Law was followed by a series of shootings that prompted questioning over the potential "sudden impact." "Does new law make them quicker to pull the trigger?" asked the *Dallas Morning News* in January. (At least one source said yes: "I think the Castle Law has more citizens thinking about fighting back, knowing they're protected from being sued later," said a Dallas man who shot and killed a man who broke into his garage, "where he stored thousands of dollars worth of tools.")

Anecdotal evidence aside, one recent government report suggests that the laws may be having some effect. A little-noticed study released in mid-October by the FBI found a spike in the number of "justifiable homicides" recorded in the past few years.

The FBI defines "justifiable homicides" as "certain willful killings" that "must be reported as justifiable, or excusable." This includes "the killing of a felon by a peace officer in the line of duty" and "the killing of a felon, during the commission of a felony, by a private citizen." According to the report, in 2007, police officers killed 391 people—the highest number since 1994—and private citizens killed 254—the most since 1997.

Although the report got little attention in the press, an article in *USA Today* quoted criminal justice experts who cited "an emerging 'shoot-first' mentality by police and private citizens" as a possible explanation.

Dressler agrees. "What's been happening is that a lot of states have broadened their homicide rules to give greater authority to citizens to use deadly force in circumstances that in the past would not have been permissible," he says. Expanding "stand your ground" style legislation "means that there are going to be, in the future, many more homicides perpetrated by citizens against other citizens—homicides that were in the past viewed as criminal now will be seen as justifiable."

"If you talk to prosecutors, the message that they're getting is, really, don't even prosecute cases that come close to the category of what is now deemed 'just homicides.'"

Whether a killing is "just" or not is currently determined by local police departments, to whom the concept is long familiar. "Police, of course, use justifiable homicide, both in self-defense and in crime prevention," explains Dressler, "but now a couple things are happening. One is the reality that … thanks to the NRA, some fairly conservative judges, Republicans, we've really become an armed nation. Far more people possess guns today than in the more distant past, and that means that when a police officer is dealing with someone, they have much greater reason to fear that the person they're dealing with is armed." This, perhaps, helps to explain the rise in "justifiable homicides" committed by police (not to mention the rise of "non-lethal" weapons like tasers, themselves deadly weapons).

The recent FBI study is not the first time the government has tracked the number of "justifiable homicides" committed by police alongside those committed by civilians as if they were equivalent phenomena. But given that police officers are, at least in theory, trained to be uniquely authorized to use force in a law enforcement capacity, to what extent do these new laws blur the distinction between police and civilians?

"I think the creed of the NRA is that citizens/civilians have the right to use deadly force because the police don't (or cannot) protect us," says Dressler. "So, under that view, yes, the distinction is blurring."

More Homicides Will Be Seen as Justifiable

Although it may be an old concept, the notion of "justifiable homicides" is itself a slippery one. Anti-abortion extremists, for example, have used the term to describe the killing of abortion providers, on the grounds that they are defending the lives of the unborn. But perhaps more alarming is the positive connotation the term holds for some. When a Memphis paper reported earlier this year that the number of local justifiable homicides "jumped from 11 in 2006 to 32 in 2007," it quoted a firearms instructor whose (admittedly unscientific) explanation was that "the thugs have started running into people who can protect themselves." It's a rather glib way to talk about murder, and the perverse effect is to cast the killings as a positive trend. In Memphis that year, the 32 "justifiable homicides" included four killings by police officers. "All were found to be what internal affairs investigators term 'good shoots,'" according to the report, which explained that "Tennessee law gives citizens the right to defend themselves if they have a reasonable and imminent fear of harm from a carjacker, rapist, burglar or other violent assailant. They can also employ deadly force to protect another person."

But what about another person's property, as in the case of Joe Horn? If a person can shoot two men in the back and get away with it—and, indeed, if he cites his legal right to do so—haven't these laws gone too far?

Dressler thinks so. "My fear is that these changes in self-defense laws will lead to a lot more homicides—and that a lot more homicides will be seen as justifiable."

The Judge Makers

Robert Huber

from *Philadelphia Magazine*

The city's abuzz about judges who go too easy on hardened criminals. But the problem isn't just the judges—it's the shady process they have to go through to get on the bench in the first place. (Pssst . . . anybody got a few grand to take care of a ward leader?)

ONE DAY IN early March 2007, at the Keystone Building in Harrisburg, there was a lottery drawing. Not for cash, but to decide who would become new Common Pleas judges in Philadelphia. Four slots were open on the city's highest court, and 27 lawyer-candidates had gotten the thousand signatures required to run. Now it was time to decide ballot position—chits of paper would be pulled from a cardboard box.

It's impossible to overstate the importance of ballot position when it comes to electing judges in Philadelphia. Nothing confirms our ignorance of judicial candidates as much as this: The first name we come to on the ballot is almost always one that is going to win.

Two candidates, Mike Erdos and Linda Carpenter, approached the drawing quite differently. For Erdos, this was a moment of truth. He was 41 years old and unemployed, having quit the D.A.'s office in January to run. His wife was expecting their second child. He had no idea what he would do next if he lost this election. Meanwhile, Carpenter, a longtime litigator who lost a run for judge in '05, had pretty much made up her mind not to run this time—she didn't even bother to make the drive to Harrisburg for the drawing. Still, she'd gotten the required signatures and was one of the 27 names that would be drawn. Who knew? Maybe she'd get lucky.

Mike Erdos, it turned out, wasn't. When he called his pregnant wife and told her his ballot spot—number 11—she cried. It was not good. He'd be lost in the pack. A couple Philadelphia ward leaders had already taken Erdos aside to tell him, "You can't do this—you gotta try and get your job back. It's just not going to work out." He agreed with them—he was probably going to lose.

For Carpenter, though, it was a different story: She was home lounging in her pajamas when fellow candidate Ellen Green-Ceisler called with the news: Carpenter had been selected for ballot position number one. Whoa! Now she was running, right now, this election. Green-Ceisler herself cried, driving home on the Turnpike, then went for a long walk along Wissahickon Creek to decide whether she was in or out—she'd drawn 19.

Mike Erdos stayed in. He felt he had no choice. He'd gone too far to back out, and if he was going to stay in, he was going to go after it. That meant spending money, a huge amount of family money, on everything he could think of: mailings, Inquirer ads, even some TV commercials. It meant paying most of the city's 69 Democratic ward leaders for the privilege of being put on their sample ballots handed out to voters at the polls.

And it meant ponying up to the real power brokers in our judicial elections—consultants. Their main job is to tell candidates which ward leaders should get their money. The best of them is a lifelong political insider named John Sabatina, who is 62 years old and calls himself The Kid.

The Kid, who might be the most powerful political player you've never heard of in Philadelphia, took on Erdos as a client.

Today, $550,000 later, Judge Mike Erdos presides over courtroom 1104 in City Hall. Meanwhile, The Kid is lining up candidates for the next election.

IF YOU'VE BEEN paying much attention to headlines lately, you know that the issue of judges—their competence, temperaments, qualifications—has been in the air. When police officer Patrick McDonald was gunned down in September, for example, details quickly emerged about the lenient way in which a Philadelphia jurist, now-retired Common Pleas Judge Lynn B. Hamlin, had handled an earlier robbery and aggravated assault case against McDonald's killer, Daniel Giddings. At that trial, an assistant D.A. had begged for the maximum sentence—up to 45 years— for Giddings, who had a rap sheet of violent crime that went back to age 10. "I have never seen an individual who presents a higher risk of re-offending," the assistant D.A. said. Nevertheless, Hamlin gave Giddings the *minimum*—just six to 12 years.

A few days after Officer McDonald's murder, Municipal Court Judge Jacquelyn Frazier-Lyde—boxer Joe Frazier's daughter—made her own headlines when she reduced felony charges against a 19-year-old defendant, who had allegedly punched a police officer, to two misdemeanors. The assistant D.A. in that case had pleaded for the felony charge: "Your Honor, it's open season on police." Frazier-Lyde reportedly responded, "It's open season on all of us, and we don't got guns and vests." She was referring, apparently, to the advantage cops have, compared to life in our toughest neighborhoods.

These are the most recent examples of what prosecutors say has long been a liberal, pro-defendant bias on the Philadelphia bench, and has spurred the Fraternal Order of Police to sit in courtrooms recently, monitoring judicial conduct. But it's not just judges' political leanings that raise eyebrows. Talk to lawyers in the city and you'll hear tale after tale of judicial incompetence, or horrendous comportment in the courtroom, or judges who are literally unable to control themselves.

There is, for example, a certain judge on Municipal Court who habitually has bowel problems while adjudicating, soiling the robe that is then passed on to other judges—we'll let the poor fellow remain nameless. There is Common Pleas Judge Renee Cardwell Hughes, whose unique courtroom demeanor, in the opinion of longtime West Chester-based defense lawyer Sam Stretton, creates a strange atmosphere. As Hughes begins her court sessions, instead of solemnly having everyone rise, she comes onto the bench like a cheerleader:

"Good morning, jurors!"

"Good morning, Your Honor."

"That's not loud enough. Louder, jurors!"

"Good morning, Your Honor!"

Stretton, who is one of the few Philadelphia lawyers willing to say publicly what he thinks about our judges, does not, to put it mildly, find this amusing, or conducive to a sober presentation of a case: "It's just insanity."

And then, also on Common Pleas, there is Leslie Fleisher, who many lawyers say is dismissive and mean. And Frank Palumbo, a nice man who, attorneys aver, can barely follow what goes on in his courtroom, let alone control it.

"Some of my colleagues on the bench," one Philadelphia court official told me, "I wouldn't hire to cut my grass."

All of which raises the question: How do people like this end up on the bench in the first place? We know the answer, of course: We elect them. But if you've ever voted in a judicial election in Philadelphia (or anywhere in Pennsylvania), you also know that in most cases, you're voting for little more than a name. Back in the '70s, a candidate for Common Pleas named William Marutani did well in South Philadelphia, an Italian scoring with the Italian-American neighborhood. Except that Marutani wasn't Italian—he was Japanese.

Which is why the real power when it comes to electing judges in Philadelphia lies with the city's ward leaders and consultants like Sabatina. And lately, the cost of getting them on your side has been rising. Much of the $550,000 that Mike Erdos spent in the 2007 Common Pleas election went to consultants like The Kid, who is also a ward leader in the Northeast, and, in $1,000 and $2,000 chunks, to most of the other ward leaders in the city. This is ethically dubious, but not, alas, illegal.

Surprisingly, given what they have to go through to get there, some judges in Philadelphia are quite good: smart and experienced and thoughtful and tough. *Judicious.*

It's a mixed bag—virtually everyone agrees on that. But you begin to wonder, when you look at the way we elect them—and the ever-increasing wads of money it requires—whether men and women potentially worthy of the honor of becoming judges might lose patience with a process controlled by the likes of The Kid.

MIKE ERDOS IS an intense, very tall ex-semi-professional basketball player who attended Yale Law and worked in the city's D.A. office for a decade. He talks convincingly about wanting to become a judge to serve, and early returns on his judicial work among lawyers and colleagues is favorable. He has nonetheless been accused of buying his seat on the bench.

But putting the blame on Erdos's profligate spending seems beside the point—he didn't create the system. Once he was running, hanging out there with no job, a second child on the way, palms so willing to be greased—*legally* greased . . . Erdos comes from money; his family was more than willing to help him out. But it seemed like a horrendous way to become a *judge*. Veteran judges say it takes two or three years to get the sordid process of running out of your system. Erdos is only a year in.

To understand what's happened—why money and consultants might have more to do with Mike Erdos becoming a judge than anything else—we have to understand how Bob Brady lost control of the process.

Once upon a time, a Democratic City Committee endorsement on a candidacy for Common Pleas was golden, because the party's ward leaders would follow in lockstep with those candidates and get the vote out. That's still partly true today. Brady, as local head of the party, keeps an ongoing list of potential candidates. You get on the list, you wait your turn—though Brady adjusts the list, depending on the needs of big-time city players like party secretary Carol Campbell, or Ed Rendell, or, at least until recently, Vince Fumo.

But Bob Brady's list no longer controls who gets elected. Three things shredded his power. In the early '80s, at a meeting of city African-American leaders, Lucien Blackwell made an impassioned speech: There were 18 spots open for judges that election, and only two of them went to African-Americans. "We'll never let this happen again!" Blackwell roared—and it hasn't. Black ward leaders banded together to support minority candidates regardless of what Brady and the party hierarchy wanted to do, which has gone a long way toward balancing the bench racially.

A second change came when Brady ran for Congress in 1997; he needed help from ward leaders, so his control over them slackened. But the third and most important difference has been the infusion of money. Ten years ago, Common Pleas candidates spent, on average, about $100,000 to get elected. Now, led by Erdos, there's considerably more money in play. Ellen Green-Ceisler spent $160,000; Linda Carpenter, even with that winning ballot position, spent more than $150,000. Nothing makes political players buck leadership like promises of cash, into either their wards or their pockets. It's called "street money." The running joke is whether you, a political operative from South or North or West Philly, can pick up enough for a post-election winter trip to the Bahamas. Except it's not really a joke.

Candidates pay individual wards $1,000 to $2,000 for the privilege of being put on their sample ballots, which ostensibly covers the cost of printing and getting field workers to distribute them, mostly at polls. This is the nuts and bolts of the elective process, since virtually none of us spend the time or know how to check judicial candidates' qualifications. Your committeeman handing out your ward's list of preferred lawyers to stick on the bench—why, it's a service.

These days, the fact that ward leaders listen to consultants instead of Bob Brady is annoying Brady to the point of moral outrage—or what sounds like moral outrage. "The problem I have," he says, "is that some people can afford to circumvent the system, spend half a million dollars. It's atrocious, and I don't understand it."

What really bothers Brady, of course, is losing control, to the point that he and Vince Fumo stood up a few years ago and said city judges should be appointed, not elected. Calling for a system that would allow them to regain their power made it obvious just how far it had eroded. Brady freely admits—in that way of his that's simultaneously refreshing and infuriating—that he isn't any better at vetting the candidates than the voters: "I'm not qualified to tell whether someone is qualified for judge or not," he says. "They all have law degrees, most are practicing law—I can't tell you a good one or a bad one."

It was inevitable that all the money floating around would bubble up into shenanigans; a state grand jury report in 2001 dipped into legendary political operator Buddy Cianfrani's methods. Back in 1997, Cianfrani worked as a consultant for six Common Pleas candidates, to the tune of $24,500. The candidates also gave Cianfrani 121 checks totaling $128,250, ostensibly to pay ward committees or leaders for their Election Day help—so far, nothing illegal. Except there was a small problem. Cianfrani had his candidates sign the checks but leave the recipient's name blank; it turned out that 30 checks, for a total of $49,500, were made out to fictitious names: "Frank Schmitz," for example, got

$2,500 from Joyce Mozenter's campaign. Frank lived at 1736 South 10th Street, which is the address of St. Maria Goretti High School. Cianfrani, who got immunity for his testimony, squirmed out of this one by claiming he had been furnished the unlikely names by other ward leaders, and it never came to light exactly where that $49,500 ended up.

Oh, Buddy, we miss you terribly. And what a tough act for The Kid to follow. But the real point of the Cianfrani story is that it barely ruffled a feather, and nothing has changed. The worst vestige of the system Cianfrani and operatives before him scammed isn't candidates' cash finding its way into pockets instead of paying for field workers to get out the vote. No, the bigger problem is the demand that our prospective judges—our *judges*—dive into a deal-making election process that becomes a test of whether they can close their eyes and hold their noses long enough to resurface with any moral equilibrium.

Benjamin Lerner, universally regarded as a smart, thoughtful, balanced judge, has an election story—every judge does. After 15 years as head of the Public Defender's office, Lerner was appointed by Governor Ridge to fill a vacant Common Pleas spot in 1996. That meant he'd have to run for a seat the next year, but candidate Lerner got some bad advice from a political operative: Since he was already on the bench, was well-known, and had the support of the Democratic city committee, he didn't need to spend much time going around to ward leaders to woo them individually.

Turns out this was a big mistake. Ward leaders don't take kindly to appointed judges to begin with, since they have no say in those picks. Lerner still paid to get on sample ballots, but ward leaders need to be personally feted, assured their one-69th chunk of political Philadelphia is important. "So they took money," Lerner says, "then cut the shit out of me." One tactic they used against him, in the Northeast and elsewhere, was to "sticker over" his name on sample ballots with the names of other candidates who'd also paid up—thereby collecting two checks for one ballot spot.

When Lerner lost, one of the first people he went to see was one Michael Nutter, then a councilman and head of the 52nd Ward. Lerner believes that Nutter cut him from his ward's sample ballot, even though, Lerner says, "Nutter knew what kind of public defender and judge I had been. If I had earned anybody's support, it was Michael Nutter's." But Nutter's ward went with other, apparently better-paying candidates. Lerner says that Nutter apologized when he went to see him.

Lerner had learned his lesson. He spent a great deal of time before the 1999 election going around and kissing up to ward leaders and their committee people. Why? It's the same answer Erdos gives: He had no choice. If he really wanted to become a judge, that's what he had to do.

I MEET JOHN Sabatina at Fluke's, a restaurant and bar just off the Cottman Avenue exit of 95; it's a couple miles from his stomping ground in the Northeast, which is how The Kid wants it—no one will recognize him here or see him talking to a reporter. He is a pasty, nondescript, cautious man who has played hardball politics as a ward leader—the 56th—for two decades. He has had his office broken into, his car set ablaze. Sabatina doesn't respond in kind. He's got a different method. A fellow ward leader who's watched Sabatina work for the past two decades explains it:

"Let's say a ward leader won't support Ellen Ceisler for judge because she looks like a woman who turned him down for the senior prom. But he can't tell anybody that, so he's against Ellen, he's *really* against Ellen. John will get on that phone, and he'll wear the ward leader down. John just keeps calling and calling. It just gets to be too much trouble, so finally. . . 'Okay! I'll support Ellen Ceisler!' Candidates get their money's worth out of John Sabatina."

I ask Sabatina how many ward leaders he has that kind of relationship with, how many he can call and badger and finally get what he wants because he's so relentless. How many?

Sabatina won't say.

Twenty? A third of the city?

"That's low."

And what if a ward leader crosses him? What if the leader agrees, say, to back one of his candidates and then takes the candidate's name off a sample ballot or stickers it over?

"They only do that once to me."

It doesn't feel tough or hardball so much as ... absurd. That *this* guy ... The other big-time consultants in the city, Carol Campbell and Pete Truman, go at it a little differently. Campbell, head of the city's 4th Ward and a former city councilwoman, is close to Bob Brady, and wields much of her power through the city committee. She's gotten into trouble: Campbell was indicted in 2001 for not reporting activities of her political action committee. No problem: Two years later, deeming herself a consultant, she didn't have to account for the $140,000 she collected from judicial candidates.

In the 2007 election, though, one of the Common Pleas candidates suggests that Campbell was playing fast and loose. The candidate was in the office of a ward leader who received a call from Campbell; he put her on speaker phone. Campbell wanted a candidate, one who had paid her to be on a sample ballot, removed from that ballot. "Take him off—take him off today! I want you to put this other person on the ballot," the candidate heard Campbell demand.

Here's another trick of the trade practiced by Campbell: Promise several wards' worth of support for some other consultant's candidate, collect a check from that candidate, and then return the uncashed check to the bewildered—and angry—candidate *after* the election. Nothing illegal there, since she didn't get paid. (Campbell has recently had serious health problems that may be diminishing her power.)

As for Pete Truman, he stages meet-and-pay events at the Airport Sheraton and other city hotels, comprising a series of get-togethers with 10 or so mostly African-American ward leaders. At the first one, prospective candidates come and speak for a couple of minutes, selling themselves; next, the ward leaders meet privately to decide whom they're going to support; then at a third meeting, the anointed candidates come back with checks for the ward leaders. Mike Erdos, for one, paid Truman $25,000.

But Sabatina, jeez. . . . A guy who at one point, when he worked for the Housing Authority, was relegated to a desk next to a soda machine. A guy with a personality "like chewing aluminum foil," says the ward leader who's known him forever. A guy who admits that "People constantly put up roadblocks for people like me." This is why insiders laugh that he's now being compared to Buddy Cianfrani. Buddy was a rascal. Buddy was fun. Sabatina is … a pain in the ass. He just won't *stop*.

John Sabatina worked with three candidates for Common Pleas in 2007, with only four slots open. All three—Erdos, Alice Beck Dubow, and Ellen Ceisler, for whom he did some pro bono work as a favor to John Dougherty—won. All three—in the sheepish description of one of the winning judges—are rich Jews. This is the sort of co-opting of his system that makes that moralist Bob Brady crazy (he calls consultants "insultants"); Brady wields his wannabe-judge list with an eye to making the bench reflect the ethnic makeup of the city.

That's not something Sabatina cares about. He wants to know two things about a prospective client: Can you afford it, and will you put in the time? Mike Erdos certainly fit the bill. He worked his butt off, going to ward functions all over the city.

In fact, that's the one *good* thing everyone points to in our system of electing judges in Philadelphia—that candidates, most of whom are well-versed in Center City, are forced to go to churches and meet-and-greets and ward functions all over town. They get a close-up view of how the other half lives.

Sabatina says Erdos spent *five years* running around the wards, building his campaign for judge—that's not literally true, but Erdos was chief of the Public Nuisance Task Force in the D.A.'s office, helping close down nasty bars and the like, so he got to know plenty of Northeast and West and South Philly community leaders. But part of the problem prospective judges have in campaigning is that they have to dance around positions on issues, because putting on the robe means you must be fair, even-handed, without a particular point of view. *Judicious.* That's another reason why ward leaders and committeemen have become so important—to separate one candidate from another. And why Erdos spent so much money.

In fact, Sabatina couldn't *stop* him from throwing his cash around. Erdos asked Sabatina one day before the May '07 primary whether he'd seen the plastic wrap around his Sunday *Inquirer*—it was printed with an Erdos ad. Sabatina replied that of course he hadn't seen it—who reads the plastic wrap around the newspaper? All Erdos really needed to do was stick with Sabatina, let him work the ward leaders. That's what it's all about. Deals.

Never mind that, Erdos guesses, maybe one-quarter of the 45,000 voters who pulled the lever for him actually knew anything about him (not to mention that he paid about $11 per vote, when you total his expenses). Sabatina thinks Erdos spent $200,000 more than he really had to, if he had just listened to The Kid.

But let's not forget the ace in the hole. Luck. Meaning ballot position, the one thing nobody controls.

Remember Frank Palumbo, the Common Pleas judge who is generally viewed as not smart enough or experienced enough or tough enough to be a judge, and who has been given a trial docket very heavy on simple procedural cases? When Palumbo ran for Municipal Court, then in 2005 for Common Pleas, he had the advantage of actually being Italian, though he didn't even need that much help. He drew the number one ballot position. Twice.

THE $500,000 QUESTION, with the system we've got, is whether the judges we elect are up to adjudicating cases from all those neighborhoods Erdos and his fellow candidates visited on their campaigns. Most court historians do believe that the Common Pleas bench has improved over the past two decades, after the Roofers scandal in the 1980s exposed judges on the take. As Gene Cohen, a retired Common Pleas judge, points out, "Judges who don't show up, or show up on the bench drunk—we don't have that anymore." Talk about a high threshold of competence.

Some lawyers who argue regularly in Common Pleas Court remain highly frustrated. Defense lawyer Sam Stretton says that too many judges get elected too young, and that the legal profession has changed in that most lawyers no longer log significant time in court, which doesn't stop them from becoming judges. Further, he says that if you go back a couple decades, the Democratic Party typically awarded judgeships to committeemen who were well-versed in the neighborhoods, who understood the lives that came before them because they were neighborhood guys themselves. (Though those neighborhoods, in the halcyon days Stretton is alluding to, would certainly be white, and the plucked committeemen would be just that: men.) These days, judges get a one-week tutorial before their initial swearing-in, but that's it in terms of official schooling before the black robe is donned.

When you watch both Linda Carpenter and Mike Erdos hear cases, it's immediately apparent how hard they're working, how intently they listen, how much they care. Again, that might seem like a laughably low threshold in rating performance, but "black robe disease"—wherein judges strike an arrogant or disdainful pose—is all too often on display.

Defense lawyer Michael Coard recently had a legal dustup with Judge Leslie Fleisher over how she treated him in court. Fleisher, infamous for bizarre, imperious behavior, pitched a fit over a minor procedural matter in the delay of a case. She forced Coard to come before her—he had to leave a Temple University class he was teaching, and put off a hearing in a murder case that same day—so she could berate him in open court for, among other things, not reading the *Legal Intelligencer*, and for his posture: "I think you'd better sit up in my room. People sit up in my courtroom. They are not lounged back like they're watching television or something."

When Coard, who is black, responded with a formal complaint, a retreating Fleisher confided to another African-American attorney she was close to that she had "no idea who Coard was"—that is, somebody who would fight back and rally support in the small legal world of the Criminal Justice Center. As if *that* would be a reason to treat him with respect.

Out of a pool of 91 Common Pleas judges, it's not a shock to come across some who act out, even outrageously. But a longtime public defender says the biggest disappointment of his career as a lawyer is the almost across-the-board inability of our city's bench to engage legal issues on a deep and substantive level.

Fleisher's behavior, for example, is not only offensive, but threatens adjudicative fairness. A buzz was set off within the Public Defender's office not long ago when, mid-trial, she demanded that police officers in her court and in the hallway— some 15 cops in all—follow her back into chambers. Fleisher wouldn't allow either the public defender or the district attorney to accompany them.

Three minutes went by. Four, five. Seven. The cops filed out.

What was that conversation about? No one, except the participants, knows. The trial continued. A defense lawyer told me that if *he'd* been working that trial, he would have gone ballistic, demanded to get what was discussed on the record, sought a change of venue, pushed to be held in contempt of court—it was, in other words, a troubling disregard of legal procedure that could corrupt a trial's outcome.

All this begins to make the strange way we elect judges infuriating. Take Fleisher. She wanted to be a judge. She had a close friend, Frank Gillen, who was a Teamster. Governor Ridge threw a bone to the union by appointing her to a vacant Common

Pleas judgeship in 2001. She still had to run in the next election, though. So in 2003, the Teamsters blanketed the city, drumming up ward support. Edgar Howard, head of the 10th, one of the big African-American wards, got behind her.

"As a favor to the union," Howard explains. Whether it's a union pulling the levers, or consultants, it's all about deals. And what's infuriating is the way operatives like Howard dismiss it with a shrug: "That's how you work."

SURPRISINGLY, IT'S WHEN I watch Benjamin Lerner—small, white-haired, 67 years old, by all accounts one of our best Common Pleas judges—preside over a murder trial one morning in early September in Courtroom 1105 of the Criminal Justice Center that the current problem is fully brought home. It's a waiver trial—meaning no jury, just Lerner hearing the case of a man who shot and killed another man in a bar because he feared that the victim, who was acting aggressively and strangely toward him, was leaving to get a gun and do *him* in. What happened isn't in dispute—but Lerner must determine whether the killer's fear was justified, which could make it voluntary manslaughter, or whether it's first-degree, premeditated murder.

That afternoon, Lerner carefully tells his courtroom how he made his decision. He says that as judge, it's his job not only "to look at the facts, but [to] look into the mind of the defendant at the time he pulled that trigger."

With that, I remember something Ellen Green-Ceisler, one of the four Common Pleas judges elected in '07, told me: After her first few months on the bench, she realized that the most important quality a judge must have is the ability to read people, to understand who is telling the truth and who is not, in a sense to look into the mind of the person before her.

It became all too apparent again recently—with that Common Pleas judge's light sentence instrumental in letting a life-long criminal back out on the street to murder a cop—just how crucial a judge's decisions can be. That judge could be Frank

Palumbo, who got elected through great ballot position. Or Leslie Fleisher—overwhelming union support. Or Mike Erdos—loads of cash. Or Benjamin Lerner, who, after getting appointed, had to run for election, lost, then kissed the rings of half the ward leaders in Philadelphia two years later, because that's the process we've got, and if he wanted to be a judge, well, he had no choice.

Back to Courtroom 1105: Lerner, careful, experienced and judicious, explains to those in his court how he considered the gunman's fear, and weighed it against his imminent danger. The man did have options: He could have called 911 on the cell phone he had with him; he could have put his .38 to the other man's head, told him not to move, and left the bar himself instead of killing him. Perhaps he was wrong in assuming the other man would even come back with a gun. He wasn't in imminent danger.

Lerner's decision is murder in the first degree. Premeditated. Murder One.

The victim's mother jumps up: "Hallelujah! Now my son can rest in peace!" The mother, with several family members, leaves Room 1105 of the Criminal Justice Center. They, at least, have gotten their day in court in Philadelphia.

In the end, there is no easy answer to what we should do about the way we pick judges in Philadelphia. State Supreme Court Chief Justice Ron Castille has been advocating for the merit selection of state-level judiciary; Pennsylvania is one of only six states that elect all judges. Merit selection—endorsements by colleagues, a certain level of courtroom experience and so forth—would seem the obvious way to go. But even there, the question becomes, exactly who decides who has merit?

One day recently, I ran into Castille in the elevator (we work in the same building), and I asked him if there is any way to select judges that is politics-proof. "No matter what system there is," he told me, "anybody who could get politics out of it would deserve the Nobel prize."

Justice after Bush: Prosecuting an outlaw administration

Scott Horton

from *Harper's*

I. The Crimes

Americans may wish to avoid what is necessary. We may believe that concerns about presidential lawbreaking are naive. That all presidents commit crimes. We may pretend that George W. Bush and his senior officers could not have committed crimes significantly worse than those of their predecessors. We may fear what it would mean to acknowledge such crimes, much less to punish them. But avoiding this task, simply "moving on," is not possible.

This administration did more than commit crimes. It waged war against the law itself. It transformed the Justice Department into a vehicle for voter suppression, and it also summarily dismissed the U.S. attorneys who attempted to investigate its wrongdoing. It issued wartime contracts to substandard vendors with inside connections, and it also defunded efforts to police their performance. It spied on church groups and political protesters, and it also introduced a sweeping surveillance program that was so clearly illegal that virtually the entire senior echelon of the Justice Department threatened to (but did not in fact) tender their resignations over it. It waged an illegal and disastrous war, and it did so by falsely representing to Congress and to the American public nearly every piece of intelligence it had on Iraq. And through it all, as if to underscore its contempt for any authority but its own, the administration issued more than a hundred carefully crafted "signing statements" that raised pervasive doubt about whether the president would even accede to bills that he himself had signed into law.

No prior administration has been so systematically or so brazenly lawless. Yet it is no simple matter to prosecute a former president or his senior officers. There is no precedent for such a prosecution, and even if there was, the very breadth and audacity of the administration's activities would make the process so complex as to defy systems of justice far less fragmented than our own. But that only means choices must be made. Indeed, in weighing the enormity of the administration's transgressions against the realistic prospect of justice, it is possible to determine not only the crime that calls most clearly for prosecution but also the crime that is most likely to be successfully prosecuted. In both cases, that crime is torture.

There can be no doubt that torture is illegal. There is no wartime exception for torture, nor is there an exception for prisoners or "enemy combatants," nor is there an exception for "enhanced" methods. The authors of the Constitution forbade "cruel and unusual punishment," the details of that prohibition were made explicit in the Geneva Conventions ("No physical or mental torture, nor any other form of coercion, may be inflicted on prisoners of war to secure from them information of any kind whatever"), and that definition has in turn become subject to

U.S. enforcement through the Uniform Code of Military Justice, the U.S. Criminal Code, and several acts of Congress.[1]

Nor can there be any doubt that this administration conspired to commit torture: Waterboarding. Hypothermia. Psychotropic drugs. Sexual humiliation. Secretly transporting prisoners to other countries that use even more brutal techniques. The administration has carefully documented these actions and, in many cases, proudly proclaimed them. The written guidelines for interrogations at Guantánamo Bay, for instance, describe several techniques for degrading and physically debilitating prisoners, including the "forceful removal of detainees' clothing" and the use of "stress positions." And in a 2006 radio interview, Dick Cheney said simply that the use of waterboarding to obtain intelligence was a "no-brainer."[2]

Finally, there can be no doubt that the administration was aware of the potential criminality of these acts. In January 2002, White House lawyers began generating a series of memos outlining the administration's motivation for torturing. They claimed that "the war against terrorism is a new kind of war" requiring an enhanced "ability to quickly obtain information from captured terrorists" and that "this new paradigm renders obsolete Geneva's strict limitations on questioning of enemy prisoners." The legal term for such contemplation is mens rea, or "guilty mind," and it is an important consideration in criminal trials. Which is perhaps the reason that John Ashcroft—when he, Dick Cheney, Colin Powell, Condoleezza Rice, Donald Rumsfeld, and George Tenet gathered at the White House in 2002 to formally approve the application of specific torture methods—asked the assembled, "Why are we talking about this in the White House? History will not judge this kindly."[3]

II. The Consequences of Inaction

The accuracy of Ashcroft's prediction remains to be determined. The United States does, in fact, have a long history of prosecuting torturers, but the punishments have varied considerably. In

1902, U.S. Army Captain Edwin Glenn confessed to and was courtmartialed for using "the water cure" on Filipinos as part of the U.S. prosecution of the Spanish-American War. He was required to pay a fifty-dollar fine. And in 1926, when the Mississippi Supreme Court declared waterboarding to be torture and overturned the conviction of a man who had confessed to another crime under its application, the police who had elicited the confession went entirely unpunished. In other circumstances, though, the consequences have been more significant. In 1983, an east Texas sheriff named James Parker was convicted of waterboarding six men in order to coerce confessions. He was sentenced to ten years in federal prison. And when American prosecutors convicted Japanese officials at the end of World War II of war crimes that included waterboarding, the sentence sought, and obtained in some of the cases, was death. Which is not to say that administration officials will or should face similarly dire sanction. But such consequences are a measure of the gravity of the crime.

Waterboarding is far from the worst that detainees have suffered under U.S. supervision. Its use is especially worthy of note, however, because it is universally understood that 1) the administration authorized waterboarding, and 2) waterboarding is a serious crime.[4]

Open criminality is a cancer on democracy. It implicates all who know of the conduct and fail to act. Such compliance presents a practical crisis, in that a government that is allowed to torture will inevitably transgress other legal limits. But it also presents an existential political crisis. Many democracies have simply collapsed as the people permitted their leaders to abandon the rule of law in the face of alleged external threats. The turn to torture was rapid, for instance, in Argentina at the time of the Dirty War and in Chile after the American-directed coup against Salvador Allende. In both cases, that turn had little to do with a perceived benefit from the use of torture in interrogation. To the contrary, the very criminality of the act had a talismanic significance. It asserted the primacy of the will of the torturer. It made the claim, for all to accept or reject, that the ruler was the law. Such a claim is, of course, intolerable to democracy, which presupposes, as Thomas Paine wrote, that "the law ought to be King; and there ought to be no other."

Reasserting the rule of law is no simple matter. A new administration may—or may not—bring an end to open torture in the United States, but it will not bring an end to our knowledge and acceptance of what has already taken place. If the people wish to maintain sovereignty, they must also reclaim responsibility for the actions taken in their name. As of yet, they have not. Pursuing the Bush Administration for crimes long known to the public may amount to a kind of hypocrisy, but it is a necessary hypocrisy. The alternative, simply doing nothing, not only ratifies torture; it ratifies the failure of the people to control the actions of their government.[5]

III. Possible Methods of Sanction

Torture is a war crime, and war crimes present an unusual legal challenge. They can be prosecuted domestically, like any other crime. But because they are war crimes, they also are subject to enforcement by all nations, under a well-established principle of universal jurisdiction. Making matters more complex, such crimes can be prosecuted not only in standing courts here or abroad but also in domestic or international ad hoc courts—like those convened for the Nuremberg trials—designed to deal with specific political concerns. Various combinations are suited to different situations:

International Criminal Tribunal

In recent years, nations have joined together on an ad hoc basis, often with U.S. support or under the auspices of the United Nations, to prosecute military and political figures from Cambodia, Rwanda, West Africa, and the former Yugoslavia. Many of these tribunals are still in progress and thus far have achieved mixed results. But they have by and large followed a predictable pattern. Rather than attempting to prosecute all potential war criminals, they have instead focused on those in positions of authority whose action or inaction had broad consequences. And they have shown a particular concern for offenses committed systematically against persons outside of combat, who in many cases have been disarmed and taken prisoner.

The precedent for all of these tribunals was the Nuremberg trials, convened at the end of World War II. Under U.S. leadership, the Allies prosecuted not only leaders of the Nazi Party but also industrialists, doctors, and prison commandants. The Americans and Soviets also wanted to prosecute the people who had created the legal framework for the Nazi regime, but British and French leaders objected. Consequently, the United States, acting on its own, convened a separate Nuremberg tribunal to try lawyers, judges, and legal policymakers. In doing so, it established the principle that policymakers who overrode the mandatory prohibitions of international law against harming prisoners in wartime could be prosecuted as war criminals, no matter how many internal memos they had written to the contrary.

The International Criminal Court, headquartered in the Netherlands, was created in 1998 to provide a permanent version of such a tribunal. The ICC bears many traces of U.S. authorship, and indeed its establishment, in one form or another, was urged by presidents from Thomas Jefferson to Bill Clinton. But American conservatives, opposing what they saw as a limitation on American sovereignty, have blocked the U.S. from joining the 108 other nations that have signed the Court's foundational treaty. And even the institution's strongest advocates agree that, although the ICC is suited to prosecuting political leaders in minor states, it was never intended as a check on the great powers. In fact, the ICC's success depends upon its gaining the support of those great powers.

As things stand it would be legally very difficult and politically impossible for the ICC to indict American policymakers for war crimes, and even more difficult for an ad hoc group of nations to do so. Moreover, any such effort would probably provoke a public-opinion backlash within the United States.

Foreign Courts

Most crimes are subject to sanction on the basis of territoriality— that is, the crime is viewed as having occurred on the soil of one particular state, and that state has the right to enforce its criminal law by prosecuting the crime or not. War crimes, however, are not subject to this territorial limitation. Any nation that has a reasonable relationship to the crime can prosecute the alleged criminal—the state where the offense occurred, any of the warring states, or a state whose nationals were harmed or mistreated. Consequently, many other nations have standing, under international law, to pursue war-crimes prosecutions against U.S. citizens.

The example of Augusto Pinochet shows how such an approach might unfold. In 1998, the onetime dictator of Chile, then eighty-two, was seized in Britain on a Spanish arrest warrant. He was charged with several crimes stemming from his seventeen years in power—including torture, illegal detention, and forced disappearances—and placed under house arrest in a Surrey mansion while diplomats from all three countries debated the next steps. After several months of complex legal proceedings, the British determined that Pinochet was medically unfit to stand trial and returned him to Chile, thus maintaining their claim to jurisdiction without actually pursuing a prosecution. Even this attenuated process would be difficult to replicate with an American political figure, however. Most nations that have a record of prosecuting war crimes are close allies of the United States and would be justifiably concerned about the practicalities of maintaining positive defense relations with the world's preeminent power. Moreover, the United States—like Chile—almost certainly would not extradite a former official for such purposes.

At present, however, one criminal prosecution is already pending. It arises from the abduction in Italy, under the CIA's "extraordinary rendition" program, of an Egyptian cleric named Hassan Mustafa Osama Nasr. Twenty-six Americans—including diplomats, intelligence officers, and a military attaché—face criminal charges in absentia in the case. For the Americans the abduction was a sensitive national-security operation. But for the Italian criminal-justice authorities it was simply the armed assault and kidnapping of a resident alien. Even if, as widely expected, the case produces convictions, the American operatives will not be extradited to Italy. They will, however, have difficulties traveling outside the United States.

Even this mild form of sanction, however, fails to address the domestic political problem. True justice cannot be compelled from without. If the United States wishes to demonstrate to the world, and to itself, that its abdication of human-rights principles was an anomaly, it will have to do so under its own auspices.

Domestic Courts

Most violations of the laws of war are punished through a military court system. Under the Uniform Code of Military Justice, which provides the tools for enforcement of the laws of war in the United States, civilians as well as uniformed service members may be prosecuted, though such prosecutions are rare and raise significant constitutional issues. Moreover, such systems are fine for punishing errant soldiers, but they seldom function properly when the culpable person is far up the chain of command. This is largely because military justice is not concerned exclusively with justice; it is also concerned with upholding command authority. There is little likelihood, therefore, that policymakers would be prosecuted before a court-martial.

Torture is forbidden by federal law as well.[6]

Could a federal prosecutor take it upon himself to enforce that law? Alberto Gonzales expressed concern in a 2002 memo that a prosecutor might display sufficient independence to do just that. But thus far none has. The scandal surrounding the dismissal of nine U.S. attorneys in 2006 helps explain why: the Bush Administration has maintained an unprecedentedly tight rein on its prosecutors, acting harshly when they depart from the prescribed political path. Indeed, so many high-level figures at Justice were involved in creating the legal mechanism for torture that the Justice Department has effectively disqualified itself as an investigative vehicle, even under a new administration.

Another major obstacle to domestic prosecution will be pardons. The exercise of a presidential pardon to protect war criminals would violate international law and would not be respected outside the territory of the United States. Under the Constitution, however, Bush's pardon power is nonetheless nearly absolute. Those advocating a pardon hope that it would put an end to questions about criminal conduct, but historical experience suggests that a pardon might have just the opposite effect. It would implicitly concede that serious crimes were in fact committed; the public would not necessarily reject a pardon, but it might well insist on full disclosure of what was done; and the president's political party likely would pay a significant price for all of this, as Republicans experienced in the election following Gerald Ford's decision to pardon Richard Nixon.

Pardons would have another unintended effect. Under well-established notions of international law, the fact that a state attempts to immunize officeholders from prosecution (such as by the issuance of a presidential pardon) would boomerang by actually conferring on other states the jurisdiction to prosecute.

Commission of Inquiry

In recent decades, the commission of inquiry, often in the form of a "truth and reconciliation commission," has established itself as the preferred means of approaching politically sensitive issues such as war crimes while avoiding the destabilization that might result from direct prosecutions. In Argentina, Chile, East Timor, Peru, and South Africa, newly elected leaders feared that the

criminal prosecution of their predecessors would wreck the fragile political consensus that had been used to establish both peace
and a legitimate democracy. A commission of inquiry allowed
these countries to move toward accountability in a slow but
deliberate way. In some cases, a bargain was struck under which
the truth about past misconduct was divulged in exchange for a
pardon, on the premise that establishing a record of historical
truth was more important to democracy than punishing individual malefactors. In other cases, however, the commission's
fact-finding process gradually built a public consensus that pros-
ecutorial action was needed. In Peru and Chile, prosecutions
occurred even after comprehensive pardons had been granted,
as the courts relied on international-law concepts to disregard
those pardons.

These commissions have not always performed as their
authors intended them to. For instance, it was anticipated that
the South African commission would widely disseminate pardons
in exchange for more detailed accounts of homicides and abuse
under apartheid. In the end, however, very few such pardons
were even sought, since many witnesses simply counted on a
sentiment of general amnesty to see them through. Such commissions also shift the balance of historical memory, which usually favors those who hold power, by ensuring that the accounts
of victims are carefully recorded. Often this occurs by taking the
victim's testimony in a public setting. In Argentina, Chile, and
South Africa, the commission process served one function especially well: the public was educated about the wretched practices
of the prior regime, and demands for a clear separation from
these practices—often including the rehabilitation of victims
and the punishment of perpetrators—changed the landscape
of public opinion.

IV. A Two-part Solution

Given the political situation in the United States, it seems clear
that the last option is the best. Although "truth and reconcilia-

tion" may strike many people as somehow too exotic a process for the United States, investigative commissions in fact have a long history here that includes the Warren Commission, which was established in 1963 to investigate the assassination of John Kennedy, and the Kerner Commission, which was established in 1967 to examine the causes of race riots in the United States. Such investigations have had a mixed record of success, but they are the best means available to the U.S. political system for investigating issues that raise broad public concern but cannot be satisfactorily delved into by such established bodies as the FBI or a congressional oversight committee.

Investigative commissions can provide truth. They can establish an important record. They can reaffirm important taboos. But they cannot provide justice. For that they are simply a first step. The second step, which I will discuss only briefly, is a formal prosecution, most likely by an executive-appointed special prosecutor. In this model—call it "commission plus special prosecutor"—the commission would find the facts, weigh them, and, if the facts warrant, make a formal recommendation for the appointment of a prosecutor, identifying the matters that necessitate further investigation. Even if the commission were to determine that no prosecutable crimes had occurred—and, given the legal complexities of such an undertaking, such a finding is possible—it would perform the absolutely necessary function of educating the public. If, on the other hand, the commission were to determine that criminal investigation was appropriate, it already would have created essential public support for such action.

From what source would the commission draw its authority? The most obvious place would be the executive branch itself. The next president could appoint a commission of inquiry with the stroke of a pen, and such a commission would have many strengths. It could be created quickly; it would answer to one master; and, since it would be created with the authority of the president, it could demand the cooperation of government actors and access to classified documents. Gerald Ford, for instance, created the Rockefeller Commission in 1975 to examine allegations of domestic spying, and it put on record a series of tawdry CIA operations and helped to impose several congressional restraints on domestic action by the agency. The problem with presidential commissions is that they can easily be accused of covering up for previous administration[7] or, conversely, of seeking "victor's justice."[8]

The alternative is a hybrid—an executive-legislative commission that would be created by an act of Congress but would draw also on the authority of the president. This alternative typically involves an elaborate process for the appointment of commissioners by both the White House and the congressional leadership. The National Commission on Terrorist Attacks Upon the United States, usually called the 9/11 Commission, is the most recent example of this approach. The hybrid commission can be challenged on constitutional grounds as an intrusion on executive prerogative, so its success still requires the president's support and cooperation.[9]

In general, the presidential commission seems a smoother, less legally problematic model, whereas the hybrid commission is cumbersome but more likely to command broad public support and confidence from the outset.

In either model, the commissioners themselves must have the right measure of integrity and commitment. Are they willing to pursue their questions to definitive answers, no matter who is embarrassed or injured by the outcome? Do they place the interests of those who appointed them ahead of their obligation to investigate the facts? A well-constituted commission is neither partisan nor relenting. It publishes the truth and leaves the prosecution to later actors.

V. Implementation

Many commissions failed to achieve positive ends because they were poorly designed. History suggests that certain structural and legal characteristics, combined with a careful definition of scope, can lead to a successful outcome.

Composition

The first action of any administration whose conduct comes under scrutiny is to claim that the process is politically motivated. The first step in addressing those claims is to separate the process of initial investigation from the process of prosecution, as discussed above.[10] But the commission itself also can be structured in such a way as to mitigate partisan concerns. This will require real wisdom, however. Simple "balancing" won't do the job.

The 9/11 Commission, for instance, was crafted as a "bipartisan" institution, with co-equal Democratic and Republican chairs, on the premise that each would counteract the partisan proclivities of the other. In the end, though, this balancing served only to provide political ammunition to both parties. Any future war-crimes commission should therefore avoid openly partisan commissioners and staff.

The political parties cannot be ignored—in order to command appropriate levels of support within the Washington political establishment, the commission will need party- affiliated co-chairs who none-theless are viewed as being consensus-builders—but the balance of the commission should be persons of established integrity whose professional backgrounds involve the skills essential to studying, understanding, and dealing critically with the issues arising from the practice of torture. A record of partisan political engagement should weigh against a candidate's selection. The experience pool should include prosecutors, intelligence professionals, retired military leaders, religious leaders and ethicists, human-rights advocates, health-care professionals, and diplomats.

Someone will have to choose those people. The 9/11 Commission legislation gave that responsibility to the secretary of defense, the speaker of the House of Representatives, the Senate majority leader, and the minority leaders in both houses of Congress. It probably will be difficult to avoid a similar delegation of authority. But to ensure that the persons selected are not simply partisan political surrogates, a further layer might be incorporated. A qualifications commission could be appointed first, consisting of a dozen members who would have the sole task of preparing a list of pre- approved candidates. The appointees would then have to be drawn from this list. This approach was taken by South Africa in its Truth and Reconciliation Commission, and it resulted in a final body that commanded broad public respect. Indeed, observers of the South African process have often cited the two-tiered appointments process as a key to the commission's overall success.

Powers of the Commission

The bulk of the commission's work would be carried out not by politicians but by a professional staff of lawyers, investigators, subject experts, and various assistants. The authorizing legislation should assume a staff roughly equal to that of the 9/11 Commission, which totaled nearly eighty. Preference would be given to persons who had previously obtained the necessary security classifications, but the new commission should also be given the power to quickly address security- classification issues. Staff members should be authorized not only to hold and deal with the most sensitive classified documents in a dedicated, secured document room but also to declassify or require the declassification of documents, redacted as appropriate, and to publish the results.

It will be essential for the commission to exercise subpoena power; that is, the ability to force witnesses to appear and testify before it with the possibility of civil or criminal penalties if they fail to appear or give misleading or false testimony. Without this power it would be very difficult for the commission to assemble the information it needs to issue its report. To invest the commission with these powers would be a somewhat complex legal matter, but not an insurmountable one. [11]

Scope of the Investigation

The commission's mandate requires definition and focus. It must also, however, provide the commission with reasonable room to pursue leads that arise in the course of its investigation. The commission's charge, therefore, should be _to examine the formation and implementation of policy concerning the treatment of detainees in operations (including intelligence operations) undertaken in connection with the Authorization for Use of Military Force Against Terrorists. _Tying the subject matter to a specific piece of legislation will keep the investigation focused on a single controlling authority even as it allows investigators to explore all of the operations in which that authority was used, whether in Iraq or Afghanistan, nearby staging areas, or other sites around the world, including Guantánamo and "black sites" yet to be identified.[12]

Such a mandate would also allow the commission to investigate a variety of non- administration actors, including Congress itself. Republicans have frequently argued that many powerful Democrats, including House Majority Leader Nancy Pelosi and Intelligence Committee Chairman Jay Rockefeller, were fully briefed on the administration's torture policy and failed to raise objections. Did Congress acquiesce to the administration's choices? Did it provide legal authority? Republicans may be questioning Democratic involvement simply in order to discourage congressional inquiries. But such questions nonetheless are completely legitimate.

Findings

The commission should conduct its work in public to the fullest possible extent. Open hearings will educate the people about the issues under inquiry and also help to build a consensus in resolving those issues. Putting the testimony of victims and witnesses on the record will be a crucial element of that process. It will be a first step toward restoring the dignity and humanity of the victims, and it will also serve to reveal, authenticate, and preserve vital evidence that may be used in later legal proceedings.

Documents, particularly the many classified documents that the administration continues to withhold from Congress and the public, will be at the core of the commission's work. The president and his advisers, like members of many regimes engaged in legally questionable actions, have placed great emphasis on creating a legal groundwork for their actions. The commissioners would examine these memos, briefs, and other records with the aid of witnesses, but it is essential that the documents themselves also be made permanently available to journalists, scholars, and lawyers. A full fact-finding process is likely to take decades. Public scrutiny can lead to the identification of important details that even the most talented investigators may miss on the first and second pass.

The commission would also be required to prepare an in-depth report. The report should provide a comprehensive narrative, setting out in detail how U.S. torture policy came to be formed and identifying the key actors and the decisions they made.

Recommendations

The report's function would be more than historical, of course. It must be forward-looking. Should laws be changed, regulations rewritten, new procedures adopted?[13] More important, the commission must look at the conduct of official actors. Were laws and policies faithfully applied or were they broken? If laws were broken, was there criminal conduct that merits study by law- enforcement professionals? This analysis would establish the background for the three most important potential results of a commission: the formal recommendation to pardon, the formal recommendation to pursue prosecution, and the formal recommendation to make reparations.

On the matter of reparations, the commission could do a great deal of good. The United States has already committed itself, under existing international agreements, to making reparations to victims of torture. Thus far, though, government action on this front has consisted primarily of efforts to foreclose recovery. Moreover, the U.S. litigation system is extremely costly and may not be an efficient means of providing redress in situations where victims are non-citizens and located outside of the United States. A commission might recommend such alternative approaches as creating a claims-settlement commission or granting special authority for *ex gratia* payments under which the United States could offer compensation without being seen as acknowledging wrongdoing. In cases in which a victim is convicted of criminal wrongdoing, the fact that he suffered torture may be considered in connection with sentencing, and some guidelines for this should be furnished.

The recommendations to prosecute or pardon would not be binding in any formal sense. Only the president has the constitutional authority to pardon at the federal level, and any indictment ultimately would have to find its way to prosecutors and the courts. The recommendations, then, would be persuasive only to the extent that the commissioners successfully made the case for them. (Many of the 9/11 Commission recommendations, for instance, have yet to be enacted.) Still, the commission would certainly be staffed with some career prosecutors. It should be in a solid position to assess whether a special prosecutor should be appointed. And that prosecutor would have a great deal of evidence and political momentum at his or her disposal. If the process is pursued faithfully, the recommendations should have considerable political influence.

The hallmark of the Bush Administration has been its tendency to rush to judgment, certain of propositions that turned out to be dead wrong. In addressing its errors, such failings cannot be repeated. The commission should proceed with care and take the time it needs to develop a full record. The process is likely to consume at least two years and possibly much longer. This is not necessarily a liability. Right now, the administration looms large and justice seems distant. That perspective will change significantly with the passage of time.

1. In addition to being illegal, torture is profoundly un-American. The central premise of the American experiment is the belief, informed by Enlightenment principles, that the dignity and worth of the individual is at least as important as that of the state. This belief weighed heavily on the minds of the Founders. The new American military was to be a force of yeoman soldiers, citizens in peacetime who were to be regarded as no less than citizens in wartime. Enemy soldiers likewise were to be treated with respect. George Washington, in the winter of 1776, sent a written order to officers overseeing prisoners: "Treat them with humanity." And in 1863, at another time of crisis, Abraham Lincoln included the prohibition of torture in the first American codification of the laws of war, which he also issued as a direct order to his field commanders. By way of such American leadership, the prohibition on torture was gradually absorbed into international law.

2. Cheney at the time declined to refer to this practice as torture, preferring instead to describe it as "robust interrogation," and that reluctance has been echoed in the press. I myself was twice warned by PBS producers, in advance of appearances on *The Newshour with Jim Lehrer*, that I could use the word "torture" in the abstract but that I was to refrain from applying it to the administration's policies. And after an interview with CNN in which I spoke of the administration's torture policy, I was told by the producer, "That's okay for CNN International, but we can't use it on the domestic feed." More recently, however, the consensus appears to be that "torture" is a perfectly adequate description of administration policy. In the vice-presidential debates, Joe Biden said that Cheney has "done more harm than any other single elected official in memory in terms of shredding the Constitution. You know—condoning torture." In the first presidential debate, John McCain said we must ensure "that we have people who are trained interrogators so that we don't ever torture a prisoner ever again." And Barack Obama, though vague, seemed to accept this formulation. "I give Senator McCain

great credit on the torture issue," he said, "for having identified that as something that undermines our long-term security."

3.   In an interview with Jane Mayer of *The New Yorker*, a former senior CIA official with knowledge of the administration's torture program summarized its attitude more bluntly: "Laws? Like who the fuck cares?"

4.   This last point is not even slightly controversial. Richard Armitage, a Republican former Navy officer who served as deputy secretary of state from 2001 to 2005, is likely the highest-ranking administration official to personally have experienced this form of torture. In the late Sixties, he was waterboarded as part of a training program—Survival, Evasion, Resistance, and Escape, or SERE—designed to prepare military personnel to resist enemy interrogators. His conclusion was straightforward. "Of course waterboarding is torture," he told the BBC in 2007. "I can't believe we're even debating it." Military lawyers agree. In a 2007 letter to Senate Judiciary Committee Chairman Patrick Leahy, four retired judge advocates general hammered the point again and again. "Waterboarding is inhumane, it is torture, and it is illegal," they wrote, adding that "it is not, and never has been, a complex issue, and even to suggest otherwise does a terrible disservice to this nation." Even Republican Senator Lindsey Graham, himself a onetime reserve military judge and sometime supporter of administration detainee policy, admits that waterboarding is illegal. "I don't think you have to have a lot of knowledge about the law," he said in 2007, "to understand this technique violates Geneva Convention Common Article Three, the War Crimes statutes, and many other statutes that are in place."

5.   It is not without justification that Bush was able to claim in 2005, "We had an accountability moment, and that's called the 2004 elections." Such taunts recall the (likely apocryphal) moment when William Tweed, the corrupt head of New York's Tammany Hall, was confronted with indisputable evidence of graft. "Well," he said, "what are you going to do about it?"

6.   18 U.S.C. § 2340 makes it a crime for any "person acting under the color of law" to "inflict severe physical or mental pain or suffering (other than pain or suffering incidental to lawful sanctions) upon another person within his custody or physical control." The penalty for this crime—as Bush's Office of Legal Counsel carefully noted in a 2003 memo on the subject—is up to twenty years in federal prison.

7. Or even their own administrations: George W. Bush formed the Robb-Silberman Commission in 2004 to look into why his administration's conclusions about Iraqi WMDs were so completely wrong, but the commission somehow failed to discover the pressure that the administration itself had brought to bear on intelligence analysts to cook their conclusions—in part, perhaps, because Dick Cheney was personally responsible for putting part of the commission together, starting with the appointment of his friend Laurence Silberman as co-chair. The Tower Commission, created by Ronald Reagan to look into the Iran-Contra scandal, was a similarly lukewarm exercise in damage control, in which the authors ultimately concluded that all that was really needed to avoid future such scandals was a modest restructuring of the role of the national security adviser.

8. This may explain why, when Will Bunch of the *Philadelphia Daily News* asked Barack Obama in August "whether an Obama administration would seek to prosecute officials of a former Bush Administration," the senator's response was guarded. "I can't prejudge that, because we don't have access to all the material right now. I think that you are right: if crimes have been committed, they should be investigated. You're also right that I would not want my first term consumed by what was perceived on the part of Republicans as a partisan witch hunt, because I think we've got too many problems we've got to solve." Obama adviser Cass Sunstein has similarly warned that pursuing prosecutions of Bush Administration officials would generate a "cycle" of partisan recriminations.

9. The leaders of the 9/11 Commission were, in fact, pointed in their criticism of the false or misleading statements that were provided by some agencies, particularly the Department of Defense and the Federal Aviation Administration. In their book, *Without Precedent*, the commission's co-chairs, Thomas Kean and Lee Hamilton, write that they openly considered recommending prosecution of some government officials for criminal obstruction, a threat that ultimately secured some compliance. They remained skeptical, however, about how much cooperation they ultimately received.

10. *Newsweek* columnist Stuart Taylor, long a defender of the administration's detainee policies, wrote in July that a war-crimes trial would "touch off years of partisan warfare. The lesson for occupants of the toughest government jobs—if the next administration could find people willing to fill them— would be that saving innocent lives is less important than covering their posteriors." Taylor has, however, embraced the idea of a truth commission.

11. The White House has forbidden several of its former employees—including former chief of staff Joshua Bolton, former counselor Harriet Miers, and former senior adviser Karl Rove—from testifying before congressional oversight panels. When a court ordered them to appear, the administration sought to appeal the ruling in a transparent, and thus far successful, effort to run out the clock. The administration has also withheld documents, citing exotic theories of privilege. In congressional hearings, White House attorney John Yoo simply refused to answer questions, on the grounds that he had been instructed by the Justice Department not to answer, even though many of the questions concerned matters that Yoo had discussed in two books and dozens of other public forums. The difference between Yoo's public discussion and his testimony was, of course, that the latter was under oath.

12. The Authorization for Use of Military Force Against Terrorists, passed into law shortly after the attacks of September 11, 2001, is the statute that has provided general authority for the conduct of military operations in what the administration has came to call the "Global War on Terror." Since the president's repeated assumptions of extralegal powers was predicated in Justice Department memoranda on his commander-in-chief authority, that military link should help define the time, the space, and the nature of the conduct that requires investigation.

13. One highly controversial area of inquiry will be the question of efficacy. The major argument for torture now is simple: It works, and therefore any state that wants to protect itself would be foolish to dispense with it. But does torture "work"? Many human-rights activists have strongly discouraged even asking the question. Doing so, they argue, transforms a moral argument—a basic respect for the dignity of all humans forbids torture—into a utilitarian argument. Such a consideration of ends versus means opens the door to all kinds of "what if" scenarios that would eventually lead to wider social

acceptance of torture. (One way to more easily assess that concern would be to substitute another taboo act—say, child rape—for torture. Would it be acceptable to rape a child if there were a ticking time bomb under the Empire State Building and you sincerely believed that raping that child was the only way to find it?)

There is much to be said for these concerns. And yet those who are against torture also have the better end of the utilitarian argument. Under centuries of the *lex talionis*, or law of retribution, if a nation inflicted indignities on its captives, others were free to do the same to its soldiers. One of the clearest consequences of the Bush torture policies has been to put American service personnel at risk. Nor is there any evidence that torture is an effective means to the end of national security. Bush has argued that "the program" he helped establish did in fact secure information that "saved American lives." But others who have looked into the incidents that Bush cites say that, in fact, what useful intelligence was gathered in these interrogations was gathered before the interrogators resorted to torture. Indeed, the techniques utilized at Guantánamo and Abu Ghraib were developed not for the purpose of gathering intelligence but rather to elicit false confessions to be used for political purposes.

This invites a number of questions: Was the intelligence collected inherently more or less reliable than intelligence gathered using other techniques? Was it necessary to turn to highly coercive tactics to secure this information? What other consequences for national security flow from the use of the new techniques in terms, for instance, of loss of intelligence-gathering channels, damage to reputation, recruitment gains for enemies, and compromised cooperation from allies? These questions, although they may suggest, perniciously, that "reasonable minds differ" on torture, nonetheless are worth asking for one reason above all. The answers, coming from administration officials, would also act as a kind of confession. Their self-justification should be part of the record.

Permissions